Miss Grundy Doesn't Teach Here Anymore

Also in the CrossCurrents Series

Miss Grundy Doesn't Teach Here Anymore

Popular Culture and the Composition Classroom

EDITED BY

DIANE PENROD

CrossCurrents

New Perspectives in Rhetoric and Composition

CHARLES I. SCHUSTER, SERIES EDITOR

BOYNTON/COOK PUBLISHERS · HEINEMANN · PORTSMOUTH, NH

Boynton/Cook Publishers, Inc.
A subsidiary of Reed Elsevier Inc.
361 Hanover St.
Portsmouth, NH 03801-3912
Offices and agents throughout the world

Library of Congress Cataloging-in-Publication Data
Miss Grundy doesn't teach here anymore : popular culture and the composition classroom / edited by Diane Penrod.
    p.   cm.
  Includes bibliographical references.
  ISBN 0-86709-438-9
    1. English language—Rhetoric—Study and teaching—United States.   2. United States—Social life and customs—20th century.   3. Popular culture—United States—History—20th century.   4. Report writing—Study and teaching—United States.   5. English language—Social aspects—United States. I. Penrod, Diane.
PE1405.U6M57   1997
808'.042'07073—dc21
                                            97–25941
                                                CIP

Editor: Charles Schuster
Manufacturing: Louise Richardson
Cover Design: Jenny Jensen Greenleaf

Printed in the United States of America on acid-free paper
00 99 98 97 DA 1 2 3 4 5 6 7 8 9

Contents

Preface

Popular culture has been linked to my education ever since my childhood days. Sometimes I think I learned more about the human condition from consuming mass culture than I did from reading all the "great works." Growing up in a rural town in southwestern New York State, I spent days and nights with my ear connected by a thin earphone wire to an old Olympic transistor radio. Homework, household chores, and the daily walk to and from grade school and junior high were spent with the AM-band disc jockeys at WKBW and WYSL in Buffalo, listening to Motown hits and the sounds of The Buckinghams, The Cyrkle, Buffalo Springfield, The Youngbloods, and other pop groups. Piles of *Mad* magazine lined the floor of my room. In high school, I whiled away hours in the art studio and in the photography lab learning how to replicate the visuals on my record albums and posters. Looking back, I experienced the pain of love, the angst of a society in flux, and the hope of a better world from those songs. *Mad* taught me about satire and cynicism in print, and the difference between the two. As a result of my childhood investment in popular culture, I became fascinated with advertising's mix of images and words; and later, as a college undergraduate immediately post-Watergate, I witnessed the incredible power of the press to influence public thought toward government. I found a vitality in learning through popular culture that was often lacking in my formal education. Music, movies, magazines, the press, and advertising spoke to me in ways that were so familiar to and yet so different from my real life. Like so many other adolescents in the mid-1970s who were fascinated with the creativity and influence of mass communication in our lives, I studied media as an undergraduate and hoped it would be my life's profession.

As one who worked in advertising, packaging design, and sales for just under a decade before returning to the university to complete my graduate studies, I participated in the creation of messages that influenced hundreds of thousands of people's thoughts and decisions. Rightly, cultural studies taught us that, indeed, the media teach and disseminate—and are financed heavily to do so—particular social policies and behaviors. At the professional level, I discovered that the innocent, romantic quality of popular culture clearly becomes reduced to economics—the language of gross rating points, costs per thousand, and household reach. For those unfamiliar with the process, making popular culture is a mentally, physically, and emotionally draining discipline. There are very few "old" (middle-aged) people in the media business. The frenetic pace of being creative under constant daily deadline burns most folks out, and many leave media for academics or for documentary/public service programming/nonprofit work. My choice was academics. When I returned to graduate study, though, I was torn between continuing my work in media criticism and moving into the teaching of writing and rhetoric. At the time, however, cultural studies became a central focus in academic study, a focus adopted by the English department but not the mass communication department at my graduate institution. Cultural studies, especially the practice of cultural criticism, appealed to me because I sensed how the different kinds of knowledge that exist in everyday life could converge with the critical thinking skills so many instructors in composition were trying to elicit in their students' writing.

I saw how a writing pedagogy rooted in cultural criticism might serve a threefold purpose: First, the topics covered in cultural studies show students in very real terms that their knowledge of themselves and of their worlds is socially constructed—produced and influenced by the rhetorical power of social institutions like schools, industry, government, and religion in subtle and not so subtle ways. Second, the college writing classroom becomes the site where students engage in questioning the language of institutional rhetoric and the power and conflict inherent in institutional discourses. Third, writing emerges as the activity where students practice the kinds of interrogation and investigation that encourage a democratic cultural literacy shared by multiple constituents rather than an exclusionary cultural literacy legitimated by "authorities." Rather than think of popular culture as a fictitious or a casual escape from dull classrooms, which is certainly how I and many others once viewed it, students now have the opportunity to consider culture as an active shaper of information. Given this, composition has the potential to educate students as to the kinds of language use, discursive strategies, and rhetorical effects at work in the circulation of public arguments.

As a writing instructor, I soon realized that course themes drawn from popular culture seemed to excite my students to write and think smartly and in ways that challenged dominant, pervasive, status quo views as compared with those instances when they employed the textual information presented in most composition rhetorics and readers. Students found that they could use what they already know about the world to discover more about the ideas and beliefs they didn't know. The results in many written papers were outstanding: students learned that writing and researching were exciting activities, and, for some, cultural criticism offered an experience of intellectual growth. From speaking with composition instructors across the United States and Canada, I found that others also discovered similar results: cultural studies content provided composition courses with the wide-ranging intellectual resources that included students in a public debate of current social issues.

The inclusiveness of popular culture is only part of what makes cultural studies so intriguing for use in the composition class, however. The dependency of popular culture on rhetoric cannot go unheeded. If the use of language is truly what marks us as being human, then we cannot discount how people effectively use language and symbols in various social contexts to influence individuals' choices. Popular culture, especially media culture, contains a broad, deep rhetorical power that compositionists and other educators are now beginning to explore in their studies. For example, the sweeping, polyphonic language contained in popular culture—standard English, street talk, idiomatic English, regionalized variations—combines with academic language in the college writing classroom to examine the multiple social environments in which we all participate. In addition, rhetorical memory as it relates to popular culture is especially important to explore in the composition classroom. Cultural knowledge, as well as individual knowledge, is shaped greatly by media technologies and messages. Questions of how people access and retain specific bits of information, or how people recognize certain ideas as valuable in society, can be addressed through the exploration of popular cultural topics. And, certainly, any composition-based analysis of popular culture demands that particular attention be given to the other classical divisions of rhetoric: invention, arrangement, style, and presentation. Critically studying popular culture not only helps students to discover how and why specific ideas and symbols become important to society, but also to come to know how and why certain ideas and symbols are given legitimacy over others in society.

I developed this collection because there is a growing number of students for whom traditional educational methods don't reach. This is especially apparent in the college writing courses I teach. These students are finding that popular culture teaches them more about the world than the classroom materials they encounter, just as I and many others did decades ago. Except that now, the excessive commodification of popular culture and its extreme lack of connectedness to historical events have made learning from music, movies, and media technology a shallow experience for most. The constant simulation and hyperreality present in much of current popular culture are apparent to many. A large number of students in our classes realize that they are constructed schizophrenically in popular culture, simultaneously portrayed in the media as sexual and chaste, violator and victim, slacker and workaholic, dysfunctional and overachieving. Furthermore, some of these students see the same pathological models being extended to other societal groups. Most students can tell us that the images are connected to whatever drives profit for the network, the movie company, the fashion designer, and so on. Many students also realize that these depictions in media culture are highly inaccurate and unfair, yet because they have few channels for arguing or opposing these constructions, the impressions become legitimated in the students' minds. The lack of educational avenues for students to develop rhetorical abilities to critique these cultural messages tends to breed cynicism rather than critical thinking about their world. It has become time, then, for more college writing teachers to develop cultural criticism pedagogies that encourage students to question this information and the kinds of knowledge it promotes in public life. The essays in this collection reflect the ranges of possibility that cultural critique holds for involving students in thinking and writing critically to address the contentions, conflicts, and social constructions that popular venues promote.

It is important to note that the authors involved with this anthology are nontenured instructors. Many are junior faculty members in tenure-track positions in American and Canadian colleges and universities. Some are teaching in these same colleges and universities as teaching assistants, adjuncts, or instructors. A few are advanced graduate students, doctoral candidates who are hoping that their work will help them to find employment in a higher education system that is under political and budgetary fire. Their voices are not privileged ones in the academy. Still, they are voices that need to be heard. Many times, these faculty embody the concept of the "public intellectual" celebrated in cultural studies. They are often the people who bring the most passion for teaching and learning into and out of the classroom space. With one foot in the realm of the university and the other in the street, the junior faculty, adjuncts, and graduate students look to share their work with larger audiences beyond the academy—friends and family, as well as coworkers in nonacademic second jobs. By maintaining positions in both educational institutions and in public life, these teachers work hard at displacing conventional images—the Miss Grundy of our title—of the college writing instructor.

The fourteen essays in this anthology move through a loose structure that addresses a host of issues about when cultural criticism and composition connect. The first seven essays present perspectives concerning the intersection of pop culture with politics. The middle four essays challenge the concept of interdisciplinarity in the writing classroom through the use of computers and other visual and aural technologies. The final three essays discuss the impact of the language of the university on our students' decisions. What is important to recognize in each of the essays is that the classroom becomes the site where changes in the students' thinking and writing take place. Without classroom interaction and the practice of writing, the discussions that occur in each of these essays remain in the domain of theory. While theory is fine, and even necessary to move us forward in our thinking, it still holds that composition requires more than theory; it demands practice to put theory into action. If teachers wish to enact a brand of composition that actively engages our students to think (theorize), then we must not lose sight of the value of writing as a way to practice the thinking process. The cultural studies pedagogies presented in this volume illustrate that composition topics can be taken up wherever students are in their lives and can be struggled with to articulate or rearticulate positions of student thought over time.

Acknowledgments

Thanks to Charles I. Schuster, editor of Boynton/Cook's *Cross Currents* series, for encouraging me to pursue the idea of creating a dialogue among instructors as to how various popular cultural media can be used to teach college writing. Thanks also go to Peter Stillman at Boynton/Cook for supporting the publication of this collection and to the entire Boynton/Cook staff for help in preparing the manuscript for production. The intersection of cultural studies and composition is an interesting, yet unpredictable, discussion. I'm glad Heinemann-Boynton/Cook was willing to advance the conversation.

I want to thank many of my students, far too many to identify by name, here at Rowan University and at my former institutions, Syracuse University and the State University of New York at Oswego, for the sometimes-too-long chats about pop culture and how it affects them as thinkers and writers. You know who you folks are. And you all thought we were just wasting time chatting between classes! I may have learned more from listening to all of you than you all have learned from me.

A special note of thanks goes to each of the contributors to this anthology. Because this work focuses on how junior faculty and advanced graduate students approach the teaching of composition through the use of popular culture, a set of voices not often heard from in the field has been given access to an "authorized" dialogue. Many of my colleagues warned me that there were risks in working with "untested" writers. Let me respond to my colleagues' caveats with this: These people have been great to work with, meeting deadlines and taking criticism well. The risks have been minimal, and the rewards from making contact with people who will make an impact on the future of college composition have been great.

I would also like to thank many people at Rowan University for their help at various stages in the preparation of this collection. I especially appreciate the help extended from Dean Pearl Bartelt of the College of Liberal Arts and Sciences and Executive Vice President/Provost Carol Matteson for their support in offering me college Probationary Assistance Grants in the academic years 1996 and 1997 to finish this book. Thanks also to Dean Antoinette Libro of the College of Communication, who has supported my work by providing me with computer equipment. Included in my gratitude for college support is Dr. David Cromie, former chair of the Communications Department at Rowan, and Thomas Kloskey, Director of the Writing Lab, who were kind enough to provide duplicating, faxing, mailing, and computer assistance when needed. Thanks also go to Janice Rowan, Chair of the College Writing Department, who worked at keeping my teaching schedule manageable while the project was in its final stages. And to Rowan's own pop culture guru, Denis Mercier, who read and commented upon various sections of the book.

Lastly, the greatest debt of my gratitude goes to Frank Panarisi and our two Chow dogs, Koan and Kuma, for providing me with the space to develop this project and for lending an ear, a pen, or a paw when it was needed most. Each day they teach me new and different ways to enjoy life. Even with all this support, any mistakes in the publication of this work are mine alone.

This book is dedicated to everyone mentioned above and to those who are trying to improve the field of composition through their teaching, their theorizing, and their interactions with students.

1

Pop Goes the Content
Teaching the
Ugly and the Ordinary

Diane Penrod

When the content of a college writing course goes pop(ular), significant pedagogical opportunities occur in the classroom. Course instructors can develop
class syllabi and assignments that tap wide ranges of compelling topics and
materials drawn from pop culture. Sources for course content can include
advertisements and marketing strategies, to provide students with a plethora of
rhetorical messages at work shaping culture; newspaper articles and/or television news coverage, to demonstrate the media's use of logos, ethos, and
pathos; and web sites, film, music videos, and song lyrics, to afford students a
rich field of opportunities to examine various aspects of intertextuality. In this
kind of classroom, students are encouraged to analyze common objects as representations of dynamic culture(s), using critical methodologies like rhetoric,
ethnography, and semiotics to question the kinds of knowledge present in their
worlds. As can be imagined, examples of learning opportunities presented by
the infusion of cultural studies into the composition classroom are endless,
and the instances presented above are now occurring in college writing
courses across the United States and Canada.

There are a number of important reasons why cultural studies' influence
is profoundly changing the college writing curriculum. The application of pop
culture to composition reveals that the boundaries among composition and
cultural studies materials often converge, if not entirely collapse into one
another. As with cultural studies, composition's intellectual identity has been
formed from a hybridization of disciplines within the social sciences. Both
composition and cultural studies often overflow their disciplinary boundaries,
incorporating ideas from across the academic spectrum to challenge the practices of academic knowledge-making.

1

Furthermore, in both cultural studies and composition, educators place a tremendous emphasis on practice. In both fields, practice and the questioning of practice take place in the classroom and extend to everyday events. The site of the classroom in either field, as readers of this collection will discover, is not a heroic and original place; it is more often an ugly and ordinary place, filled with discussions grounded in quotidian topics. The ugliness and ordinariness of the classroom space and the discussions contained within it are quite important for the development of critical thinking, however. Many of the practices that composition and cultural studies instructors outline to their students are inextricably connected to the shaping and producing of thought and experience. The topics and assignments students write about usually relate to their identification and experience with various objects and events in the world. In these classroom spaces, students learn to focus on the social construction of texts and how texts are used rhetorically to reflect the values, positions, social relations, and histories of the community for which they are produced.

The influence of cultural studies upon composition through the use of pop culture, then, frames the complex rhetorical relationships audiences establish with cultural objects. Beyond the standard academic discussions of persuasive and informative rhetorical relationships that occur in the composition classroom, a course that utilizes pop culture exposes the adversarial, diplomatic, institutional, political, instructional, and conciliatory rhetorical associations that exist between an artifact and its audience. The complexity of the rhetorical and semiotic codes and their connections maintained in common objects provide multiple opportunities to engage students' critical consciousness in the writing class. By focusing on everyday items as topics of written inquiry, teachers and students can decelerate the rapid pace of popular messages and critically examine the rhetoric that shapes daily life.

The Movement Away From the Heroic and the Original

Decades ago, significant developments in pedagogical practices related to the making of knowledge began to coalesce throughout the arts and humanities, resulting in the rise of interdisciplinary approaches to teaching and thinking. The teaching of writing, for example, moved away from concentrating solely upon making sure students dotted all their i's, crossed all their t's, and parsed their sentences perfectly. These are the kinds of educational practices once presented in pop culture by the *Archie* comic book character Miss Grundy.[1] In the wake of the changes made in the academy, composition's early contributions to the connections between writing and ordinary culture began to include the discussion of commonplace elements—such as advertisements—as source materials for assignments. This move started to forge a dialogue between teaching practices and isolated skills that once seemed to alienate many students from writing pedagogy. The result of this dialogue was that by the mid-1980s, pop culture no longer merely reflected the staid events of the academy;

rather, the academy began to look at popular icons and practices as serious subjects of study. Thus, a different kind of dialogue emerged between the popular and the academic: a discussion that linked the ordinariness of everyday topics to the rigors of disciplinary investigation. In the field of composition, the result was the increasing influence of rhetoric, ethnography, semiotics, and popular cultural topics as methods and sources for inquiry.

Investigating the popular icons, images, and texts of various segments of society allows students to interact with the rhetorical intentions and needs of others through the exploration of how a cultural artifact is (or is not) sanctioned by the mainstream. Years ago, architect Robert Venturi reasoned that the influence of mass culture on mainstream American life is evocative: full of societal messages and propaganda, a hybrid mix of high and low forms of culture. Moreover, Venturi believed that pop culture starts from a system of values and diffuses across society, shaping consciousness. In his early explorations linking the influence of democratic forms of culture to everyday life, Venturi often looked to the rhetoricians I. A. Richards and William Empson to explain the kinds of ambiguity, irony, and complexity found in cultural icons. Venturi ultimately came to believe that the rhetorical influences inherent in mundane cultural objects have important connections to how people react to what they see and hear.

Venturi called the product of the influence of pop culture on architecture that of "the ugly and the ordinary."[2] "The ugly" are those objects that are common in the culture, while "the ordinary" are those items which are distinctly conventional. According to Venturi, ugly and ordinary items in culture represent the democratic segment of society, as they embody mass consciousness. Venturi's concepts were offered as an antidote to architecture's then reliance upon what he called the "heroic and original,"[3] or a scale of representation that resulted in making timeless, grand-scale, heraldic associations between building and space. Heroic and original work had only a single meaning, a single view. But popular culture, in the form of the ugly and the ordinary, developed more localized and multiple meanings.

For Venturi, the process of creating becomes evolutionary rather than static: the ugliness and ordinariness contained in the popular item evoke certain rhetorical tropes, which arouse various meanings and associations in individuals. These meanings and associations almost inevitably change over time. Therefore, popular material has the potential for shaping the meaning-making processes—and, by extension, the knowledge—of an entire culture or of a specific group of individuals within that culture. What this means for composition, in the words of Henry A. Giroux, is that the study of pop culture encourages us to make "a claim to particular memories, histories, ways of life, identities, and values that always presuppose some notion of difference, community, and the future."[4]

Drawing upon the ugly and the ordinary as a foundation for written inquiry offers student writers a way to incorporate a richness of meaning not always found in heroic and original topics. The use of contemporary cultural material in a composition class authorizes student writers to demonstrate their particular cultural associations and levels of knowledge about the world in their own texts. The unlikelihood that they will share a single view of an assignment grounded in pop culture opens the way for students to provide numerous interpretations and arguments. Inquiry, then, can become much more rhetorically-, semiotically- or ethnographically-based, as the cultural artifact draws out multiple levels of response from student writers.

Venturi's study provided the groundwork for the academy to examine how pop culture estranges familiar images, thereby providing perspective on social tensions, icons, and events. As compositionists, we can build upon this frame to encourage critical writing strategies in our students. The use of rhetoric or semiotics in the composition classroom to alienate students' comfort with familiar articles, for example, somewhat slows the rapid pace of the evocative messages sent by many cultural artifacts. This gives students time to develop a level of critical awareness to engage with the complex rhetorical dimensions contained in ugly and ordinary materials like corporate logos or cult figures. Since most writing activities outside of the academy produce truly nonheroic and nonoriginal forms that often reflect a profit-over-quality approach—E-mail, corporate web sites, gossipy and/or formal information-loaded memos, reports that require sophisticated phrasings to mask intended meanings to various constituencies, vitae and resumes, and brochures and television spots that sell an image or a mission to an audience—there are many more sophisticated rhetorical and semiotic appeals at play than persuasion or information to which students may be blind. Teaching the rhetoric of the ugly and the ordinary in college composition courses, then, means asking students to examine the complexities and tensions in writing that exist in everyday culture, not so that they become better persons or create a better society, but rather so that they learn to recognize that conflicting messages, struggle, intervention, and influence are very much a part of living, thinking, and writing.

The Challenges for Composition

As I outlined earlier, just as Venturi's research held new promise for architecture, his influence can yield new and exciting ideas to as well as highly visible challenges for composition. A cultural studies approach to writing encourages both writing instructors and student writers to move beyond status quo expectations in their thinking, as it demands each of us to reveal our preconceptions, values, and resistance to as well as standards for learning, thinking, and writing. Moreover, cultural studies methodologies sometimes require educators to set aside the methods they were once taught. For compositionists, this may mean that some instructors need to retire Miss/Mr. Grundy's pedagogical ways. In place of a current-traditional model for teaching writing that often uses top-down ideas for writing instruction, a critical-dialogic pedagogy has to be established and maintained with students to advance transitive exchanges of information. This kind of classroom exchange does not suggest a lessening of student accountability for producing solid written work, as one could suppose. On the contrary, if anything, what a cultural studies model for composition argues for is *increased* student accountability, as students must develop critical and rhetorical skill in analysis as well as the ability to write clearly and cogently about their findings.

To move toward a critical-dialogic pedagogical model, some composition educators also may have to set aside what Ira Shor has called "normative views"[5] concerning writing instruction. Normative views do exist in composition, such as the teacherly heuristic, "Students have to make the [writing] assignment their own," a good idea that becomes normative when student writers are pushed by the instructor to think only in terms of what is acceptable in mainstream culture—or worse, what is acceptable to the professor— even if the students' alternative views offer greater insight. When writing teachers retain normative views in their teaching practices related to media culture, for example, they reinscribe a trendiness and superficiality in students' critical thinking processes that the cultural studies model of learning works to counter.

The decision of whether to select trendiness or timeliness in the course content is perhaps the most daunting challenge facing compositionists in their use of pop culture. Pedagogically, it is more advantageous for educators to use cultural artifacts in a timely way. Timeliness refers to using popular objects as indicators or examples of how rhetorical and/or compositional elements function in society. The timeliness of a cultural object tends to demonstrate the adaptability of an icon, event, or image across multiple rhetorical or composition principles and has the advantage of showing students the various ways an artifact can be represented to different segments of society. Timeliness contributes to the development of a dialogic pedagogy with students because it checks the potential resistance some students have about studying pop culture as an academic topic. Many students view contemporary cultural subjects cynically, a form of resistance that envisions areas like the media, cyberspace, sports, and fashion as being something *done to them* rather than as topics to explore. Often students do not realize that pop culture has a distinct pedagogical aspect; it educates them to think and to act in very prescribed ways. By presenting how these items can be decoded for discussion from various rhetorical and/or semiotic perspectives, however, progressive educators can show students ways of examining underlying social relationships that connect profoundly to language use and the construction of identity. This is important knowledge for students to investigate. As Henry A. Giroux points out, many popular or cult figures in our society, such as Howard Stern, Rush Limbaugh, and others, legitimate "a new form of public pathology dressed up as entertainment."[6] The entertainment quality of much of pop culture often obscures deeper public beliefs and values contained within the rhetoric; for students to think critically about the ideas supported by society, writing instructors need to push students' analyses beyond obvious surface messages.

Trendiness, in contrast, occurs in composition courses when the rhetorical or writing aspects of the courses are subsumed by a noncritical study of popular images, icons, or events. Trendiness also plays into normative thinking by providing a false sense of security to the class, a feeling that everyone is the same in representations forwarded in pop culture. In a sense, trendiness promotes a consumerist mind-set that leads the students and the teacher to construct dishonest dialogue. A noncritical or trendy approach to pop culture that views this subject as providing innocent, fun topics to explore in the writing class dismisses the kinds of affective, ideological, and rhetorical influence public culture maintains in society. Trendy views deny the differences, contradictions, implications, antagonisms, and complexities that exist for each of us when we absorb pop culture. Furthermore, trendiness glosses over the important ethical and social questions, such as, Whose agenda(s) is/are represented in this object? Can one enjoy aspects of this icon, image, text, or practice and still recognize potential contradictions? What specifically about this artifact gives rise to certain forms of cultural knowledge while repressing other forms? Such questions move students beyond a superficial, or what some of my students have called a "politically correct,"[7] look at the topic. Without asking these, or similar, questions in the cultural-studies-based composition classroom, the instructor—even a well-intentioned one—does little more than put a clever spin on her pedagogy.

Undoubtedly, cultural-studies-based composition courses take much planning and effort to enact. An example of the difficulty writing teachers encounter when balancing timeliness and trendiness in composition classes occurred during my graduate school teaching experiences. Early in my studies, each graduate teaching assistant (GTA) in English was required to participate in ENG 613, a seminar/practicum devoted to the teaching of college composition at the university. Part of fulfilling our course requirements was to develop design overviews and syllabi for the 200-level sophomore composition class we would teach the following term, a class focused on argumentation and rhetoric, with an emphasis on contrastive cultural rhetoric and cultural studies.

What most often emerged in our seminar discussions of the design overviews and syllabi was topic trendiness generally based on the individual instructors' interests: the rhetoric of MTV, the rhetoric of Beatles or Bruce Springsteen songs, the rhetoric of *Batman* (*Superman*, *Spiderman*, etc.) comic books, the rhetoric of talk shows. At the time these courses were planned, a wave of late-1960s nostalgia filled our campus, and many GTAs and adjuncts tried to design courses to ride the crest of student interest. While connecting course materials to student interest is an important and necessary component in any course, the materials chosen need to correspond to the focus of the class—in this instance, the teaching of writing and rhetoric—and not neces-sarily to personal interests with the serendipitous hope that the selected pop artifacts relate to important course information. This is, I believe, one of the important constraints writing instructors face when adopting a cultural studies pedagogy: It is easy to think that "anything goes" in the classroom. However, this is not an accurate view. Selecting cultural items as the foundation to teach writing and rhetoric requires instructors to comprehend how the material will benefit students learning the practices of writing and rhetoric. Trendy topics, such as the meteoric rise of a musical group or a new look in fashion, do not generally capture the public's attention long enough for us to grasp the full influence a topic has in society. Instructors' reliance on trendy topics to teach writing and rhetoric defeats the purpose of cultural studies, which is to explore the range of historical, political, social, and communicative structures that exist in everyday life and to examine how this range affects each of our ways of thinking about the world. Selecting topics for study based solely on trendi-ness reduces the potential for critical exploration, for determining meaning, and for creating knowledge through writing.

Timeliness of course content can be achieved when a writing class goes popular. The 200-level class I designed for my ENG 613 seminar project, for example, also drew upon the 1960s nostalgia movement on our campus. Instead of basing the entire course on a single popular object's position in time, like Beatles songs or *Batman* comics, I first outlined the contrastive cul-tural rhetoric principles and fundamentals of argumentation I wanted to teach, including tropes, irony, Burke's pentad, ethos, logos, and pathos. Then I used popular artifacts as demonstrations for the principles the class studied and as the grounding for contrastive rhetorical situations in American society. For this class, cultural references were used to expand and to challenge students' textbook understandings of rhetoric and writing.

Clearly, timeliness in selecting objects of inquiry drawn from pop culture requires instructors to preplan and to carefully consider how these materials are to be used in their courses. As Ira Shor notes, students are often highly resistant to the territory explored in a cultural-studies-based curriculum because the content is not often considered "serious."[8] Student resistance to a perceived lack of *gravitas* in course content can be countered, however. As I have argued earlier, successful popular content presents the opportunity for students to read, inquire, and write from multiple viewpoints. In my 200-level course, for instance, the topic I chose was the rhetorics of Vietnam. The emphasis on the plural *rhetorics* is important here, as its use attempts to show the multiple contrastive rhetorical positions many societal groups expressed during this era. The impetus for the course was to motivate student investiga-tion into how a culturally perceived monolithic event like the Vietnam War ini-tiated various rhetorical stances. America's preparations for the Gulf War also contributed to the course's timeliness. On campus, students' interests regard-ing Vietnam were piqued because of both the 1960s nostalgia and the media's rhetorical maneuvers of continually comparing and contrasting the Gulf action with Vietnam.

As a basis for examining how people argue in cultural contexts, the four units of my course paralleled the rhetorical experiences of four distinct groups who shared the Vietnam experience. The class moved throughout the semester reading primary documents like the Students for a Democratic Society's "Port Huron Statement," viewing documentaries such as *Letters Home: A Soldier's View of Vietnam* and *Incident at My Lai,* and observing file film footage of Lyndon Johnson's press conferences concerning the Gulf of Tonkin and Tet Offensive incidents. Students used this information as a foundation for rhetorical inquiry into the daily CNN coverage of the Gulf conflict, the televised military briefings, and George Bush's press conferences on various military actions. The rhetorics of Vietnam estranged the familiar, current military discourse enough so that students could actually match verbatim political phrasings between U.S. presidents elected nearly thirty years apart, which made them question the sincerity of the politicians' messages in both eras; the various rhetorical positions studied by the class also showed students that the "minor players" in a military action, such as college students, soldiers, and even "the enemy," display a rhetoric filled with logos, ethos, and pathos.

From teaching this course, I learned that timely cultural objects establish frames of reference and expand student understanding. These items expose students to how groups, individuals, and ideas are categorized by society. Because of students' everyday connections to popular items, they have a knowledge base from which to work. As the class begins to question the contexts in which the artifact appears, instructors begin to notice students questioning the status quo, challenging official knowledge, and expanding inquiry into writing assignments beyond normative views. Through rigorous critical inquiry, many students gain intellectual empowerment after years of "square-peg thinking" in the educational process. Students start to understand that their writing matters, and that their voices count when they enter into discussions both in and out of the classroom. After an initial phase of resistance in cultural-studies-based composition classes, students often find a dialogic, critical exchange of ideas to be liberating. For these students, this application of critical inquiry to pop culture marks the first time they have been motivated to participate in their own learning. Sometimes, this interconnectedness of course work and culture gives students their first opportunity to connect academic learning to daily living.

Interdisciplinary approaches in composition have been followed by instructors for some time now to produce strong student writing assignments. While the critical perspectives of an interdisciplinary focus can be helpful in composition, cultural studies demands a methodology that encourages students to engage in a broader examination of pop culture. To accommodate the multiplicity of rhetorics, codes, literacies, and practices found in these artifacts, however, another approach is needed. A *transdisciplinary* approach, one that reveals the movement of an item across the informational lines of disciplinary study, proves more useful. Applying the words of Lawrence Grossberg, Cary Nelson, and Paula Treichler, "culture is understood *both* as a way of life—encompassing ideas, attitudes, languages, practices, institutions, and structures of power—and a whole range of cultural practices: artistic forms, texts, canons, architecture, mass-produced commodities, and so forth."[9] In writing classes, then, a transdisciplinary analysis of cultural studies works as a teaching strategy precisely because writing, as a critical activity, involves ideas, attitudes, and language practice. Furthermore, to introduce students to the theoretical concepts of rhetoric and semiotics is to invite them to initiate a critique of institutions and structures of power. The shape of the texts studied in composition classrooms can follow the transdisciplinary range of practices in culture that Grossberg, Nelson, and Treichler outline because these are also the situations found in the ugly and ordinary aspects of writing and using language in daily life and in the academy.

It must be noted here that critics often point out that cultural studies approaches to composition sometimes can look like, on paper and in practice, disciplinary courses. And it is a point educators must consider as a serious challenge in our argument to include cultural studies as an important addition to the teaching of writing: When using cultural objects, how does the teacher distinguish between teaching composition and rhetoric and teaching other allied disciplines, such as history, law, linguistics, sociology, anthropology, political science, art, and communications? Even though our objects of inquiry are transdisciplinary, how do writing teachers shape their courses to retain the look and feel of a composition class? These are questions that all of us cultural studies faculty must continue to address in our pedagogical practices, since the simple and naive answer is that all composition teachers must focus on the writing and the rhetoric contained in the cultural material. As Henry Giroux noted in his book *Disturbing Pleasures*, writing is important in cultural studies pedagogies because it "challenge[s] certain dominant assumptions about the meaning of schooling, the discourse of authority, the relationship between language and experience, and the role of social responsibility."[10] It is hoped that with more extensive teacher-talk concerning transdisciplinary and cultural studies methods for writing instruction, our critics' charges will be substantially reduced.

Some critics charge that writing instructors also face a challenge maintaining focused or accessible discussions when enacting cultural studies practices in their classrooms. Some composition teachers who opt for popular topics in the composition class complain that students become easily bored and apathetic. While student boredom and apathy tend to be symptoms of something going awry, the students' signals may not be necessarily related to the topic. The underlying problems that can occur in a cultural-studies-based composition class are several: the students may feel too challenged by the material and their boredom or apathy is a form of resistance to the discussion;

they may decide that cultural-studies information isn't appropriate for college study; they may adopt a "cool pose" in discussions so as not to expose themselves to criticism from their friends. Short of scrapping the topic and selecting a more conventional pedagogy, I recommend trying some options to overcome these problems.

Keeping the class focused on the writing is important for every instructor. When we draw upon pop culture in composition classes, it is very easy for the class to move away from discussions of rhetoric and writing and toward interesting but tangential conversations related to superficial qualities embodied in the cultural artifact. While certainly these tangents can be made into useful rhetorical inquiry—as in examining the audience values in the reception of a music video or cartoon or the questioning of ethical language used in an advertisement—teachers need to guide their students away from trite responses and toward more probing questions. Otherwise what may occur is a seventy-minute discursive tail-chasing session, the outcome of which is that students aren't clear as to what rhetorical or composition criteria the pop objects illustrate. The result of classes that do not forge a relationship between composition and cultural materials is boredom and apathy or—equally bad—student misunderstanding of the class's purpose.

Generally, student misunderstanding of the course's aims arises from precisely this kind of breakdown. Teachers have to direct student commentary toward the relationship between rhetoric and the pop icon or image; otherwise, the discussion spins uncontrollably into an "I like/I don't like" reaction. After several classes where students discuss popular items without focus, it is understandable why many might not be able to articulate what it is they are doing in their writing class. In the upper-division writing classes I've taught, I have heard and read many student descriptions of their previous college writing courses as being filled with "great discussion" about "cool topics," but these students have missed out on what constitutes critically engaged rhetorical practices in a writing course. Instead of these students' experiences with pop culture emancipating their mainstream thinking, their writing reflects an entrenchment of dominant, usually consumerist, views.

These student reactions make sense, though, if the instructor hasn't developed clear instructional aims and goals for the use of cultural material. Writing teachers have to remember that, for the most part, their students' prior school experiences have been lacking in critical analysis. Students may indeed believe they are being critical in their discussions when they state personal preferences, and, as a first pass into critical discussion, the personal-preference perspective works. Without recasting those statements into deeper critique, however, class discussion remains at a trendy, superficial level and replicates the status quo, which is exactly what we're trying to avoid. The guiding process teachers must employ to help students learn how to question cultural material is a mix of what Ira Shor outlines as "patience, experimentation, negotiation, and careful observation of student learning."[11]

The last challenge educators face in bringing cultural studies into the composition classroom is helping our students develop meaningful evaluative criteria. In our professional training, each of us learned how to evaluate the strengths and weaknesses of a literary piece, an argument, or a theory. Moreover, we could test our critiques against well-established disciplinary conventions, based on authority, references, style, genre, and so on. But no clear evaluative criteria exist for pop culture: How does a person compare the merits of a musical group like the Beatles to those of the Fugees or Pearl Jam, for example? The predetermined boundaries we take comfort in to evaluate information are collapsed in ordinary cultural forms; there is no professional governing organization which can rank musicians or their songs. To help our students critique cultural productions, composition teachers have to think about ways of collaboratively generating criteria in their classrooms to encourage student inquiry.

Much of the difficulty in applying criteria in evaluating cultural forms arises from the hybrid, or mixed, quality of pop culture. The hybridization of the popular with elite cultural elements creates a normative implosion. Qualities like "good" and "bad" become outdated, irrelevant terms because so much of what popular items do is shape how individuals and groups recognize themselves and others. We should be aware that in popular messages, individual and group identities are constructed in highly complex ways and often contain conflicting characteristics. Part of thinking critically in public culture, then, is a matter of sorting out the whys and hows of message construction and transmission when there is no obvious answer located in the icon, event, or image. Given this confusion, it is often an arduous task for teachers and students to achieve consensus. Such conflicts produce student resistance, characterized by silence, reliance upon personal taste, or evaluation based on individual—not cultural—values, as well as "cool poses." If the development of criteria to evaluate the cultural material is not established with the students beforehand, the discussion can turn from the interrogation of ideas to the contemplation of personalities, a move that tends to produce self-indulgent discourse in both conversation and writing.

To move students into informed critique, we must learn to accept pedagogical risks. A pedagogical risk for some educators may involve experimenting with media culture or technology as teaching tools. It may mean deploying cultural studies methodologies to improve the quality of the assignments given to students. As the essays in this collection demonstrate, there are numerous places in writing pedagogy where pop culture and cultural studies can enhance the writing curriculum. The next move is for compositionists to consider how they can incorporate these elements successfully into their own courses.

The willingness to take pedagogical risks rests on the critical-dialogic exchange in the cultural-studies-based composition classroom. Writing teachers must acknowledge that our students have expertise and intelligence in a wide variety of areas where we do not. Those areas of expertise may be obscured by the standardized college entrance tests students take to measure their preparedness for post–secondary school education, but they are all the more real and relevant to our students' lives. As a topic for inquiry, pop culture often inverts the traditional professor-student relationship, leveling the playing field so that instructors and students share equal footing in the learning process. Sharing the control for what is learned in the classroom may be an uncomfortable position for some faculty to take, but we all need to recognize that our students can possess authoritative knowledge about a wide variety of cultural practices, from music to local histories. On other issues, our students may be partially informed or not informed at all.

Topics drawn from pop culture can make composition classes matter to students, moving the course beyond the official category of "required course taken" on the graduation checklist. To understand better why this happens, teachers should initially look at their students' precollege learning experiences.

Why Popular Culture Matters in the Composition Class

As Leslie Savan makes clear in *The Sponsored Life*, we are all bombarded by some sixteen thousand media messages per day.[12] Using Savan's statistic as a rough estimate, the average eighteen-year-old entering our college composition classroom on the first day of the term has encountered *over one million media impressions* in his or her lifetime. Undoubtedly, the influence of these messages on our students has great importance for those of us who teach college writing. Students do not come to us as "blank slates" waiting to receive our knowledge; rather, they possess an immense amount of knowledge about lifestyle consumption, sound bites, and popular images. While this internalized public culture clearly has an influence on student writing, it may not be one of the primary causes of the decline of written literacy as many critics argue. Educators and critics like Herbert Kohl, Jonathan Kozol, Stanley Aronowitz, Michael W. Apple, and the Boston Women's Teachers' Group have argued that there are many more important factors affecting students' abilities to read and write than pop culture. Because the problems these educators address aren't as glitzy, sexy, or controversial as topics drawn from pop culture, it is far simpler for some teachers, politicians, and pundits to bash movies, music videos, song lyrics, television programs, and computers as the contributors to the decline of student literacy scores rather than to find solutions to more perplexing socioeconomic problems that vex education, like child poverty, hunger, and corporate downsizing affecting many regions in North America.

As teaching tools, media, technology, and popular culture can serve as a corrective to bring about benefits from the "damage" pop culture is often charged with wreaking in our society. Popular culture is a natural subject for composition because it greatly shapes the way cultural memory is formed, how public and private identities are constructed, and how lifestyle decisions are promoted.

In fact, pop culture can counter what Michael W. Apple calls "official knowledge," the select body of information (political, social, cultural) that holds dominance over other kinds of information and limits and/or constrains how individuals perceive what is reasoned, just, fair, and acceptable within society.[13] Our students overflow with official knowledge. Deploying popular culture as a topic of writing inquiry invites students to interrogate ugly and ordinary objects in order to discover how they subvert and support official knowledge. There is both a resilience and a resistance in common objects that simultaneously attract and repel the audience(s) for which they are intended. Resilience keeps the everyday and conventional elements of the topic in the cultural forefront—even when political and social movements try to squelch them, with no questioning or critiquing of the object and its context. Resistance in objects, in contrast, creates the opportunity for an "oppositional response," whereby individuals situate themselves counter to the surface value(s) of the message. Students need to learn to negotiate both the resilient and the resistant sides of pop culture in their thinking and writing practices, especially since they so powerfully influence our values and our identities.

Most students, after all, construct their views of pop culture based on dominant corporate economics (i.e., "what sells"). This dominant corporate view is what depicts much of pop culture as being trendy and lacking in substance. However, to take an oppositional response to public culture in the composition classroom requires students to suspend their investments in the mainstream messages and to reexamine their positions related to the everyday object(s). As students begin to reposition themselves in relation to these topics through the writing process, an estrangement with the familiar, mainstreamed view of the object occurs and constructs moments of reflection and critique. This repositioning is an important *unlearning* process that helps students move toward critically thinking about the rhetoric and the content of the materials they examine.

As readers will discover in later sections of this anthology, from something as mundane as the lyrics of a rock 'n' roll song or the images offered by a cartoon, a host of critical social issues emerge: censorship, sexuality, economics, race, aesthetics, class. These artifacts have the potential to show students that simple, pat answers often have far more complicated implications for individuals. For example, the freedom of speech Snoop Doggy Dogg enjoys in his rap lyrics may be called into question by female students who feel victimized by the sexual characterizations of women in the music. Students might have to decide whether a person's freedom of speech contains the right to have others feel victimized, or whether the economy of music is such that the scarcity of the "banned" lyrics drive the demand and cost of the music higher. By investigating—and estranging—familiar topics, students can use their knowledge of popular music to interrogate less familiar topics, such as censorship and social equity.

Additionally, while many students tap into pop culture on a regular basis, few, if any, rigorously examine their use of videos, music, television narratives, movies, store catalogs, advertising, or popular fiction. Even more so, students rarely study how culture influences them to participate in the teenage consumerism critiqued by Juliet B. Schor in *The Overworked American*.[14] And, as many of us have found when we teach from cultural topics, it is the rhetorical strategies used in popularized culture that often blind students in their critical decision-making. To reduce this blindness, we must help our students destabilize culturally coded meanings so that they may become critical consumers.

Another significant advantage to a popular culture emphasis is that the author becomes less important, less privileged in the writerly arena. It is not so important to know *who* produced or created a cartoon, an ad, or a song as it is to know *how* the cartoon, ad, or song is being received and rescripted by the audience. Content drawn from pop culture is plural, fluid, and multiple. It is fundamentally rhetorical. Composition in this context becomes actively critique-based because students must learn how to apply criteria they construct in class to evaluate the object and its effects upon society. To focus on the outward effects and influences of pop culture precludes the expressivist approach, which often limits the student to one perspective of many. This reining in of the personal view is quite the opposite of what is often found in students' writing, where the individual's perspective dominates. Furthermore, instead of writing for imaginary or ideal communities of readers (those readers the writer perceives to be most like herself), students begin to address audiences who have some connection to a real image, icon, or event. When readers take on real identities, students become more actively engaged writers.

Drawing upon ugly and ordinary topics moves composition toward the ethnographic, since students attempt to represent the various cultural groups connected to the icon or object studied. But localizing rhetoric and composition in particular pop culture events seems to raise challenges for the student writer that are not necessarily shared with the professional ethnographer: How does the student name who or what is included or excluded in public culture given her limited experience? How does she create the identities which emerge from interacting with things that are ugly and ordinary? What memories are invoked in people across generations who view these ugly and ordinary objects? How does the student writer represent these memories, which are maintained, transformed, and set aside? How does the writer *communicate* her insights? Rhetorical though these questions may be, their answers hold important implications for students and teachers.

So, why does teaching ugly and ordinary topics matter in college composition classrooms? The answer lies in our culture itself. For many of our students, pop culture is displacing traditional text-based material as a source of knowledge. A quick examination of today's typical college composition classroom informs us that most of our students are more televisual and teleliterate than they are print-oriented. Contrary to what some may believe, these students' televisual orientation and teleliteracy are not completely derived from recreational viewing. Increasing numbers of students derive their elementary-

and secondary-school learning from commercial sponsorship and media sound bites implemented through programs such as Channel One and Cable in the Classroom (and now CNN Interactive on the World Wide Web).[15] Moreover, the use of popular video adaptations and comic book versions of canonized literature in junior high and high school courses, such as Franco Zeffirelli's *Romeo and Juliet* and Kenneth Branagh's *Henry V*, and the "classic comics" comic book series, have replaced reading the original works for most of our students. As I have mentioned earlier, the entertainment aspects of these cultural forms often outweigh the historical, political, linguistic, and social importance of the works in the secondary-school curriculum and do much to reinforce the kind of "public pathology" in our students' rhetoric that Giroux argues currently exists in media culture.

While others have debated elsewhere the numerous fiscal and political reasons for the turn to televisual programming in our elementary and secondary schools, college composition instructors face growing challenges teaching writing to a population that is becoming decreasingly print-literate and increasingly teleliterate, if not in some cases highly icon-literate. The question composition instructors face is a perplexing one: How do we teach critical inquiry to students increasingly steeped in powerful, visualized, commercialized readings of the world? A Burkean response to this question might be to practice homeopathy and apply, in small controlled doses, those elements that have created the "illness." In other words, instructors can use pop culture as a "corrective" by injecting controlled doses of it into the intellectual world of the composition classroom.

From Bored Youth to *Border Youth*

The first day of the new academic term is not far off. I can picture the next generation of twenty-two College Composition II students sitting at their desks. At my college, College Composition II is the completion of the first-year writing sequence. It is required by the university for graduation in most departments. The students taking the class range from Advanced Placement newcomers to last-semester seniors. No longer first-semester students, for the most part, the excitement of being at college has worn off long ago. Many are cynical about higher education, partially because of the media reports they take in and partially because they have dealt with college bureaucracy first hand. Others in the room don't want to be in college, but someone somewhere told them that a lack of a college degree means little hope for a decent job. One or two in the class really want to experience intellectual inquiry in their university experience, but these students don't seem to find it in their course work. The students all wait patiently for the time when their degrees are in hand so they can move on with their lives. They are bored youth, bored by the boundaries they assume exist in the learning process, bored by not seeing connections between learning and living in their education, bored because active learning is not like changing the channel selector on the TV in the dorm. Now these students expect me to bore them for sixteen weeks.

I tell them in my introductory comments that College Composition II is our university's rhetoric/argumentation/research course. They groan. I hand out a six-page syllabus for the course. More groaning and some wincing is evident. Yes, there is a text in this class. Several texts, actually. I believe I see tears welling up in some students' eyes. Then we start to discuss the class outline. This term the class is studying the rhetoric of the Internet. Last term, the fall class studied the rhetoric of *The Bell Curve* and the spring class examined ethnography.

"The Internet? Cool."

"I don't know anything about computers. I'll probably break one and have to pay for it."

"Can we check out the sex sites?" Lots of men in the class turned their heads when this line was uttered by a woman sitting in the back of the class.

"I already know this stuff. Do I have to stay here?"

And so the class moved slowly into a state of inquisitiveness. Boredom, for the time being, was set aside for most of the students. The Internet, like *The Bell Curve* and other topics I've used for classes in the past, contains elements of pop culture that cut across various social, political, and intellectual interests. Drawn to the topic because of the media and cultural hype, these students will discover that there are histories, values, politics, and inequities deeply connected to a technological brand of cultural knowledge seldom presented in the official mainstream information outlets. As the students progress through this class, they will find that their own intellectual work in this area does matter, that their writing practices matter, and that boredom in the learning process is grounded in maintaining the rigid borders that we, or others, have set for education. By the end of the term, many of the bored youth who faced me on the first day of class will leave as border youth, individuals who investigate the print-driven literacies of Western culture as well as the visual and electronic literacies of postmodern culture, and who interrogate their experiences in culture and find ways in their writing to give active voice and criticism to their discoveries.

Henry Giroux's recent work in cultural studies points composition instructors toward ways of reaching students intellectually through the use of pop culture. His article "Slacking Off: Border Youth and Postmodern Education," for example, raises an important point for the infusion of cultural studies into composition: The tension inherent in cultural objects "become[s] . . . useful pedagogically when it provides elements of an oppositional discourse for understanding and responding to the changing cultural and educational shift affecting youth in North America."[16] This is, I think, a critical observation. The influence of postmodernism on citizenship and literacy has been to emphasize the diversity and fragmentary quality of voices, experiences, and languages in flux. Postmodernism, for all its liberating qualities, creates chaos in the existing order of things, literacy and higher education notwithstanding. One potential outgrowth of the disruption of a systemic social order like education seems to be a belief that "anything goes" and that no standards exist in the curriculum, a position continually articulated by scholars and pundits opposed to cultural studies and postmodern pedagogies. This criticism is inaccurate and promotes the cynicism and disconnectedness to learning that some of our students possess. As I pointed out earlier in this discussion, "anything" is not useful in a cultural studies pedagogical model, especially for composition. Today's youth are far more savvy to "anything goes" messages through their media consumption than through their traditional educational experiences; a corrective is needed to counter the material-driven foundations of their thoughts—represented by the one-word response "whatever"—in order to encourage critical inquiry. This attitude of "whatever" shared by many of our students isn't something new; it has been building silently for a long period of time. What seems to make these students' attitudes new to us is that the beliefs underlying their positions are so pervasive.

Over the last thirty years, the literacies of North American youth have been indelibly marked by electronic media and advertising. In fact, most of us reading and writing in this anthology have been steeped in media culture. In 1966, for example, the literacies of youth were shaped by television programs like *Star Trek*, which, to the horror of the Grundys throughout the continent, glorified the use of the split infinitive with its classic line, "to boldly go where no man has gone before," and a host of teen magazines that published the lyrics from music produced by the Beatles, the Rolling Stones, and the Doors. In 1996, however, the literacies of youth are shaped not only by mass transmissions from television and radio, but by the electronic media of the computer (World Wide Web and cyberspace, hypertextual books and games, MOOs and MUDs, international and national E-mail, etc.), as well as by the video and film industries. The introduction of even more speed and motion to the elements of visual time and space has further fragmented syntax far beyond Miss or Mr. Grundy's imagination—perhaps even beyond the expectations of cultural theorists like Paul Virilio, Gilles Deleuze, and Felix Guattari, all of whom describe the ways speed, motion, and film fragment language.[17]

The speed and constancy with which our students obtain informational messages indicate shifts in knowledge production and in literacy, as Giroux rightly notes in his article.[18] But rather than claim, as Giroux does, that these students are the "border youth" between "a modernist world of certainty and order, informed by the culture of the West and its technology of print, and a world of hybridized identities, electronic technologies, local cultural practices, and pluralized public spaces,"[19] I tend to think the accelerated volume of information pressed on students in contemporary society has created "bored youth," who quickly grow tired of the influx of messages and who are on a quest for increased mental and emotional stimulation.

We can, however, convert "bored youth" into Giroux's "border youth." The key to doing so is to decelerate temporarily the rate of speed and motion with which the messages enter our students' lives. In those moments of deceleration, educators can provide opportunities for students to learn how to decode the overt and the subtle language used to shape and transmit contemporary cultural knowledge.

A cultural studies curriculum in composition promises to enhance and transform our students' literacies. Intrinsic to such study are questions related to race, gender, the economy, politics, and emotions. As they engage in this inquiry, students interrogate the ways a culture invokes "the popular." The knowledge produced from this inquiry is what E. D. Hirsch has called "cultural literacy," the "translinguistic knowledge on which linguistic literacy depends."[20] But it is here that I want to reclaim the term "cultural literacy" from its infamous connotations. Studying pop culture in the composition classroom demonstrates that cultural literacy need not only be identified with canonical or official knowledge. Contemporary literacy requires all of us to be cognizant beyond a superficial level of the varieties of cultures that comprise our nation and their differing influence upon the values, judgments, logics, and evaluations embedded within popular artifacts. The kind of cultural literacy I am proposing resists standardization by national curricula boards or government legislation, as Hirsch once called for.[21] The cultural literacy I am arguing for is the kind of literacy-as-parking-lot that Robert Venturi discovered for his architectural style: Let's look out upon this vast public space and see the differences that make up its inhabitants. Then let's see what the differences tell us about who these inhabitants are and how they live, work, and think. It is a cultural literacy based on the use of ugly and ordinary topics, rather than the heroic and original ones Hirsch wants, and it requires a pedagogy of writing that dismantles many of our assumptions about how we teach composition and rhetoric.

As writing instructors, we need to help students see that writing is mostly, in the words of Jim W. Corder, an "argument . . . emergen[t] toward the other."[22] As we argue, we engender new views that rewrite master narratives and old, static visions. In their places, we refashion cultural meanings. The numbing messages that now short-circuit the minds of so many youths offer the possibility of becoming the living arguments that will transform those youths into critical, literate, civic-minded participants in our culture. The question that arises is, how do we as composition teachers accomplish this in our classrooms?

What This Book Attempts to Accomplish

In the essays that follow, each author demonstrates possibilities for using popular cultural artifacts as living arguments to transform the ways students make knowledge in the writing classroom. The instructors' accounts of what occurs in their classrooms are more ugly and ordinary than heroic and original, as the writing classroom becomes a site for the examination of self and object in composing rather than a transformation of self through writing.

Following postmodern fashion, there is a pastiche quality to the essays found in this collection. Pastiche encourages a dialogic exchange when cultural studies interacts with composition; it is as if we are standing in the corridor and overhearing snippets of teacher-talk. Some essays in this volume are praxis-driven discussions of classroom activities; others are theoretical in scope and present challenges to the politics of writing and of composition. A few essays contain instructors' personal connections to classroom events and writing assignments. There are several discussions to challenge the discipline's ideas about writing and reading in an increasingly more iconic age. Many authors offer teacher lore, classroom activities, and readings for those instructors who want to begin using popular cultural topics in their classes but don't know where to begin. What unifies these essays, though, is that each asks us to think about what it means to teach writing from a cultural studies perspective.

This anthology is designed to open a dialogue about the ways composition teachers can help their students develop critical thinking skills in a time when students' literacy skills are perceived to be declining. Part theory, part lore, the discussions in this collection reflect a movement to a genre of teacher-talk we might call "theory-lore," in which newly trained composition instructors move beyond simple anecdotal talk of classroom practices to more theoretically informed ideas about how those classroom incidents affect student writing and the production of knowledge. Theory-lore offers one possibility for responding to the genuine and interesting problems that occur in the classroom as students engage ideas and images that lie outside the borders of the traditional pedagogical beliefs many teachers hold about writing. Theory-lore as teacher-talk also helps us connect our discussions of the teaching of writing to a cultural studies emphasis because it rigorously interrogates practice through a theoretical lens, articulating how the analysis of practice informs us of our own language and motives. In sum, theory-lore opens a kind of dialogue that privileges neither theoretical nor practical approaches to the teaching of writing; rather, it assumes that both have an important, and mutual, effect on what teachers do in their classrooms when the doors close and the lessons begin.

Notes

1. Miss Grundy is used here as a representation drawn from popular culture and not as a sexist reference to women teaching college writing. I acknowledge that there are as many, if not more, *Mr.* Grundys working in composition as there are Miss Grundys. In the teaching of writing, Grundyish behavior is certainly not gender specific. Therefore, in future references to Miss Grundy, I have also added "Mr."

2. Robert Venturi, Denise Scott Brown, and Steven Izenour, *Learning from Las Vegas.* Rev. ed. (Cambridge, Mass.: MIT Press, 1977), 6.

3. Ibid., 8

4. Henry A. Giroux, *Fugitive Cultures: Race, Violence and Youth* (New York: Routledge, 1996), 83.

5. Ira Shor, *Empowering Education: Critical Teaching for Social Change* (Chicago: University of Chicago Press, 1992), 72.

6. Giroux, *Fugitive Cultures*, 194.

7. *Politically correct*, as my students generally use the phrase, is an abstract shorthand for decorum in mainstream college-level discourse. It is often used by my students to dismiss or resist any topics that they feel challenge the values taught to them by family, friends, religious outlets, or the media. I find that students who use the "PC yell" most frequently are those who see a four-year college education and its subsequent degree as an "instrument" (to borrow a term from Ira Shor) for turning economic profit later in their lives. For these students, college is understood as a tool for future earning potential rather than as an intellectual investment. A more detailed discussion of students viewing higher education as an "instrument" can be found in Shor's *Empowering Education*, 72–84.

8. Shor, 73.

9. Lawrence Grossberg, Cary Nelson, and Paula Treichler, eds., introduction to *Cultural Studies* (New York: Routledge, 1992), 5.

10. Henry A. Giroux, *Disturbing Pleasures: Learning Popular Culture* (New York: Routledge, 1994), 133.

11. Shor, 73.

12. Leslie Savan, *The Sponsored Life: Ads, TV, and American Culture* (Philadelphia: Temple University Press, 1995), 1.

13. Michael W. Apple, *Official Knowledge: Democratic Education in a Conservative Age* (New York: Routledge, 1993), 59.

14. Juliet B. Schor, *The Overworked American* (New York: Harper Collins, 1994), 25–27.

15. As evidence of the depth and breadth of the influence of television-in-the-classroom on our future students, let me point to a recent article by Marianne Manilov, "Channel One, Joe Camel, Potato Chips, and ABC: Meet the Largest Corporations Taking Over the Classroom with Commercials" (EXTRA! July/August 1996, 18–19). In her article, Manilov outlines the major players in the commercialization of American schoolrooms. The big corporate player besides ABC/Disney Television is Kohlberg Kravis Roberts & Co (KKR), the leveraged buyout wizards of the late 1980s. According to Manilov, KKR maintains a subsidiary, K-III Communications, that owns the properties Classroom Channel, Films for the Humanities and Sciences, Macmillan Early Science Program, and the Katharine Gibbs Schools. K-III Communications purchased Channel One from Whittle Communications in 1994. Under K-III, Channel One now boasts of a "captive audience" of *eight million* students a day, a site on the World Wide Web (with countless numbers of hits), and advertisers like McDonald's, M&M/Mars, Pepsi, and Reebok vying for classroom attention. Perhaps what is most ironic about K-III's influence in the classroom is that its major investors, according to Manilov, "are teacher pension funds and educational institutions—like the State of Oregon [teacher] retirement fund, the State of Washington investment board and the Massachusetts Institute of Technology." It seems as though the common phrase bandied about in mainstream reports on education, "education's investment in our youth," car-

ries a double meaning. For more analysis on the influence of Channel One on American youth, see the special issue of *EXTRA!* (May/June 1997) devoted to the lessons Channel One teaches.

16. Henry A. Giroux, "Slacking Off: Border Youth and Postmodern Education," *Journal of Advanced Composition* (Spring 1996: on-line version). Ellipses mine.

17. See Paul Virilio's *Speed and Politics* and *The Lost Dimension* (New York: Semiotext(e), 1977 and 1991, respectively) and Gilles Deleuze and Felix Guattari's *Cinema One* and *Cinema Two* (Minneapolis: University of Minnesota Press, 1984 and 1992, respectively) for discussions related to how the introduction of speed and motion have constructed fragmented grammar and syntax in film and discourse.

18. Giroux, "Slacking Off."

19. Ibid.

20. E. D. Hirsch, Jr., "Cultural Literacy" in Theresa Enos and Stuart C. Brown, *Professing the New Rhetorics: A Sourcebook* (Boston: Blair Press, 1994), 370.

21. Ibid., 372.

22. Jim W. Corder, "Argument as Emergence, Rhetoric as Love" in Enos and Brown, 423. Ellipses and brackets mine.

2

Meaning Is Cool
Political Engagement and the Student Writer

David M. Weed

> Beavis: This video's got, like, words and stuff in it.
> Butt-head: Words suck. If I wanted to read, I'd go to college.
> Mike Judge, *Beavis and Butt-head*

Students discussing Beavis and Butt-head in my classes generally begin by expressing contempt for much of what its eponymous heroes represent. The pair can readily be classified as dysfunctional, brutal, and unkempt: their physical ugliness reflects their social ugliness, a side of suburban America that its residents hesitate to recognize because something may be inadvertently set on fire.[1] Some of the upper-middle-class students at the institution where I have taught *Beavis and Butt-head* initially dismiss the cartoon as nothing more than humorless, juvenile programming; I allow them to voice their criticisms before leading the discussion toward Beavis and Butt-head's running commentary on the music videos that they incessantly watch. Invariably, at least one student understands that Beavis and Butt-head, despite their personal shortcomings, are perceptive critics of a medium that targets him and others in his age group as its principal audience. After all, the duo's problems derive largely from their attempts to translate the MTV ethic of sexism and violence—the things that they think are cool—into the larger world. Their functional illiteracy, however, is matched by the very particular literacy they bring to readings of White Zombie and Madonna. As generic parallels to televised tag-team film critics such as Gene Siskel and Roger Ebert, Beavis and Butt-head rule the couch in the same way that their counterparts control films' fates from the balcony.

I use *Beavis and Butt-head* here and in my classes as a touchstone for my principal method of teaching composition; in my courses, I focus on popular culture as a means of developing students' literacy about the effects of culture on social personality. This kind of investigation makes students more incisive writers and, equally important, more astute citizens. I suggest in this essay that the notion of citizenship has been neglected in American colleges because of the historical relationship between social classes and the university system. In the name of familiarizing students with the great works of Western civilization, colleges and universities have disdained teaching students to interpret meaning in ways that allow them to understand that they have an immediate political stake in representation. This issue is critical because composition students differ in one important respect from Beavis and Butt-head: in large measure, students attend college in order to learn to work with words and with meaning. Of course, one of the ironies of Mike Judge's cartoon is that, although Butt-head pronounces that words suck, he and Beavis continually manipulate the words and meanings transmitted into their living room (especially when they resonate sexually). Student writers, I suggest, generally possess a similar latent facility with popular culture. From the moment that Big Bird, for instance, introduces them as children to the letter *a* on *Sesame Street*, students begin developing a literacy about popular culture that may be deepened and refined in a composition course so that they can perceive the way that representation shapes culture and influences their lives.

The legitimacy of employing popular culture in the college classroom becomes an issue only in the contexts of the history of English studies (of which composition is traditionally considered a province), the goals of the traditional liberal arts curriculum in American postsecondary institutions, and the political agenda of conservative thinkers. The practice of reading the classics literature and "Great Books" in English courses (a process that often begins, in fact, by connecting writing to reading in lower-level "composition and literature" courses) suits the conservative agenda well. Lynne Cheney, chairman of the National Endowment for the Humanities during the Reagan and Bush administrations, asserts that the great works of Western literature constitute an apolitical, objective, and universal representation of truth.[2] Cheney attempts in particular to show that, because the great works are universally true, they demonstrate the excellence of Western civilization, especially as it is manifested in the United States. She defends this elitist and nationalistic reading of Western civilization against the postmodern "radical relativism"[3] of contemporary scholars, whose understandings of the connection between politics and culture she deems subversive. Although Cheney never explains precisely what she means by the term "Western civilization," she claims that French philosopher Michel Foucault's work, for instance, constitutes "nothing less than an assault" on it.[4] She makes Western civilization and truth equally vague, insubstantial categories that radical "ideology" somehow threatens to extinguish.

Cheney primarily invokes Western civilization in order to deny that the humanist tradition is anything less than egalitarian: its "truths pass beyond time and circumstance . . . transcending accidents of race, class, and gender."[5] In this formulation of Western civilization as the secular equivalent of a mystical religious experience, however, Cheney conveniently ignores the way that discourses such as truth and objectivity operate politically, particularly in the service of upper- and middle-class interests. In connection with the university, these discourses provide professors with access to objective truth, which students may not refute because it is objectively true. Thus, tautology becomes a rhetorical means of stifling opposition. The traditional mission of the American university's liberal arts curriculum, then, is to instruct the upper-class, the middle-class, and the upwardly mobile (who prove their worth in part by their acknowledgment of the truth of the discourse of truth) in the knowledge that signals their membership in the dominant classes. In composition courses that use literature as a basis for writing, for instance, professors transmit a set of shared cultural experiences and vocabularies, which in turn permit the college-educated to recognize themselves and their economic peers as socially superior. William Shakespeare's *Romeo and Juliet*, then, accumulates an exchange value among those who are familiar with it, differentiating them from members of the working and lower classes, who are culturally marginalized because they have not studied Shakespeare's timeless message. The furor that emerges when *Beavis and Butt-head* supplants *Romeo and Juliet* on the syllabus derives in part from the challenge that popular culture presents to the upper- and middle-class investment in the university's liberal arts curriculum.

Popular culture disrupts the ideological "class work" that the literary text traditionally performs. Attempts to dismiss popular culture as trendy or to vilify it as part of a radical subversion of principles of objectivity mask institutional and cultural fears that the conglomerate of Western tradition will be exposed as a position crucial to the legitimation of powerful class interests rather than as truth. Indeed, popular culture's value in the composition classroom lies precisely in its capacity to clarify the way that words and meaning, in the texts that students read and the texts that they write, emanate from their authors' positions, which involve the "accidents" of race, class, and gender, as well as, among other things, their relationship to truth and to Western civilization.

Cheney fails to recognize, for example, that the attack on the humanist tradition involves more than a question of whether the great works themselves are transcendent and universal: it also asks who has access to, and who benefits from, discourses such as truth. Indeed, the value of "radical relativism," including the study of popular culture in writing classes, lies precisely in its sharp concentration on the specific circumstances that give rise to a text rather than on broad "universal" themes. Especially in composition, students benefit from understanding that each text emerges from its author's position in time and culture. No writer, and thus no text, is objective. That is an important lesson for writing students to learn about the works they read and, equally important, the papers they write. Meaning issues from a writer's particular circumstances. If the principal goal of composition is to teach students to argue—a process of recognizing, refuting, and defending positions—then merely assuring students that the truth of Western civilization underpins their writing is less productive than directing them toward an understanding of their location in a dialogue between competing interests and discourses.

Of course, literary works may—and should, I think—also be taught as examples of arguments rooted in politics and in history, which in many cases influence us in the present. To divorce Samuel Richardson's *Pamela* (1740) from the shifting discourses of class and gender in eighteenth-century England, for instance, strips it of much of its value. To teach *Pamela*, however, involves familiarizing students with emerging eighteenth-century notions about men's and women's natures, and with relations between the English aristocracy, gentry, and servant class. The advantage of using contemporary popular culture (which was, of course, the status of Shakespeare's and Richardson's works when they were written) lies precisely in its immediacy: students rapidly interpret the discourses that influence representations in contemporary popular culture because they already are familiar with the codes embedded in these works and the positions that their authors occupy. Contemporary popular culture heightens students' awareness of the way that all representation involves argument.

In my composition courses, therefore, I stress the ability to discern the arguments implicit in popular culture texts. Science fiction, for example, provides a useful lens for examining the way that contemporary culture projects itself into the cosmos. Inhabitants of other planets are never merely aliens; instead, they express immediate social concerns. The abundance of alien life forms in the *Star Wars* trilogy, for instance, gives students ample material for writing and discussion. The films work well in part because almost every student has seen them, and some have seen the films several times. Even students who have watched the trilogy repeatedly, however, have not necessarily investigated the reasons for its appeal. Once students—especially the men, who are eager to work with one of their favorite productions—begin to see that the trilogy's representations of masculinity in particular address them as a late-twentieth-century audience, they find new territory to chart in a galaxy that they imagined to be thoroughly familiar. In classroom discussions, I help students to refine their understanding of *Star Wars* as simply "good versus evil" by examining the particulars of "good" and "evil" masculinity. Building on a common understanding of the Empire as a militaristic organization reminiscent of German fascism, we investigate the film's deployment of the faceless male figure encased in armor—especially Darth Vader and the ranks of storm troopers—whose evil is represented as a loss of social personality in their subservience to the state. Good masculinity, on the other hand, permits a splendid variety of personality (C-3PO's metallic, overcivilized delicacy and Chewbacca's hairy savagery make the extremes) working together in a democratic common cause.

The most readily available and widely disseminated popular culture texts often work best in the classroom, then, because students are already prepared to engage in the specific concerns that are a hallmark of good writing. In order to make this kind of composition class work, the instructor needs only to realized that she and her students are involved in the same project of reading and analyzing a culture that depends heavily on media to give it coherence and meaning. After almost fifty years, for instance, television has produced enough images that important changes in American culture can be traced through individual series. Returning to science fiction for an example, the ships' crews in the various incarnations of *Star Trek* reflect shifts in American capitalism's relationship with the rest of the world between the mid and late twentieth century. As models of corporate leadership, for example, Captain Jean-Luc Picard's managerial presence in the 1980s series *Star Trek: The Next Generation*, differs from James T. Kirk's entrepreneurial spirit in the original series from the 1960s.[6] Instead of promoting transhistorical categories such as truth, then, through which students are tacitly induced to defend the civilization in which they occupy (or are attempting to occupy) a privileged position, I ask students to locate and to evaluate the competing forces of power and production that texts communicate.

A classroom analysis of *Star Trek* in particular suggests the fruitfulness of investigating the role of capitalist organization in the dissemination of contemporary culture. Students generally already understand the critical role of wealth and money in our society, which provides a basis for developing their sense of the connection between capitalism and representation. The emergence of college football and basketball as multimillion-dollar enterprises, for instance, raises questions about whether an education and the slim possibility of a professional sports career constitute just compensation for the surplus value that the student athlete's labor creates for the university, for the communications industry, and for advertisers. Engaging students in the politics of popular culture, then, embroils them in problems that are not easily resolved and that cannot, certainly, be reduced to the matter of the truth of Western civilization. The liberal arts curriculum in general and the writing class in particular function best as educators (rather than as reproducers of class divisions) when they ask students to probe and to elucidate positions in association with the politics of culture: teaching students to advocate and to exalt Western civilization, a practice in which students are directed unwittingly to include themselves in "our" history and "our" traditions, serves primarily to persuade them that their role consists of participating in and obeying tradition.

I encourage students to distance themselves from the cultural representations that they investigate, not to deceive them into thinking that distance equates with objectivity, but in order to help them discover the way that cul-

ture situates both producers and audiences in systems of meaning. This dual-
ity—a question of maintaining a critical distance when one is unavoidably
also part of the culture—informs one of my student's essays, which was written soon after Nirvana lead singer Kurt Cobain committed suicide in 1994.
Mike Magnuson's "Ripped Jeans, White Blood Cells, and Capitalism" con-
nects Cobain's life and the manner of his death to capitalism's dominant position in the production and dissemination of American culture. Magnuson
argues that the relationship between capitalism and the individual is fraught
because capitalist organizations such as the fashion industry and the music
industry "take meaningful expression and twist it until it no longer has meaning. It instead has commercial value."[7] Anticapitalist, counterculture symbols
such as the flannel shirts and ripped jeans worn by Cobain and other "grunge"
frontmen such as Pearl Jam's Eddie Vedder, for instance, shift from being
expressions of "apathy, if not violent rage, towards commercial fashion" on
the bodies of the artists to commercial items purchased by "teenage mall rats
who [have] no idea what ripped jeans [are] all about."[8] The fashion industry
translates the clothing worn by "struggling musicians forced to buy second
hand" into "designer grunge" available at hefty prices: "The same shirt that
Kurt Cobain bought for two dollars at the Salvation Army was now available
at The Gap for $50. What was borne of financial necessity was transformed
into a mainstream trend by the same capitalist machine that brought Nirvana
to suburbia."[9]

Magnuson contradicts the media accounts that attributed Cobain's suicide
to drug use and to personal difficulties by insisting that Cobain died because
he could not reconcile himself to a capitalist structure that made him a mil-
lionaire and a pop icon at the same time that it distorted and trivialized his
meaning. The music industry in particular, Magnuson recognizes, has a history of absorbing counterculture threats—jazz, rock 'n' roll, punk, and rap—
in order to neutralize them. Magnuson argues that Cobain was not willing to
be a spokesman for white, middle-class members of Generation X who rebel
superficially against corporate America while they value material possessions
even more than the baby boomers before them. Cobain, he writes, was never
speaking for Generation X: "If anything he was speaking to it. He was speaking against it. As Nirvana's popularity grew, the same people that . . . Cobain
wanted to kill in high school were now Nirvana 'fans.' He hated these people
for what they were—part of the system."[10] Magnuson ultimately suggests that
the Cobain created by the culture industry became so representative of all that
he disdained that he could no longer live the lie. Cobain writes in the lyrics to
"Dumb" that "I'm not like them, but I can pretend,"[11] but eventually, Magnuson claims, he could no longer pretend: "The real Kurt Cobain no longer mat-
tered, so he was out of his own control. Despite his efforts not to be like
'them,' he was pretending to be like 'them' simply by living."[12]

Magnuson's investigation of the relationship between capitalism and the
individual talent shows one way that composition courses organized around

popular culture can develop students' awareness that the cultural representations permeating their lives are not innocent and without consequences. Meaning shapes them, and can involve matters as critical as life and death. As a method for teaching composition, popular culture provides a bridge to the generally more distant historical concerns of the English classroom and to the rest of the liberal arts curriculum by encouraging students to see themselves as active participants in cultural issues rather than as passive recipients of truth and tradition. The virtue of employing popular culture figures such as Beavis, Butt-head, Captain Kirk, or Kurt Cobain, therefore, lies in their capacity to make students more thoughtful citizens. To rejuvenate the notion of citizenship for postmodernity, I think, involves arguing for the idea that individuals have a stake in culture and a responsibility to understand its social and political implications. The kind of analytical, critical voice that Lynne Cheney deems subversive in writers like Foucault I foster in students so that they learn to discern and to evaluate the meanings embedded in culture instead of simply taking their place among an oligarchy of the degreed.

Meaning, and the student's place in structures of meaning, becomes not only cool but also valuable to a university that needs to reconsider its mission if its goals are indeed the promotion of a democratic and egalitarian society. That mission begins in places like writing classrooms, which can challenge students to think about their relationship to complex systems of meaning instead of repeating the truth. The category of truth, finally, is not inherently corrupt, but it becomes dangerous when distorted into a secular religion based on a blind faith in Western civilization. Then it becomes a perversion, useful as a tool of indoctrination rather than education, compelling students to believe that adherence to tradition makes their privileged position an unequivocal right.

Notes

1. In separate 1993 incidents in Ohio, Beavis and Butt-head's antics with fire in early episodes were blamed for provoking children to start blazes in their homes. In August, two sisters burned their room with matches and an aerosol spray can, and in October, a five-year-old boy playing with matches destroyed his family's mobile home in a fire that killed his younger sister.

2. Lynne V. Cheney, *Telling the Truth: Why Our Culture and Our Country Have Stopped Making Sense—and What We Can Do About It* (New York: Simon and Schuster, 1995).

3. Ibid., 17.

4. Ibid., 91.

5. Ibid., 14.

6. The 1990s production of *Star Trek: Voyager* focuses on a crew lost in a hostile, faction-ridden quadrant of the galaxy. I think the show suggests concerns about America's role (especially as a "peacekeeper") in distant parts of the world, such as Bosnia and

the Middle East. Much of the publicity about *Voyager* revolved around the fact that the captain was a woman. The show's producers battled parent company Paramount over the gender of Voyager's captain and won, finally casting as Captain Kathryn Janeway actress Kate Mulgrew, whose physical and vocal resemblance to Katharine Hepburn suggests that the woman in command is as forceful and commanding as the renowned film actress. I also understand, however, that the show's weak ratings in its first season are being blamed on the casting of a female captain.

7. Mike Magnuson, "Ripped Jeans, White Blood Cells, and Capitalism: Nirvana and the Defense Mechanisms of Mass Culture." Unpublished essay, 1994.

8. Ibid.

9. Ibid.

10. Ibid.

11. Kurt Cobain, "Dumb,"on *Nirvana*, Geffen Records, 1992.

12. Magnuson, unpublished essay.

3

Expatriating Students
from Their Television Homelands
The Defamiliarization
of Pop Culture

Sanford Tweedie

*This instrument can teach, it can illuminate, yes, and it can even
inspire. But it can do so only to the extent that humans are
determined to use it to those ends. Otherwise it is merely lights and
wires in a box.*
— Edward R. Murrow on television, 1958

*Let us never cease from thinking—what is this "civilization" in
which we find ourselves? What are these ceremonies and why should
we take part in them?*
— Virginia Woolf[1]

Several years ago, I taught writing and American culture at Justus Liebig
University in Giessen, Germany. Self-exiled, I caught up on many books I had
long intended to read. One was John Irving's novel *A Prayer for Owen Meany*.
In what I find one of the most insightful and, at the time, personally relevant
statements, Irving emphatically asserts,

> Every American should be forced to live outside the United States for a year
> or two. Americans should be forced to see how *ridiculous* they appear to the
> rest of the world! They should listen to someone else's version of them-

selves—to *anyone else's* version! Every country knows more about America than Americans know about themselves! And Americans know absolutely *nothing* about any other country![2]

Since first reading this, I have agreed with Irving's charge. He articulates what was for me one reason among many why I ventured to Europe for my two-year teaching stint. I wanted to see the U.S. from a perspective other than the one offered by living here. I wanted to see the U.S. through the eyes of the Other.

But how can I get my students to make a similar move—not physically, to another country, but mentally, to seeing American culture from the perspective of a foreigner, an outsider? The obvious answer—obvious for this book—is through the examination of popular culture. We teachers who use pop culture want our students to develop distance, to be critics, not simply consumers. We want them to become more like us, to develop more sophisticated viewpoints, to reach an epiphany and see that, while pop culture is "popular," it is not necessarily what we consider "cultural." Certainly, these are worthy ambitions. However, it is not enough to simply deliver pop culture to the classroom and expect, because students know it well, that their writing will therefore be successful. Consider the following example.

When I asked a former student who stopped by my office about his current writing course, he showed me an assignment with which he was struggling. Ostensibly, the assignment concerns the impact of pop culture on moral decision-making. Students read a text, apparently about the ill effects television viewing has on children. Then they are asked to address the following issue:

> The article "Glued to the Tube" discusses the controversy over television programming. What can parents do to counteract the dangerous effects of television on children?

This appears a straightforward assignment: pop culture and family values all wrapped up in one, a connection often drawn in the current political climate.

But the question is a loaded one. Potential responses are limited. Either because of the instructor's personal beliefs and/or something stated in the article, the assignment requires the student to accept that television viewing has "dangerous effects" on children. Given the assignment's phrasing, how could the student not respond along the lines of: "We need to better control what our kids are viewing. When I become a parent, I will be sure to monitor the shows my kids watch, never use the television as a baby-sitter, and write complaint letters to all those companies who advertise on shows I find morally repugnant"?

While students who attempt to project themselves into the scenario presented may meet with limited success, most at our college—traditional students, age-wise—are likely to find even playing the role of parent quite difficult. Few are parents, and thus they will have trouble adopting a parental mind-set. A significant minority will never have children, for various reasons, and may have no predilection to envision themselves as parents. Furthermore, many students—who have recently moved out of their parents' home or, worse in their view, live at home while working and going to school—are still coming to terms with their independence vis-à-vis their parents. In other words, the student is to write a paper arguing "parents should . . ." while being situationally disinclined to think like a parent. Further, students may see themselves as still aligned with the television-watching children about whom the article and assignment speak, and for whom television is seen as dangerous. Thus, the assignment requires not only a censuring of television but, in so doing, of the students' past experiences and evolving identities, as well.

Because the writer is only allowed to rehearse future societal roles within the confines of a desired response and must first buy into the dangers of television in order to evaluate the medium, this assignment, and others like it, often fails to overcome the students' inability to look critically at culture. Students find it easier to assimilate the teacher's perspective, rather than attempt to rearticulate the terms of the assignment. This leads to writing that will likely not be engaging. The assignment will remain, for most students, an academic exercise. It certainly does not permit the perceptual reconsideration of society that Irving calls for.

Instead, our assignments should postulate the writing situation as an opportunity for students to envision themselves and their subject matter in ways they have not previously considered. To promote such repositioning requires the instructor's careful consideration, for our assignments not only enable but also limit students' perceptions and abilities to write about themselves and their realities. Intended or not, our assignments authorize particular student worldviews. One method for allowing students a role in constructing the worldview of their writing involves introducing cultural studies via informal ethnographic research, in which students record, describe, and reflect on an aspect of society so culturally pervasive as to be critically invisible. In doing so, students will find themselves, as anthropologist James Clifford says of postmodern ethnography, making "the familiar strange, the exotic quotidian."[3] In his introduction to a collection of essays marking ethnography's shift from scientific to literary phenomenon, Clifford describes the ways in which writing about cultural objects invests them with meaning created by the writer. For the remainder of this discussion, I will focus on an assignment that again uses television but draws students' attention to it as a cultural object which is impacted by their writing about it. Further, I use my own situation to compel students to "listen to someone else's version of themselves." I have never owned a television. My students, not surprisingly, find this peculiar and indeed downright "foreign." As I explain my perspective as a non-television-viewer to my television-watching students and respond to their attitudes toward television, I disrupt their acculturated acceptance of this icon.

I prompt this repositioning by first asking students to focus on what it means to have, rather than not to have, a television. For a week, they keep a journal of their own viewing habits. This exercise gives them a basis to judge television's role in their lives in two ways. First, students can compare their actual viewing time to that of classmates. Second, because I ask them to record their reason for seeing each program (weekly or daily habit, out of boredom, because others were watching it, etc.), they increase their awareness of why they watch television. Next, students read and write a reaction to an article concerning how inhabitants of a remote mountain community dealt with the introduction of satellite dishes, expanding their viewing options from three or four part-time stations to seventy-seven channels.[4] I then provide the students with a questionnaire concerning their perceptions of television and the role it has played in their lives. Based on the journal and responses to the reading and questionnaire, we have a far-ranging class discussion on television and its impact on individuals and families. For students, the culture of television becomes "a newly problematic object of description and critique."[5] Simply by studying the television in ways they had not previously, students become aware of its role in their lives and begin to question, without direct prompting, its worth. While the writing assignment I eventually give does not ask for an ethnographic study per se, it does incorporate this ethnographic "research" concerning television.

When it is time to begin the larger assignment, I hand out a sheet explaining my situation. This description further articulates my role as a foreigner in the eyes of students. While I watched a lot of television as a child, its importance diminished during my adult years. The televisions I did watch belonged either to my parents or to the roommates with whom I shared an apartment. When I lived in Germany, I all but quit watching. Coincidentally, soon after I returned to the U.S. and met the woman I would marry, her television was stolen during a burglary. She did not replace it. Like me, she has no great desire to buy one. Neither of us is anti-television, nor are we pro-television: we simply do not miss it enough to purchase a new one. By refusing to do so, we realize that we are, in a sense, out of touch with an integral facet of American culture.

But we are faced with a dilemma. My wife's daughter—my stepdaughter—who was seven years old when I first gave this assignment, enjoys television and sometimes wishes we had one. Her friends are at the age where they occasionally discuss what they have seen on TV. We expect that these TV-based conversations will only become more frequent. Thus, my wife and I wonder if we aren't being too drastic in our approach, if we aren't depriving her of some sort of cultural literacy necessary to be a full participant in society, if we are doing our daughter wrong by not buying a television and monitoring her viewing time.

My assignment explains these concerns and our lack of resolution. I then ask the students to write me a letter in which they either support my position or argue for my buying a television. As I tell my students, I am sincerely interested in hearing their reasoning. My wife and I often feel torn over this issue. Even we would like to watch a movie on occasion! Regardless of which position they claim, however, students must—implicitly or explicitly—critique their own television viewing habits. They must, in an Irvingesque flight of imagination, envision what it means to live without a staple of American culture, and with an ethnographer's eye, they must assess television's significance as a cultural object. Television understood ethnographically requires more than simple observation; it demands that the ethnographer actively concern him/herself with "contexts of power, resistance, institutional constraint, and innovation."[6] In the case of this assignment, given to students in the lower level of our college's two-course basic writing sequence, the issues that arose included obligations within families, social expectations, and the possible multiple uses of television.

Many students argue for my family's maintaining its current situation while many others argue, equally adamantly and persuasively, for our purchasing a television. Below, I provide an example of each position that I find convincing in its own right. The papers were, in my estimation, the strongest work produced by each student during the semester. This is not to say that *every* student produced his/her best writing for this assignment. Instead, I offer these essays as representative of students who were able to improve their writing because of the assignment, not in spite of it. I begin with the opening paragraphs of each (reproduced exactly from student papers). Jenn's paper opens:

> Dear Mr. Tweedie,
>
> Hello, How are you? I am writing in regards of the importance of owning a television set for your family. Purchasing a television set for your daughter, Tara, should be on the very top of your Christmas List. Not only will Tara will love her new gift, but it will serve as an educational experience as well as for entertainment purposes for the whole family.

Amy's paper begins:

> Dear Professor Tweedie,
>
> A television set is just one way of getting information about what is going on around the world. I believe that your seven-year-old daughter, Tara, is not being deprived by not having a television set. Having your television set stolen two years ago maybe the best thing that could have ever happened to your child.

I ask for this assignment to be written as a letter for several important reasons. By using the epistolary form, students are writing for a specific audience. Although written to me, the teacher, I have become, through the circumstances created by the assignment, interested, rather than the usual dispassionate observer and evaluator. Not only the writer, but also the reader, has a stake in the cultural meaning the text creates. The academic paradox of having students imagine an audience while still, in reality, writing for a teacher is circumvented. Both Jenn and Amy bring an engagement to the page that they might not have felt had they begun by writing to an indeterminate, generalized, "academic" audience. Like the diary form, the epistolary form frees people to speak in ways not generically feasible otherwise, allowing for intimacy and revelation students do not see as possible in the academic essay genre.

This specificity extends to the context of the assignment itself. Because of the level of detail provided in the assignment and because of their knowledge of me through class contact, students are not required to create a hypothetical scenario, as in the assignment discussed earlier, but can instead respond to my circumstances. For example, Jenn emphasizes the situation's immediacy by pressuring me to buy a television in time for the then-upcoming Christmas holiday. Not only does she argue from the child's perspective of how special receiving a television on Christmas morning would be, she also plays on my guilt as a parent who could make my child very happy with this gift. In essence, Jenn has entered a dialogue with me, demonstrating her ability to visualize the audience to whom and circumstances within which she writes.

Despite this unconventional academic form, rhetorically each introduction provides a thesis statement declaring the writer's position in relation to the question—should my family purchase a television?—and focusing on the effects such a decision will have on our daughter, Tara. Each then goes on to offer support for the claim. These papers, then, maintain some of the traditional apparatuses of academic writing. Despite the syntactical errors/irregularities present in the introductions and throughout the papers, each writer produces carefully considered and convincing arguments for why my family should or should not buy a television.

When taken together, Jenn's and Amy's papers clearly demonstrate how through ethnography, one "see[s] culture as composed of seriously contested codes and representations."[7] Jenn underscores the potential benefits of owning a television. In the paragraph quoted below, she not only demonstrates that a television brings into one's living room things that could not otherwise be experienced, but she also shows how her example, watching the Cirque du Soleil, served her academically:

> TV lets you experience everyday or special situations that you would not
> have the chance to otherwise. For example, there was a special on HBO, a
> cable channel which featured, "Cirque DE Soliel", a circus which is very
> famous around the world for it's unique performances. Through TV I got to
> watch it even though it was being performed in Canada. This took place two
> years ago, but since I was so impressed by their performances, I had a good
> base to do a presentation for my dance class on this particular circus. If it was
> not for the TV I would not have been able to have watched it, and not gotten
> an A+ on the presentation.

Jenn's paper's effectiveness is further increased because she again writes to the actual audience of her professor, whom she knows will value such direct applications to college work. She refines her argument in the later paragraphs, emphasizing the control one can and should exert over the television. As long as television's use as a recreational device is kept in perspective, Jenn asserts, my family will understand the values and limitations of this medium.

Amy draws upon personal experience to a greater degree than does Jenn. She clearly laments a childhood spent addicted to television and discusses the potential benefits of growing up without it. Amy also argues, convincingly, that were my family to own only one television, we might find it divisive. She demonstrates through her experience that when people want to watch different shows, having one television can cause arguments and resentment among family members. Amy also imagines possible implications of not owning a television and advises that we ignore a sort of societal peer pressure encountered by those who don't own televisions.

Such acumen could not have resulted from the original assignment on television presented earlier in this discussion. We see in Jenn and Amy's work the ways in which "the writing of cultural descriptions is properly experimental and ethical."[8] Their writing is experimental in that they have been asked to investigate their attitudes about television, then apply these findings to my own situation; they have been asked to write a reasoned, academic argument in the form of a letter; they have been asked to play a role in a professor's decisions about his personal life. And the writing is ethical in a way that the first assignment presented did not permit. Instead of assuming a predetermined position, these writers were able to delineate their own values, then use them as a basis to persuasively alter my value system. The personal stake students find in this assignment can be seen when, two years later, I run into one of these former students and am asked, "Did you get that TV yet?"

In closing, I wish to return to an Irving-like critique of Americans. In the United States, when a plane lands, everyone sits quietly, staring out the window. A few recalcitrant folks will stand up and reach for the overhead compartment despite the flight attendant's procedural admonishments not to. In Europe, when a plane's wheels hit the ground, the passengers erupt in a loud cheer. They applaud for the pilots, for the crew, for the airplane, for the whole assemblage of humans and machinery that has brought them to their destination intact. Europeans do not assume that the safe arrival of their plane is a birthright, but instead the result of carefully constructed planning and execution. Through their display of gratitude, they show a realization that their circumstances are controlled by others. My assignment attempts to produce a similar denaturalizing of television for students. No, I don't mean that I want my students to cheer each time they hit *on* and the screen lights up, but I do hope, as some have later confided, that they now consider the influence of television on their lives whenever they reach for the remote control. I want to dispel the acceptance of television as culturally inevitable.

For teachers, I hope I have initiated a reexamination of our flight plans, those assignments we give students. I have suggested that we foster student engagement by creating assignments that highlight the differences between our students and us, whether it be demographic markers, cultural upbringing, geographical relocations, experiences, perceptions, or, as in my case, life and lifestyle choices. Writing assignments that incorporate informal ethnography can invite students to reconsider those orthodox and bounded viewpoints assailed by Irving.

Notes

1. Quoted in James Clifford, "Introduction: Partial Truths," in *Writing Culture: The Poetics and Politics of Ethnography*, ed. James Clifford and George Marcus (Berkeley: University of California Press, 1986), 2.

2. John Irving, *A Prayer for Owen Meany* (New York: William Morrow, 1989), 203.

3. Clifford, 2.

4. Richard Zoglin, reported by Stacy Perman, "The Town That Television Forgot," *Time*, 31 October 1994, 46.

5. Clifford, 3.

6. Ibid., 2.

7. Ibid.

8. Ibid.

4

Using Advertising
in First-Year Composition
A Rationale and Practice

Lynn Burley

First-year students come to the composition class already having been exposed to hundreds of thousands of advertisements in the form of media such as television commercials, magazine ads, and billboards, as well as other types of advertisements such as posters, T-shirts, and the labels on their jeans. They are also already experienced consumers, whether as direct purchasers themselves or as indirect influences on their parents' purchases. However, many of these students will say that advertising has little effect on them; they buy what they like anyway, or at best, advertising just lets them know what their choices are. The students' viewpoint supports a similar critique made about consumer sovereignty by Sut Jhally, media critic and author of *The Codes of Advertising*, who argues that "if the market is like a voting machine then it will most reflect the 'choices' of those who have the most to spend."[1] However, as Jhally points out, what students, like most consumers, do not realize is that advertising shapes and directs consumer choice in certain directions for the benefit of the producers of the goods.[2]

As part of my class at Purdue University, I attempt to challenge students to identify and analyze the ideology of advertisements as encoded in the language and images used, and to reflectively consider the cultural values promoted and valorized by them, particularly concerning gender, age, race, and class.

Rationale

The study of the language of advertising is appropriate for the first-year composition class because it offers a way for students to analyze the dominant social structures in our society through texts which affect us all. Examining

38

advertisements enables students to begin to see how many of their beliefs have been shaped and reinforced by those groups with power. By decoding and discussing language, students have a starting point whereby they can examine certain aspects of their convictions in an effort to understand how socially-dominant ideology has succeeded in molding their consciousness.

In addition, working with advertisements offers a textual genre students already know much about; often they feel comfortable and capable talking about advertising. While the class introduces new ways of looking at ads, focusing students' attention on the issues of gender, age, race, and class, class members can choose the particular ads they want to analyze. This way, students can build on knowledge they already have. The class does not require any expertise in advertising techniques; though the issue of technique often comes up in class, the goal is not to learn about how ads are constructed or deemed successful, as might be the case in a media class. The knowledge students need is what they bring to class as consumers. The goal is to learn to decode ads in order to better understand what ideology is prevailing in our society and analyze its effects.

Students accomplish this analysis through a process approach to writing, including freewriting, multiple drafts, peer evaluation, and peer editing. And by using texts that all students can relate to, the process seems to facilitate better peer groups. Not only do students discuss such aspects as development and organization in their drafts, they seem more likely to discuss content as well, voicing opinions as to both how a particular student's thoughts are written and what is written. In the process model, it is important to a writer's development for students to participate in critical response—giving their opinions in a thoughtful manner as well as learning ways to deliberate their classmates' responses. Peer discussion, often rather heated, leads the student writer to reexamine her position and, ultimately, to revise, either incorporating others' suggestions or anticipating and refuting future readers' arguments.

This part of the writing class is crucial, because in the peer group students become aware of the privileged ideologies portrayed in advertisements as they defend and refute their arguments. Students must write about the advertisements from their own positions, which inevitably yields a statement about themselves and their ideologies. The peer groups are a means to help each writer discover her own agenda, her own privileged ideologies, and examine how her beliefs have been shaped, in part, by the thousands of seemingly innocuous ads permeating her life.

What makes this class different from more traditional classes is not in the writing process itself, which has become common in the first-year composition classroom, but that the students must examine and critique their own experiences, which often leads to resistance. In my class, student resistance takes the forms of outright hostility and challenge of the teacher or of other students, or a total unwillingness of students to participate in the class. Instructors must recognize that asking students to critique the cultural codes that are often the basis of the students' own beliefs is difficult, sometimes even frustrating, for the class. For example, students will say that a particular advertisement is sexist and degrades women, but that that is the way it is in the "real world" and advertising merely reflects this idea. Even the women in the class will say that if the idea sells the product, it is a good ad. When the teacher or other classmates push these students to reevaluate their positions, anger is often the result.

Students must commit themselves to a particular position in this exercise, a task that is often very difficult for them to do, and then they must explain the position they take. The writing instructor must encourage, and practice, tolerance of diversity in the students' views, yet push reluctant students to critique their own convictions. Students must know that they can disagree with the instructor's ideology without fear of negative consequences in discussions or in the grading process. Encouraging resistance to the ideology of the ads is often seen by the students as permission to resist the ideology of the instructor, to disagree with her views, and this is good.

Practice

I introduce students to cultural codes by first examining Purdue's mascot, Purdue Pete. Students are instructed to first list words which describe Purdue Pete, focusing on how he looks. The students begin with *tough, fierce, muscular, rugged,* and *skinny* (Purdue Pete has muscular arms and chest, but skinny legs). Next, the students are asked to think of words that describe the image that Purdue Pete evokes. They list *school spirit, loyalty, winner, Purdue, college,* and *football*. The purpose of this exercise is to think about not only what we see in the text, but also what the text connotes. Cultural codes, then, are the denotative and connotative meanings with which we associate the text. As Jhally has observed, "Objects lose any real connection with the basis of their practical utility and instead come to be the material correlate (the signifier) of an increasing number of constantly changing abstract qualities." [11] The code, then, becomes what controls demand for a product and the socialization process promised by the product.[12] The codes demonstrate what is privileged and valued in our community, and it is this that the students are expected to be able to recognize and explain.

Given that the focus of the class is on race, gender, age, and class, students are next asked to list words relating to these aspects. The students decide Purdue Pete is white, male, young, and working class as signified by the hardhat he wears and the sledgehammer he carries. Students seek to explain why the mascot is male, young, white, and why he is working class. Even if a mascot appears gender-neutral—an animal figure such as the University of Wisconsin's badger or even something like Ohio State's buckeye—the mascot is made masculine. Thus, Ohio State's mascot becomes "Brutus Buckeye." Students quickly get the point when asked to picture Purdue University's mascot as "Purdue Patty" instead of "Purdue Pete" leading the football team onto the field.

Now that students have an idea of cultural codes and how they are represented, they can begin looking at advertising. Some students may need more convincing evidence for advertising's pervasiveness in their lives and the degree to which advertising affects them. A simple assignment such as having students log, for just one day, the number of ads they see, including television commercials, magazine ads, billboards, and posters, as well as the number of brand names, sports teams, and college logos they see on clothing, shoes, baseball hats, book bags, notebooks, and other accessories of their friends, classmates, and acquaintances, will usually raise their awareness of the impact of advertising. Not only does this assignment raise students' awareness, it also opens the way for students to question what constitutes advertising, as students start to realize that it is not always the case that the advertiser must pay to advertise a product.

When I begin discussing cultural codes with students, I introduce them to cultural codes in texts with which all of them can be expected to be familiar. Mattel's Barbie doll and the school mascot are easily accessible means for first examining cultural codes. These specific icons lend themselves particularly well to discussions of gender, race, age, and class because students have firm ideas about them. The gender codes signified in these two icon genres are so widely accepted that students are often not even willing to question them. I have to challenge the students to look for the contradictions between their experiences and the ideology of the icons.

With Barbie, students are asked to visualize her, then to describe her. Inevitably, the majority describe the quintessential Barbie—blue eyes, blond hair, thin, beautiful Barbie. Some students will point out that Barbie comes in several models, but ultimately, the doll has the same figure, the same "look," regardless of the model selected. The discussion of cultural ideology begins when students start to question why this is so—why most of them envision the blond, blue-eyed Barbie and why she later came in different, yet similar, models. Students then examine her personality, her intelligence, her profession. Students consider why her hair is long and blond, why her waist is so small, why she is white, why she owns the particular accessories she is packaged with, and this generates a lively discussion. At this point, some students will offer resistance, believing that Barbie is "just" a toy and has no value as an object of study. This is to be expected, but these students will be continually challenged throughout this course to problematize the ideology they encounter. It is often difficult for them to respond critically to texts they have always viewed as neutral or insignificant. Through class discussions, it is hoped that by questioning what may seem insignificant, students will learn to question for themselves and to contemplate the diverse opinions they will continually find in a society striving for equality.

To begin looking at print advertisements, students are asked to bring in some of their own magazines. They are asked to list the cultural codes they find and we examine these as a class. Usually, if any language is found in the ad, it provides the dominant codes for interpretation, such as in an ad for Lady Stetson cologne. The text reads, "Lady Stetson—How the West was Won." Students should pick out the codes directly from the wording—lady, West, and won. From these "megacodes," most of the other codes will follow. Students can discuss why these codes are used to sell a fragrance—why the term "lady" instead of any other female reference such as "woman," "girl," or "dame"; why the use of the word "West," particularly when considering our cultural ideal of the West and the codes associated with it, such as individuality, ruggedness, and the cowboy; and finally, the competitive term "won," especially since the image accompanying the text shows a man embracing a woman.

Besides the language, students need to be directed to look at the entire ad, including the models—what they are wearing, how they are posed, their expressions, colors, and so on—the background, the product, or any other details they can find. They need to trust their impressions and learn to think about what they are seeing. For instance, the color red has many connotations attached to it—it can signal alarm, a warning, bravery, sexiness, danger, blood, sportiness, and so on. If a red car is featured in an ad, it probably is a sports car instead of the family station wagon, and the red signifies sportiness or maybe sexiness, but probably was never intended to make the reader think of blood. Most students do this exercise well; however, they often see or interpret words and images differently from the instructor, who is more than ten years older than they are. This is one reason why they must not only identify the codes of the ad, but also explain and analyze them.

After spending time in class, practicing together in small groups with ads, students are given their assignment, which is to identify and analyze the cultural codes in an advertisement of their choice. They must first explain how they determined what the codes are—through the language, the images, colors, expressions and position of the models, and the background. The second part of the assignment is to analyze how these codes have functioned in their own experiences. Students are to consider what values are set up as positive, as desirable, and for whom these values are intended. In the assignment, students must answer the question, What conceptions of gender, race, age, and/or class are promoted through this ad? The most difficult part of the assignment is for students to make a leap from what is presented in the ad to explain how it affects their lives and the communities in which they live. Students then write two drafts, each of which is presented in small group settings and commented on by the instructor, before submitting a final draft for a grade.

The following is representative of several class discussions concerning four ads—three for WonderBra and one for WonderBody—and demonstrates how students can resist examining the ads when pushed to define their own positions. All four ads appeared in various magazines, but were also for sale as wall posters in a catalog distributed on campus. Shot in black and white, three of these posters feature head and chest shots of the same thin, white, blond model in a black, lacy WonderBra, staring directly into the camera. Accompanying each picture, directly underneath her bust, is one of three captions: "Double Major," "Newton Was Wrong," and "Engineering 101." The fourth poster features the same model in a mini, black, one-piece slip with the caption, "Mind Altering and Legal, Too." In each of the ads, the model's bust is most prominent and her hair is disheveled. In three of the ads, she faces the camera directly, with lips parted; in the fourth, she gazes out to the side, her arms raised, her hands in her hair, her head tilted down.

As a class, we used these ads to practice finding the codes and discussing what their significance might be. The ads were passed around class as students worked in groups of two or three, writing down at least ten codes. First, students were asked to supply codes surrounding the model, which were then listed on the board. These included *beautiful, sexy, slender, mysterious, alluring, provocative, feminine, pouty, sassy, challenging, messy (hair), well-endowed, smooth, clean, black, white, lace, bare,* and *lingerie.* Second, students were to list codes suggested by the captions. These included *college, students, history, engineering, freshmen, drugs, prison, Newton, physics,* gravity, *breakthrough, masculine,* and *female.* (The codes *drugs* and *prison* refer to the ad copy that suggests the product is "mind altering and legal.")

Next, the students were asked if they disagreed with any of the codes or wanted a particular code explained. This discussion focused not on the ads, but on how our culture views some of the codes found in the ads. For example, several students asked those who had volunteered the codes *masculine* and *female* to explain them. How could the ad be both? The simple explanation, one student said, was that these ads used femininity to appeal to men, but she found the captions to be geared toward men, since they invoked the sciences, a field dominated by men. Several women disagreed, stating that there were many women in the sciences and that it was no longer a male-dominated field. The students debated back and forth, but I eventually stepped in to ask what it meant that, at Purdue at least, only 27 percent of the academic year 1995's first-year engineering class were women and only 25 percent of those graduating with an engineering degree that same year were women. Most agreed that while the field is changing, the sciences are still considered masculine. Still, two women refused to accept this point. They stated that they knew women engineers, that they had female science teachers in high school, and that they knew of famous women scientists. When another student asked them to name these scientists, one of the women students became so angry, she yelled at the class, telling them that they were a "bunch of close-minded pigs" and that she did not have to defend her position to them. The other female student retreated, saying that maybe the class was right; she then remained silent for the rest of the discussion.

Another point that sparked debate was the class's attempt to justify the codes *beautiful* and *feminine*. One of the men said that this model was not his idea of beautiful, that she was "just average"; many of the women agreed. Another said that the model looked too aggressive to be called feminine. A third student, a woman, believed that because the model's bust was perfect, it was probably surgically enhanced, and most agreed with this assessment. Because of the model's possible breast enhancement, about half the class thought the cosmetic surgery detracted from her femininity because the model was not "real." The rest thought it made her more feminine because, as one male student said, the bigger the breasts, the more womanly, or feminine, she is.

This discussion provided the opportunity to point out that we each have different opinions about such subjective attributes as *beauty* and *femininity*, as well as different experiences or conceptions involving such ideas as the masculinity of the sciences, but that the students needed to learn to be more critical about the codes. I asked the man who had stated that the model was not beautiful if he thought the model was intended to be only average. He said no; he thought that she was supposed to be very sexy and desirable so that men would want to buy their girlfriends the bra and slip. So while the model may not be beautiful to my student, she does represent what our society has learned to value as beautiful—flawless skin, full lips, straight, white teeth, big eyes, slender build, ample bustline, white skin.

In a subsequent class, we talked about why these particular codes were used by first discussing who the intended audience was for these ads. Students considered where the ads were placed. Since they were found in a catalog distributed specifically on college campuses, it was likely that the audience was intended to be young, single students. The class debated whether these ads were intended for males or females, since the ads also had been placed in women's magazines. Some of the students said they thought both men and women were targeted for the ads because some women would buy this bra, thinking they would look like the model. Men would want to buy the bra for their girlfriends so that their girlfriends would look like the model. Several women spoke up, saying that the ads insulted women and that any woman with a brain would never buy this bra. The women's response initiated a heated exchange. Some students felt that only those women who were jealous or unattractive would be insulted by the ads, and others tried to convince their classmates that these ads were insulting to anyone. Some students felt that the ads implied that women have to have cleavage, have to be sexy, have to be the ideal beauty, because that was the only way women are valued in society. One woman pointed out that the references to Newton and to an engineering class in the captions made it seem as though the best use of scientific knowledge is to make women's breasts look larger, or as though real or perceived breast enlargement was the most important accomplishment of physics and engineering. Others shot back that there was just too much some people were reading into these ads—after all, one student said, it's no big deal.

It is precisely the "no big deal" attitude this class is trying to overcome, however. These ads, taken all together, *do* matter, because our values and beliefs are reflected in them. It is obvious, then, that this class is overtly political, because notions of race, gender, age, and class have to be examined. Students must look at the cultural codes of an ad, determine what they are and why the codes are portrayed as they are. These ads shape our consciousness by invoking certain privileged ideologies concerning race, gender, age, and class that are seen as the prevailing view of the communities within which the ads exist. Students will often resist participating because they do not want to critique what they feel is right and okay.

At the end of this assignment, the class moves from advertising to critiquing cultural codes in fairytales, in the workplace, in school, and finally, in our concept of individuality. Students come to analyze and to know that there are many interconnected relationships between a person and an object and between the symbolism an object contains and power.[3] I have had students come back years after they have taken my class to tell me that they can no longer look at a magazine or watch a television commercial without looking for the codes and trying to decide what ideology is being promoted by the ad. Students have learned to question what they once thought was either not worth questioning or not permissible to question. That is what makes this first-year composition class a rewarding experience for all of us.

Notes

1. Sut Jhally, *The Codes of Advertising* (New York: Routledge, 1990), 15.
2. Ibid., 15.
3. Ibid., 22.

5

Woman[ly] Teaching
Gender, Pathos, and Politics in the Writing Classroom

Gail Corning

When we enter the writing classroom, we encounter not only the ideas of our students but also their feelings. We encounter, that is, not only minds, but bodies. Yet as academics, we tend to act as if feelings do not or should not intrude into intellectual pursuits. Disregarded as a strategy for making knowledge, emotion lurks largely ignored at the bottom of the academic hierarchy, partly, at least, because it's gendered female; even the word "discipline" implies a male domain of rigorous, orderly, rational, and pure mental process. Emotion languishes on the female side of that dichotomy: it is loose, sloppy, sensual, contaminated, fleshly, and not a process at all, but a morass. In fact, I am uncomfortable even writing about it in a scholarly essay.

But I had a classroom experience that forced me to interrogate emotion in the same way I would demand to understand the "logic" of a situation. That self-interrogation prompted me to tack a figurative sign on my classroom door—CAUTION: WOMAN TEACHING—so I could test whether emotion could be used to learn and teach how our values are not just constructed, but embodied. I wanted to see what it would feel like to be a woman teaching, and to explore what it might mean, politically and ethically, to practice in the writing classroom a womanly teaching that pays attention to emotions and to what the body has to tell us through emotion.

A few years ago, I taught an advanced writing class. In it, a group of students presented to the class Douglas Park's article, "Analyzing Audiences," in which Park argues against a demographic notion of audience in favor of a situational one.[1] At some point in the discussion, one young man opined that he didn't care what Park had to say, if *he* were to speak to a predominantly female audience, he would use mostly emotional appeals. A few gasps issued from the feminists in the classroom, and I clearly remember my response:

Intellectually, I decided not to intrude, but to leave responsibility for the discussion to the presenters; physically, I felt as if I had been kicked in the stomach. In fact, the force of my physical-emotional reaction so astonished me that my intellectual reaction, while probably pedagogically correct, was also a convenient cop-out—I needed time to theorize about why my body had reacted so disproportionately to an event that was, after all, just a fairly ordinary expression of phallogocentrism.

Thinking about my reaction to the student's remark, I realized that on one level he was simply being observant: women are socialized to respond to arguments from pathos. But on another level, his statement, which he seemed to regard as self-evidently reasonable, relied on an ideology that denigrates pathos and elevates logos as the way to think and know, and therefore also denigrates women as "emotional" and ergo inferior (and not only as thinkers) to men. Well, there it was, that ancient, destructive bugaboo, grossly insulting; no wonder I experienced it as a bodily assault.

As a woman with a number of roles (the wife of an academic, the mother of two sons, a graduate student, and a teacher of writing), all of them complicated by this young man's remark, I was not about to let it go by. I felt the complications in my body, as a set of marked indexes that could be read. What I read there were the theoretical and political issues that enabled this student's statement, and my resistance to their implications. I was also delighted to discover that my body knew instantly what my mind had taken some time to figure out. Interrogating the emotions I experienced as a woman teaching gave me the chance to validate my body's knowledge and reveal the social constructedness of value systems at the same time. But how could I address these issues in a way that would be meaningful to students' practice as thinkers and writers? Given the force of my own emotion, I wanted the students not merely to sit passively through a lecture on theory, but actually to experience how emotions and values are linked and how social meanings are materially embodied. It took me a few days to come up with a plan, but this is what I did.

During the course of that teaching term, the newspapers had reported a number of cases of child abuse. In the class following the one I've described, I recounted one particularly gruesome case and asked the students to write, in one word, their reaction to the story. I then asked each student for his or her response, and wrote those words on the board, separating them (without the students' noticing, I hoped) into two lists: the responses of the women in the class, and those of the men. Predictably, they were all emotional responses: disgust, sadness, revulsion, anger, and so on; and the content of the lists was alike, regardless of the gender of the respondent. I asked the class to identify whether they had responded from logos or pathos; when all agreed on the latter, I asked if they could tell me why. The same young man who had unknowingly prompted the exercise answered instantly, "It's because of our morals."

I have to admit I didn't expect to get the answer I wanted so quickly. But his observation opened a space for me to help the class members connect their own emotional responses with their "morals," and with the larger issue of the social construction of value systems: how we come to decide what the commandments of our culture are, and how we react to the violation of those commandments, primarily with our bodies. I asked the students to consider what bodily sensations they had had when they wrote down their one-word emotional responses, and asked them to consider as well why, given that emotion signals us to what we consider important, emotion has become, in Richard Weaver's word, a "liability"? By answering for them the more explicit question, "How did emotion come to be displaced by reason as a determinant of intellectual, social, and political power?" I narrated Weaver's story about the nineteenth-century evaluative shift toward an image of humanity as "scientific,"[2] and how we came to believe "that to think validly was to think "scientifically."[3] I offered Chaïm Perelman's construction of what and how something comes to achieve "fact status,"[4] and suggested how tenuous that status can be when everything we believe or believe in is couched in language. I emphasized that language is an act we wield as forcibly as a club on one another, chiefly to establish certain versions of reality, including the "reality" that emotion is inferior to rationality and that therefore women, the "emotional" gender, are inferior to men. Through language, I proposed, we create a reality that is not given but socially constructed, a reality that is subject to change, a reality that may be no more than the playing out of implications of the very terms with which we choose to discuss it. [5]

My point in all of this was to encourage my students, who were in this class because they wanted to learn to write better, not just to think about, but to *feel* how words matter, so they could then consider how, if they wanted to be ethical writers, they needed to recognize that the words we use can be not just abstract tools, but actual weapons for expressing or sustaining power; and to consider how potentially devastating those words and their implications can be. So I ended my narrative by reworking a familiar children's retort against hurtful language to "sticks and stones can break your bones, but words can *kill* you." And I followed by listing every racial or religious epithet I could think of, ending with "woman": not to imply some parity between the *reality* of being called a "woman" and being called, for example, a "kike," but to illustrate how we load some terms with meaning until they *are* mean, until they are potentially lethal.

What I was trying to do of course was make explicit for the class the way language works as a symbol system and how we use and misuse it to define situations[6] and then "forget" that those situations are language constructs; how, in other words, language is never free of motive although the motive is usually not recognized.[7] These are theoretical suppositions with which we are all familiar. But what I had forgotten—forgotten, that is, until kicked in the stomach by words—was that where there is motive, there is emotion, emotion embodied in us by language. Since language is the major symbol system by which we construct and divide up our world, and since emotion is inextricably bound up with language, it seemed useful to me to try to figure out whether and on what basis emotion could be rehabilitated as an epistemic asset.

I found my own epistemic asset in Satya P. Mohanty's article, "The Epistemic Status of Cultural Identity: On *Beloved* and the Postcolonial Condition."[8] In his attempt to find "a better way to think about identity than might be suggested by the alternatives provided by the essentialists and the postmodernists,"[9] Mohanty argues that experience, if it is interpreted through theory, can yield reliable and genuine knowledge. He first claims that "'personal experience' is itself socially and 'theoretically' constructed, and it is precisely in this *mediated* way that it yields knowledge."[10] He then develops this idea by reference to an essay by feminist theorist and philosopher Naomi Scheman in which Scheman focuses on the anger that women who have been members of consciousness-raising groups may come to feel. Scheman and Mohanty assert that the emotion is not an individual matter with a private significance to which only the woman has access. In fact, the emotion itself may be recognized for what it is only through the mediation of the group, which provides an environment in which emotional, social, and political support constitute an alternative narrative of the woman's relationship with a sexist world against which the emotion of anger can be tested for appropriateness. This alternative narrative provides a critique that "involve[s] notions of what a woman is supposed to be angry about, what she should not tolerate, what is worth valuing, notions that are not merely moral but also social-theoretical in nature."[11]

In other words, our emotions come to count as knowledge when they are tested in a social-theoretical context and validated against the various narratives or accounts that may be available. Mohanty rescues emotion from both essentialist and postmodern attacks when he posits that "our emotions provide evidence of the extent to which even our deepest personal experiences are socially constructed, mediated by visions and values that are 'political' in nature, that *refer* outward to the world beyond the individual."[12]

The advantage of womanly teaching, which pays attention to emotions, is that emotions are never in short supply and, because they are both intimately linked to our values and refer outward to our social and political life through their constructed nature, we can teach and learn from them. They are "ways of paying attention to the world,"[13] and if we listen for emotion in the classroom (even our own), chances are we will hear an opportunity to call into question suppositions that claim to be self-evident representations of the world. We can do this by subjecting personal experience to validation by public meanings—that is, we can insist that the personal is political and use the political link to "make sense" of experience. When we make personal experience available to public scrutiny, we suggest to our students that there "are different ways of making sense of . . . experience, and the way we make sense of it can in fact create a new experience."[14] For example, the male student who assumed it "made sense" to rely on emotional arguments with a female audience holds that position from the personal experience of growing up in a sexist social structure, a political erection that pretends not to be there. And his acting on that assumption furthers a sexist social narrative that will have effects in the real world. Under my scrutiny and that of the class, I wondered if this student might reevaluate his experience to create a new one for himself and those he acts upon.

In complicating his assumption by subjecting it to the exercise with which I began the class period, I wanted to achieve four things. First, I banked on this male student's reacting as emotionally as the women in the class so he would confront the disjunction between what he said and what he felt. Second, I hoped to offer the entire class a social, theoretical, and political context in which they could make sense of experience differently from this student's relation to the world. Third, I wanted to stress that our experiences do not have self-evident meanings, for, as Mohanty says, "our access to our remotest personal feelings is dependent on social narratives, paradigms, and even ideologies."[15] And fourth, because our experiences do not have self-evident meanings, I wanted to alert students that their emotions are important clues to their relation to the world because they have epistemological significance.

When I experienced anger at the student's statement and later asked myself whether my anger was justified, I recognized that both my personal feelings and the student's were dependent on different ways of making sense of the same social narrative. Although my anger in class was immediate, it had not sprung fully formed from some secret well of self; just as the woman did in the consciousness-raising group that Scheman studied, I also had come to recognize the emotion through the mediation of a group. And I could validate that emotion as justified according to feminist views about the world. But another emotion followed the anger: a discomfort that, only after the mediation of a group of female colleagues, did I recognize as shame. What was I doing being so emotional, being a woman, in the classroom? Academia leaves emotion *out* of the classroom: by womanly teaching, I had transgressed. Academic discourse, spoken or written, should be "detached," "objective," "logical"; we teach our students not to write "I feel," but to "describe" or "analyze," to bolster their reasoning with facts and arguments from authority. Teaching writing involves teaching students to recognize disciplinary boundaries, and most stay inside them to avoid risk (I refer back to my own discomfort in writing about emotion and recognize how relieved I am to find Mohanty *theorizing* about it—he purifies emotion so that it becomes reputable and I may discuss it without my body's shrinking with guilt.). But as teachers of writing, we deal with language, and language, slippery with emotion, is always sliding over the boundaries, taking risks. It will not be kept out.

Although I am always a woman teaching, what I call "womanly teaching" is not a gendered construct. It depends only on encouraging students to pay attention to their emotions because emotions signal when our deepest values are being called into play. If students interrogate their value-based emotions in a public forum, they may come to know that no knowledge exists outside of social contexts of justification. The epistemic consequence of womanly teaching may be that students will "try on" different versions of reality and work out different relations to their world, relations that *feel* right. If we leave emotion outside the classroom, do we also leave out ethics? As my student recognized instantly, we respond from pathos "because of our morals."

Notes

1. Douglas Park, "Analyzing Audiences," *CCC*, 37, no. 4 (December 1986): 478–488.

2. Richard M. Weaver, "Language is Sermonic," in *Language is Sermonic: Richard M. Weaver on the Nature of Rhetoric*, ed. Richard L. Johannesen, Rennard Strickland, and Ralph T. Eubanks. (Baton Rouge: Louisiana State University Press, 1970), 203.

3. Ibid., 204.

4. Chaïm Perelman, *The Realm of Rhetoric* (Notre Dame, Ind.: University of Notre Dame Press, 1982), 24.

5. Kenneth Burke, *Language As Symbolic Action* (Berkeley: University of California Press, 1966), 46.

6. Ibid., 16.

7. Kenneth Burke, *A Rhetoric of Motives* (Berkeley: University of California Press, 1969), xiii.

8. Satya P. Mohanty, "The Epistemic Status of Cultural Identity: On *Beloved* and the Postcolonial Condition," *Cultural Critique* 24 (spring 1993): 41–80.

9. Ibid., 42.

10. Ibid., 45.

11. Ibid., 46.

12. Ibid.

13. Ibid., 49.

14. Ibid., 46.

15. Ibid., 47–48.

6

Multicultural Semiotics
Race, Class, Gender, and Sexuality in American Popular Culture[1]

Ann Garnsey

The following essay discusses the design of an argumentative writing course entitled Multicultural Semiotics: Race, Class, Gender, and Sexuality in American Popular Culture. I outline and explain the course objectives and then demonstrate the application of these to the course paper assignments. The course focuses not only on argumentative writing skills but on specific textual, methodological, and thematic components. It asks students to analyze texts from popular culture, to take a semiotic approach to those texts, and to look at multicultural issues in them. This essay, then, describes the theory underlying the use of multiculturalism as a theme and semiotics as a method, and argues for attention in the college writing classroom to the discursive practices of popular culture.

Objectives of the Course

The course objectives reflect a foundational assumption that popular culture ideologies and debates provide an ideal environment for exploring the discursive grammar of argumentative writing. I want my students (1) to expand their conception of argumentative discourse to include the languages and motifs of the popular culture around them, in advertising, magazines and catalogs, television, and films; (2) to analyze and evaluate critically the arguments that are implicit in this culture using semiotics; (3) to examine cultural arguments critically by focusing on issues of race, class, gender, and sexuality; and (4) to sharpen their ability to write persuasive and supported prose in a primarily interpretive context.

Explanation of Course Objectives

This course leads students onto the stage of argumentative writing by directing their gaze outward toward the audience, toward the rich tapestry of popular culture texts. I suggest two tools to guide that gaze: I ask students to take a semiotic approach to popular culture texts and to be aware of the multicultural issues confronted or concealed in those texts. I take this approach because I believe that our "reality" is constructed through the exchange and negotiation between discursive texts or practices and "material" conditions. In other words, a person's material conditions of race, gender, sexuality, and class—being an African American lesbian of middle-class origin, for example—interact with the discourses produced by popular culture texts such as television programs. Such a person's consciousness or notions of what is real (including notions of race, class, gender, and sexuality) come from this negotiation between cultural discursive practices—television discourses in this case—and the material conditions of being black, a lesbian, and middle-class. Of course, negotiations are not always apparent, clear, or consistent, because discursive practices and material conditions are very seldom clear-cut and often exhibit contradictory meanings. Despite these difficulties, this course asks students to analyze and interpret specific discursive practices in relation to specific material conditions. Inviting students to investigate the discursive practices in the culture around them plays to their strengths and addresses their needs in a world of complex, multiple literacies, while an emphasis on semiotic analysis helps students see popular culture as a system of signs with socially constructed meanings that warrant interpretation.

The Textual Focus: Popular Culture

This course focuses on the discursive reality of what has been known traditionally as popular culture—advertising, catalogs and magazines, television and music videos, and film—because these texts are most accessible to contemporary students, many of whom are the postmodern successors to Generation X, and because such studies are still undervalued and much needed in academia. A primary feature of postmodernism, according to theorist Fredric Jameson, is the destruction of boundaries. Jameson notes that the disintegrating wall between "high" and "low" culture is the "most distressing development of all from an academic standpoint, which has traditionally had a vested interest in preserving a realm of high or elite culture against the surrounding environment . . . of TV series and *Reader's Digest* culture."[2] Even if we, as academics, do not fully change or release our notions of high and low culture, we certainly need to realize the value of theoretically analyzing popular culture texts and of teaching these strategies to our students. Like film scholars Jim Collins, Hilary Radner, and Ava Preacher Collins, I believe that mass culture texts "have the most powerful impact on how we envision ourselves and each other, on how we imagine our present, past, and future," and thus present the "most pressing need for intensive critical analysis."[3]

Who better to help fill that need in cultural studies than our students? Many of our students are young and very literate in the vernacular languages of popular culture. Jim Collins, in "Genericity in the Nineties: Eclectic Irony and the New Sincerity," notes that "cinematic cultural literacy" is growing and becoming more and more sophisticated primarily because a new generation of filmmakers and film viewers has grown up with television, which frequently airs older Hollywood films.[4] In addition to the background or history of movies, intertextual commodities are now part of the cinematic cultural system. According to film theorist Thomas Schatz, films create "a cultural commodity that might be regenerated in any number of media forms" such as pop music, children's books, novels, and so on.[5] These commodities refer back to the original text—the film—and thus become part of an intertextual system, which actually occurs throughout the webs of popular culture meaning, not just with film.

Our students are often skillfully versed in the significative nuances of popular culture texts and in their intertexts and backgrounds; they write and think more critically and more effectively when their discursive projects are woven from the material of their own literacies. Having begun from a position of contextual and intertextual competence or mastery, students spend less time teasing out pieces of meaning with strategies we might consider unsophisticated—summarizing, describing, aphorizing—but which are, more often, simply survival tactics for those who sojourn into unfamiliar discursive territory. Instead, students are more likely to embark on more critical academic ventures, such as analyzing signs in the popular culture system and constructing arguments about these signs. In other words, using popular culture in the composition classroom creates a bridge between our students' multiple vernacular literacies and the formal or "academic" literacies we attempt to teach them.

The Methodological Focus: Semiotics

Because this course intends to help students sharpen their ability to write persuasive and supported prose in a primarily interpretive context, they need a method that helps them, as textbook editors Sonia Maasik and Jack Solomon explain, to go beyond "descriptive reviews or opinion pieces."[6] Maasik and Solomon's reader, *Signs of Life in the USA: Readings on Popular Culture for Writers*, explains to students what semiotics is and how to use it as a critical tool in interpreting the "signs of life" around them. Maasik and Solomon rightly argue that using semiotics as a methodological tool allows students "to formulate cogent, well-supported interpretations" of popular culture texts.[7]

A semiotic approach in this course involves looking at popular culture as a series of signs. Importantly, semiotic analyses look not only at the signifier, but rather at what the sign means, its signified. Signs can generally be seen, as Maasik and Solomon explain, as "message[s] to be decoded and analyzed to discover [their] meaning[s]."[8] Meaning changes and is thus a "social construct, not a simple reflection of truth or reality"; in fact, it often reflects the ideological interests of the meaning maker.[9] Hence, semiotic analysis involves looking at meaning, and at what is entailed in the construction of meaning. According to cultural critic David Morley, one needs to examine not simply the content of what is being said or shown but also the "assumptions that lie behind that content." He advises looking at "latent messages," which can be brought to the fore by asking questions such as: "What is taken-for-granted (what 'doesn't need saying') . . . what kinds of assumptions are made, what kinds of things are *in*visible."[10] This type of instruction can be labeled, in Henry A. Giroux's words, "radical pedagogy," or pedagogy that helps students place cultural texts within a "complex and often contradictory set of ideological and material processes through which the transformation of knowledge, identities, and values takes place."[11] Metacognition on this level is the overarching goal toward which each of this course's objectives is designed.

It is also important in a semiotic analysis to realize that the "meaning of a sign is to be found within the system to which it belongs."[12] To illustrate this, teachers might explain to their classes that a classmate's haircut may not signify much on its own. When the haircut is seen as part of a system of 1990s hairstyles made popular by television—the sitcom *Friends* offers a famous current example—then the meanings of the classmate's haircut become clearer. This clarity derives from the fact that a sign's meaning does not reside essentially within the sign or object itself; a sign derives meaning from being similar to and different from other signs in a system.[13] A person who is very literate in or knowledgeable of the system of TV hairstyles in the mid 1990s, for example, would be able to distinguish the classmate's haircut as either being a Rachel (Jennifer Aniston) or Monica (Courtney Cox) knockoff and would be able to discuss the connotations of glamour and popularity this hairstyle signifies.

Semiotics enables students to see the complexity of culture and to write about it using analytical strategies which are conventionally valued within the multiple universes of academic discourse. Culture becomes for students a web of signs which warrant interpretations, interpretations that catalog underlying assumptions and values. Maasik and Solomon assert that the skills students need to interpret culture, particularly the act of supporting interpretations with evidence, are the same skills that students need to become writers of "critical essays that present a point of view and an argument to defend it."[14] Argumentative writing is also facilitated, I would contend, by semiotic analysis because semiotics emphasizes placing signs within overall systems of meaning. This process pushes students to think analytically and to synthesize information by making connections between signs and their signifying relationships.

The Thematic Focus:
Race, Class, Gender, and Sexuality

The thematic focus for this course is the material realities or social processes of race, class, gender, and sexuality. I focus on these material realities because American culture is really many cultures laced with racial, gendered, class, and sexual differences. It therefore does not have a single or universal narrative. Developing among students the interpretive skills to negotiate and appreciate these multiple narratives represents a significant step toward the realization of Giroux's radical pedagogical goals. In addition, many cultural studies focusing on these material conditions or processes have overemphasized or simply looked at only one condition instead of conceptualizing and thus studying them as intersecting processes.

America is a multicultural society with many differing cultural codes. Hence, cultural texts, according to Giroux, "must be examined as part of a broader discourse that takes up the circuits of power that constitute the ideological and material dynamics of capitalism (or any other social and economic system)."[15] In addition to capitalism, other systems of power such as patriarchy, white hegemony, and heterosexual hegemony need to be considered as interrelated and intersecting contexts for cultural texts.

In the past, many critics who were interested in understanding cultural circuits of power began looking at certain material conditions. Morley, for instance, explains that his study on television audiences looks at "the relations between socio-demographic factors (such as age, sex, race, class) and differential interpretations of the same programme material."[16] But in his critical postscript, Morley acknowledges that

> Although reference is made to the effectivity of the structures of age, sex, race and class, only the latter is dealt with in anything resembling a systematic way. Race is invoked as an explanatory factor on a rather *ad hoc* basis, as is sex/gender; age is mentioned but not explored as a structuring factor. Evidently this is a severe problem—as the age and sex/gender dimensions are particularly important. . . . this is a case of the overemphasis of one structural factor at the expense of all others.[17]

Other critics admit encountering this same problem of being unable to discuss and theorize fully more than one material condition. Janice Radway comments: "Many of the problems Morley identifies in his work with respect to this problem are also present in mine." She explains that while Morley's work was preoccupied with class, her work overemphasized gender.[18]

These critics' afterthoughts suggest that we, as scholars and teachers, need to take an approach that looks at more than one material condition and that conceptualizes them diachronically and in multiple dimensions—as processes that intersect. In this view, race, class, gender, and sexuality (as well as age, disability, etc.) are processes because their meanings are continually being formed and negotiated. Their meanings affect and are involved in everything we do, whether we are conscious of it or not. Therefore, we cannot understand one process without considering the others. Radway explains, for example, that in order to make the study she did on romance novel reading better, she "would now want to organize an ethnography of romance reading comparatively in order to make some effort to ascertain how other sociological variables like age, class, location, education and race intersect with gender to produce varying, even conflicting engagements with the romance form."[19]

Guiding students to work on the intersections of race, class, gender, and sexuality helps them to explain more thoroughly and precisely cultural identities and texts, and provides them with a window from which to see the power relations that construct such texts and identities. By looking at multicultural issues, students can see who has the power to construct cultural codes, and whose gender, sexuality, race, and class profits from such codes, and whose does not. Students realize that there is no universal or essential view of identity, that, in Stuart Hall's words, the " 'grand narratives' which constituted the language of the self as an integral entity don't hold."[20]

Course Paper Assignments: An Overview

Each paper assignment focuses on a different medium of popular culture in this order: ads, catalogs and magazines, MTV and television, and film. Each assignment is very similar in focus and in method: the students are asked to perform a semiotic reading of a particular medium, an ad for example, with special focus on multicultural issues. To this end, I pose several questions to my students in the assignments. General questions that can be asked in relation to any of the cultural mediums include:

- Who is the intended audience? How are they constructed in regards to race, gender, sexuality, and class? How do you know this?

- What color and gender are the people you see? What sort of people are not there?

- Why are you being shown or told certain things? Why are you not being shown or told certain things?

- How are you responding to the cultural text? With pleasure? Disdain? Why?

- What things about race, class, gender, and sexuality are taken for granted?

- What cultural myths are being plugged into? Do these myths privilege some people and not others?
- What gender, racial, sexual, and class roles are portrayed? Why?
- What do you now think is really being said?

Because each paper concentrates on a different medium of culture, each assignment has additional questions specific to the cultural medium at hand. For example, in the ads assignment I also ask: What relationship is there between the ad and the magazine in which you found it? And perhaps, Why is there not a clear view of the product? In the catalog assignment I add: What relationship is there between the ads and the feature stories? Because students can talk about plot in relation to television and film and often get enmeshed in the details of explaining "what happened" in a specific film or television program, I remind them in those assignments to be careful not to oversummarize. I reiterate that their main purpose is a semiotic one—to look at the television show or film as a sign with many messages and make a complex argument about the values and ideologies underlying those cultural representations.

Each assignment also gives examples of certain concepts or issues that the students can focus on, but these are usually derived from the course readings. A popular concept for students to use, for instance, is women as Other. Because this concept can be applied easily to images of women in advertisements and magazines, we read Simone de Beauvoir early in the semester.[21]

Although concepts such as women as Other are suggested in the assignment sheets, the student ultimately chooses the multicultural issue(s) on which he or she wishes to write. Similarly, even though each unit and resulting paper focus on one medium, such as film, and although we watch and discuss specific movies in class during the unit on film, the student ultimately chooses the film(s) on which she or he will write.

While the four paper assignments require that students explore only one cultural medium at a time—ads, for instance—I encourage them to look at a series of the medium's outputs as a strategy for making their analysis and argument more persuasive. The students do not necessarily write masterfully about the popular cultural sign system, since they are looking at such a limited representation of it. I believe, however, that this approach helps students write more focused essays, especially since they are tackling a new medium every three to four weeks and perhaps a new social process or processes (i.e., race and gender) in each paper. Since I want my students to look at systems of meaning and intersections of social processes, the semester is organized so that the first four essays build up to a final paper assignment which is more comprehensive in nature (discussed more fully below).

The frankness of images persuading us to consume forms the guideline for how my assignments are sequenced. My class looks at ads first because they are most explicit about consumption. We then look at catalogs and magazines because they contain many ads and can be seen as an extended ad. We then analyze MTV, where, as television theorist Ann E. Kaplan shows, videos can "function like advertising," and we also study television in general.[22] If one disregards the commercials throughout its programs, television does not overtly sell things—its purpose is entertainment. We then move on to another seeming entertainment genre—film—which can also function as advertising. Schatz comments that "movie and ad techniques are intermingling. In fact, one might argue that the New Hollywood's calculated blockbusters are themselves massive advertisements for their product lines."[23]

Paper #1: Advertising

The first unit of the course focuses on advertisements. Why start the semester with ads? As Roland Barthes says in "The Rhetoric of the Image," "We will start by making it considerably easier for ourselves: we will only study the advertising image." Barthes begins his venture into "the semiology of images" by looking at ads simply because the signs in advertising are overt and thus easier to identify and analyze: "In advertising the signification of the image is undoubtedly intentional; the signifieds of the advertising message . . . have to be transmitted as clearly as possible. If the image contains signs, we can be sure that in advertising these signs are full, formed with a view to the optimum reading: the advertising image is *frank,* or at least emphatic."[24] Because of the overt messages in advertising, it is a suitable medium to use when introducing students to semiotics.

The first assignment on advertising, then, is meant to introduce students to the actual practice of semiotics and to help them begin thinking about multicultural issues. The unit on ads includes various readings that look at multicultural issues in advertising; it also includes exercises that help students work with and understand various semiotic theoretical practices and concepts, such as "denotative" meaning (explicitly showing something) and "connotative" meaning (suggesting something). For instance, my class and I bring in a variety of ads gathered from common, accessible sources, and we puzzle over which ones are trying to look denotative. Ads that emulate newspaper articles or editorials are particularly useful to illustrate this concept. On the back of a box of chocolate chip granola bars, for example, my students found what appeared to be a short article on the history and current quality of granola. It seemed like a newspaper article because it had a title, "Granola— It Just Keeps Getting Better," and encircling the text were the words "Extra— Extra—Extra." In analyzing this ad, the class and I discussed our reactions to newspaper articles in general and discovered that we expect them to explicitly show or tell us something. In other words, we expect articles to be denotative. In the case of the granola bars box, however, the "article" is really an ad trying to exploit all of the connotations surrounding newspaper articles, such as objectivity and truthfulness, in order to lend more credibility to the product.

Like the granola ad, most ads are overtly connotative—Nike, for instance, spends millions of dollars each year expanding the vague aphorism "Just Do It," the connotations of which are limitless. Many of these ads nowhere depict shoes nor a corporate name, but rather make a suggestive statement about personal ideology and end with a display of the corporate logo (the swoosh); in the final analysis, these vignettes play (and perhaps prey) upon a polysemous process of meaning making where "It" never adheres to any particular antecedent, where the semiotic anchor, ironically, is not in any word(s) but rather in the materially denotative swoosh. In addition to highlighting semiotic concepts such as "denotative" and "connotative," the in-class exercises we do, when coupled with class discussion, bring out various advertising techniques such as exploiting society's insecurities (as can easily be seen in any ads for breath mints or deodorant).

By the time the unit on advertising is done, students have a grasp of at least a limited number of multicultural issues and models of essays which address those issues. They also understand and are able to use certain key semiotic terms such as *sign* and *denotative/connotative*. They also understand that ultimately an ad's mandate is to persuade; it is an argument that can be analyzed, its meanings decoded. Many students focus on the meanings surrounding gender in advertising, particularly how women are portrayed. It is fairly easy for them to discuss the objectification of women that is so prevalent in magazines such as *Vogue* and *Mademoiselle*. When the issue of gender is coupled with another social process, such as race or physical ability, the students' arguments become much more complex. One female student in the class investigated the meanings surrounding female beauty in fashion magazines and came to the conclusion that only able bodies are portrayed as beautiful. She skillfully used her own personal perspective as an African American woman to direct her insights into the often invisible assumptions of advertising. A male student similarly used his perspective as a father to guide his interpretation of images of women in advertising. He critiqued the recurrent image of a middle-aged woman as the ideal parental caregiver, arguing that this image reinforces the traditional notion that men are less capable of being nurturing parents. This semiotic approach of analyzing gender roles, specifically the dominant meanings surrounding parenting in advertising, made for an interesting and unique essay.

Papers 2–4: Catalogs/Magazines, MTV/TV, and Film

The objectives for the next three units—on catalogs/magazines, MTV/TV, and film—are very similar to the ones stated above for advertising. The readings get more difficult and theoretically sophisticated throughout the semester. We read, for instance, about whiteness and its attending privileges and anxieties. Analyzing the J. Peterman Company mail-order catalog brings these issues to the fore. Looking at the catalog as a sign that carries many racialized meanings, we investigate why it divides the world geographically into "Western, industrialized societies" and non-Western places.[25] Students are able to recognize easily the negative connotations the catalog places on the West, such as the "creeping homogenization" that is associated with industrialized countries in contrast to the positive connotations surrounding "diversity" that non-Western places supposedly possess.[26] We discuss how this fear of homogenization relates to anxieties that many whites have about their supposedly empty cultural identities, which is, arguably, what the J. Peterman Company is trying to exploit by marketing its products as culturally diverse.

As we move into the entertainment mediums of television and film, we discuss how entertainment is not innocent, even though its rhetorical practices may seem less overtly persuasive. TV and film still appeal to certain cultural dreams and desires, and this is why we find them engaging; in class, we discuss the relationship between the complex meanings underlying these dreams and desires and the pleasures we associate with entertainment.

The Final Paper

The final paper assignment prompts students to bring many of their previous thoughts and written ideas together in a longer and more comprehensive paper. In this assignment, the students have to look at the larger system of popular culture, because they are required to talk about two or more mediums (instead of one, as in the previous papers). This requirement may lead to papers examining the intertextuality of popular culture mediums. This assignment also requires that the students work with more than one social process, such as race and sexuality or gender and class, and write about how these processes intersect. They may have been doing intersection work all along (usually, some students find at the beginning of the semester an intersection— typically race and gender—that they are particularly interested in, and on which each of their papers can focus).

My goal is that by the end of the semester, the students are sophisticated enough as scholars of individual parts of popular culture that they can successfully put the parts together in order to see larger wholes or meaning-making processes. One student, who wrote about Calvin Klein's CK One cologne in her first and final paper assignments, illustrates this progression in thinking. This student wrote quite positively about Klein's ads for CK One in her first assignment. In analyzing these ads on her own, she concluded that the advertising strategy was for the cologne to appeal to anyone, man or woman, black or white (as is reflected in the name of the cologne, the use of androgynous male and female models as well as models of different races, and the use of black-and-white photography). She interpreted this strategy as not only plugging into our society's need for individualism, but also as overcoming gender and racial inequalities. Her positive assessment of CK One changed, however, in her final paper when she compared it with other signs within the larger popular culture meaning system. Specifically, in juxtaposing *Boyz N the Hood,* a film we watched in class, and CK One, she was able to discern two very different approaches to race and gender issues. John Singleton's film, she argued, targeted race and gender as primary issues to be dealt with, while Klein evaded those issues with the concept of oneness. The student ultimately concluded that although images of race and gender are not necessarily affirming or positive in *Boyz N the Hood* (and she actually problematized Singleton's representation of women), they are nonetheless portrayed as processes which have an impact on daily lives. Klein's ads, she asserted, suggest that gender and race do not make a difference in our lives, and thus create a false sense of equality in American society. The curriculum worked for this student, leading her recursively through analytic loops of increasing complexity; by semester's end, she was a self-aware semiotics sophisticate, recognizing the extent to which a sign's meanings can increase in complexity when it is analyzed in relation to other signs within a larger system.

Notes

1. I would like to thank Eric Miraglia and Kay Westmoreland for their valuable suggestions and comments on this article.

2. Fredric Jameson, "Postmodernism and Consumer Society," in *Studying Culture: An Introductory Reader,* ed. Ann Gray and Jim McGuigan (London: Edward Arnold, 1993), 193.

3. Jim Collins, Hilary Radner, and Ava Preacher Collins, introduction to *Film Theory Goes to the Movies,* ed. Jim Collins, Hilary Radner, and Ava Preacher Collins (New York: Routledge, 1993), 1. Collins, Radner, and Collins are speaking specifically of popular cinematic texts.

4. Jim Collins, "Genericity in the Nineties: Eclectic Irony and the New Sincerity," in *Film Theory Goes to the Movies,* ed. Jim Collins, Hilary Radner, and Ava Preacher Collins (New York: Routledge, 1993), 244.

5. Thomas Schatz, "The New Hollywood," in *Film Theory Goes to the Movies,* ed. Jim Collins, Hilary Radner, and Ava Preacher Collins (New York: Routledge, 1993), 29.

6. Sonia Maasik and Jack Solomon, ed., *Signs of Life in the USA: Readings on Popular Culture for Writers* (Boston: Bedford Books of St. Martin's Press, 1994), 4.

7. Sonia Maasik and Jack Solomon, ed., *Editor's Notes to Accompany Signs of Life in the USA: Readings on Popular Culture for Writers* (Boston: Bedford Books of St. Martin's Press, 1994), 2. Maasik and Solomon's reader, *Signs of Life in the U.S.A.,* is one of the primary textbooks used in the course.

8. Maasik and Solomon, *Signs of Life,* 4.

9. Maasik and Solomon, *Editor's Notes,* 5.

10. David Morley, *Television, Audiences and Cultural Studies* (London: Routledge, 1992), 84 and 82 respectively.

11. Henry A. Giroux, "Reclaiming the Social: Pedagogy, Resistance, and Politics in Celluloid Culture," in *Film Theory Goes to the Movies,* ed. Jim Collins, Hilary Radner, and Ava Preacher Collins (New York: Routledge, 1993), 39–40.

12. Maasik and Solomon, *Editor's Notes,* 4.

13. Maasik and Solomon, *Signs of Life,* 14.

14. Ibid., 9.

15. Giroux, 52.

16. Morley, 75.

17. Ibid., 125.

18. Janice Radway, "Reading *Reading the Romance,*" in *Studying Culture: An Introductory Reader,* ed. Ann Gray and Jim McGuigan (London: Edward Arnold, 1993), 68–69.

19. Ibid., 69.

20. Stuart Hall, "Minimal Selves," in *Studying Culture: An Introductory Reader,* ed. Ann Gray and Jim McGuigan (London: Edward Arnold, 1993), 137–38.

21. See Simone de Beauvoir's "Women as Other," in *Writing About the World,* ed. Susan McLeod (Fort Worth, Tex.: Harcourt Brace Jovanovich Inc., 1991), 242–47. This is an excerpt from de Beauvoir's classic 1949 text *The Second Sex.*

22. Ann E. Kaplan, *Rocking Around the Clock: Music Television, Postmodernism, and Consumer Culture* (New York: Routledge, 1987), 17.

23. Schatz, 32.

24. Roland Barthes, "The Rhetoric of the Image," in *Studying Culture: An Introductory Reader,* ed. Ann Gray and Jim McGuigan (London: Edward Arnold, 1993), 15.

25. The J. Peterman Company, *The J. Peterman Company Owner's Manual No. 29* (Summer 1994), 11.

26. Ibid., 67.

7

Making Spaces for Pleasure
Literacy and Popular Culture
Kay Westmoreland

When Raymond Williams defined culture as "ordinary, " as "a whole way of life," he was looking back to his boyhood experience growing up in a remote village in South Wales and thinking of the ways in which ordinary people there had the capacity to experience culture each day. Williams's inclusive definition of culture as "a whole way of life—the common meanings" as well as the arts and learning[1] has in the four decades since it was propounded been a touchstone for considering how the examination of an increasing variety of texts in numerous mediums by scholars in diverse fields might benefit society. The astounding proliferation of texts, from popular entertainment forms to diverse consumer practices, and the lightning-fast changes in communication technology, make especially pressing the need for close examination of the kind of literacy to be gained by analyzing these texts.

The opportunity to think closely about this began for me two years ago when using a number of popular culture texts in a new graduate seminar in cultural rhetoric, a course that introduced students with limited theoretical backgrounds to current rhetorical practices in various fields of contemporary cultural studies.[2] My aim in the course was for members to increase their understanding of signs in the world around them each day by focusing on the production and the reception of those signs in a variety of media. My emphasis on semiotics was for its flexibility as a tool of analysis. The choice was also based on my response to Terry Eagleton's call in 1984 for a return to the traditional function of criticism, which has always been the province of rhetoric, the examination of "symbolic processes of social life, and the social production of forms of subjectivity."[3] Recently, Henry Giroux has warned that we need to be aware of how the dynamics of culture and politics are changing with the growth of electronic media; Giroux calls for a critical pedagogy that would expose the way power is organized through the circulation of signs in

64

newspapers, mass-circulation magazines, movies, music videos, advertisements, and television programs.[4]

The tools for the critique of representation that Giroux finds so important are readily available in the work of Roland Barthes, who initiated modern cultural studies by looking closely at the indexical quality of advertisements—their seeming to point to and announce themselves as ads—a trait Barthes shows makes them especially lucid models of semiosis.[5] As early as the 1960s Barthes was treating fashion magazines as elements of popular mass culture and showing how they are a rich social text for semiotic analysis.[6] Barthes always brought a playfulness to his analyses, and something of this play and delight in even blatantly commercial forms no doubt influenced my selection of one issue of the J. Peterman Company catalog, *The J. Peterman Company Owner's Manual No. 29* (summer 1994), as a popular culture text for analysis in central writing and discussion assignments for the seminar.[7]

Because of the relative isolation of our campus from commercial centers, catalogs are a mainstay in this area of eastern Washington State, so it was here that I was first introduced to *The J. Peterman Company Owner's Manual* by several subscribers who had been among its loyal readers since the first issue in the fall of 1988. Advertising leisure clothing for both women and men, as well as a smaller selection of collectable knickknacks, the Peterman catalog stands out from the clutter of other retail catalogs stuffing our mailboxes. It is an impressive, five-by-ten-inch, one-hundred-page pamphlet on heavy white bond paper with clothing styles simulating early-twentieth-century fashions. This is one piece of advertising that immediately claims your attention because it looks expensive, probably was, and the consumer doesn't immediately have to pay for it. The catalog has also been attracting the attention of reviewers. Reviews can be useful extratextual cultural materials because they give students a chance to hear professionals discussing other professionals whose work they admire, a much needed perspective from outside academia that helps students think of writing as the creation and product of the work people do each day. Not surprisingly, most responses from these writers have been positive, praising Donald Staley, whose Manhattan advertising agency designs the catalog.[8] In a feature article on American catalogs in the November 1993 *New York Times Magazine*, Holly Brubach says that the J. Peterman catalog is "like someone who, on first acquaintance, strikes you as the kind of person who would make a good traveling companion—witty, entertaining, a bon vivant and a raconteur." Compared with his mail-order competition, the narrator of the J. Peterman catalog is "a merchant poet."[9] This position, however, has not been uncontested. Gary Trudeau's Doonesbury took "J. Pretensions" to task for flimflam rhetoric romanticizing pseudo-artifacts of exotic cultures. The "nostalgia gear" of Trudeau's Boopsie—the Giverny Beekeepers Bonnet, the Fletcher Christian Sarong, and Joe DiMaggio's Chest Protector—she says make her "feel like a schoolgirl again, dreaming of Key West, Paris and Khartoum." [10] Refusing to see Peterman's catalog from the retail business perspective, Marjorie Ingall, a columnist for *Sassy*, is one of few so far to point out the obvious racist and sexist grounds for Peterman's motifs. This is "bad" writing, at the least "pretentious and over-written." For Ingall, Peterman's clothes "wear their overblown race-obsessed, imperialist male fantasies on their creamy white, starched linen sleeves."[11]

This chasm between critical responses to the catalog proved useful in focusing discussion on contradictory views of popular culture we often hold but seldom examine. We may, for example, find ourselves enjoying movies and still be aware that they have been shaped by commercial pressures that cause the audience to be narrowly, even inhumanely, defined. This is potentially why the class had little trouble describing the subject space of many of the J. Peterman catalog layouts. The ideal consumer for the text would be someone who is at home at garden parties, or a traveler en route to the Big Sky country of the American West or to exotic-sounding international spots. Occasionally tossed in to the product names and descriptions are references to incongruent geographical locations in the media spotlight—the (now-defunct) Waxahachie, Texas Particle Physics Shirt, for example, which produces cultural capital through the *mysterium* of science it initiates. Always the vignettes invite the reader to imagine herself or himself in positions of power signified by an almost comic exaggeration of the media's signifiers of excessive material wealth. Students noted that the actual writer of the catalog copy, Mr. Staley or his associates, is someone like themselves who has done extensive graduate work in the humanities. On the other hand, they could not identify with the narrator the writer had created, a figure noticeably attracted to the fictional romance in the lives and works of Isak Dinesen, Hemingway, and the Fitzgeralds for the same reason he would not likely be attracted to those of Bobbie Ann Mason. Peterman's narrator poses in many different guises, all pointing to the fulfilled middle-class lifestyle, a blatant overcoding that was useful in the classroom because it enabled students to talk about this highly textualized traveling narrator who speaks to readers in a pastiche of conventionalized voices of other media. He is the "scriptor" Barthes says is born at the moment the narrative begins.[12]

The class noticed that in whatever guise, the narrator is in control and offers that control as a symbolic commodity. This control itself seems to be parodied by the aggressive exploitation in another J. Peterman catalog entitled *Booty, Spoils and Plunder*®, first released in October 1991. Instead of clothing artifacts for the body, this catalog deals in cultural artifacts for the home and office: sixteenth-century porcelain plates recovered from the South China Sea, baseballs signed by Babe Ruth, actual letters of Winston Churchill and Edward III. A single-page ad consisting of the traveler's itinerary for the "Exclusive J. Peterman Co. 11-day Deluxe Tented African Safari in Kenya" offered "your own private tent. Hot shower, outstanding table d'hôte meals, open bar."[13] This piqued a discussion of the ways in which the copywriter's play with movie stereotypes of early-twentieth-century luxury travel promises both a direct encounter with untamed wilderness and protection from such an encounter. Several people found that this heavily mediated experience of nature recalls the catalog's consistent gestures to the real as a simulation. What was for sale here, one student noted, was assurance of having the correct sensibility, the disengaged, depoliticized "camp" sensibility Susan Sontag diagnosed in a more favorable light three decades ago.[14] It's not surprising that in plugging us in to groups of signifiers, Peterman's narrative signs in his *Owner's Manual* teleguide us along semiotic chains rooted in the Edwardian period, the last days of European colonial power. One of the most productive uses of the catalog was its out-of-joint appeal, which the class noted early in our discussions. The actual audience for the numerous literary and theoretical allusions might be, they speculated, middle-aged academics, who would on the other hand be likely to reject the exploitative colonialist rhetoric. Because this fact could not be made to fit the commercial motivation of a retail catalog, spaces for analysis were opened up.

Among the most powerful signifiers in the Peterman catalogs are direct references to romantic movies from the 1930s up until the past decade. In the *Owner's Manual No. 29* the most sustained cinema motif is a four-page spread entitled "Out of Africa," based ostensibly on Isak Dinesen's *Letters from Africa, 1914–1931* (1981), a paperback edition of which appears for sale at the bottom of page 28 of the catalog. The merchandise, hand-rendered in the fashion of turn-of-the-century retail catalogs, appears on human torsos—the faces of which do not appear—surrounded by verbal text that turns out to be a stripped-down plot outline recounting the influx of Western European settlers to East Africa between 1906 and 1939. We began our discussion by reading several interviews with John Peterman, who is open to talking about the inception of his Lexington, Kentucky-based company. Peterman claims that the catalog is intended for people who enjoy reading. With only about one-fourth of the page layout taken up by the actual garment, the remaining space filled by verbal text, the catalog provided materials for analyzing the ways verbal texts work to "anchor" or control the much more expansive area for connotative meanings of the purely iconic sign. Comparing the catalog with other fashion advertising, the class could dismantle the way Peterman's "written garment" worked symbolically by providing the context for the item's use, therefore controlling the cache of possible meanings for the buyer.[15]

Because of this section's placement among other layouts referencing Hollywood's movie industry, a semiotic chain of associations and cues sends readers back to their memories of *Out of Africa*, Sydney Pollack's 1985 movie production starring Meryl Streep and Robert Redford. We watched the video in order to make close observations on the ways reseeing it or seeing it for the first time mediated our experience of reading Peterman's ad. Several students could remember, as I did, that the year after its release the movie won seven Academy Awards, among them those for cinematography, original score, art direction, and sound. For us the memorable visual and auditory associations created powerful semantic spaces that are invaluable to the merchandiser. Many in the class would have just passed into adolescence in 1985. We also had class members from other countries who had not seen the movie, and who because they had little exposure to recent American cinema were in an interesting position to reflect on the difference between technical and cultural conventions in Hollywood and those in their countries. Even as I returned to watch *Out of Africa*, I was struck by the vastly different historical and political contexts I found myself bringing this narrative representation into now. Back in 1985 I had not noticed the lack of any mention in the credits of the indigenous peoples who contributed to the production, or that the only recognition given there was to Ker & Downey Safari Transport Services of Kenya. The film now appeared to me to be filled with what Mary Louise Pratt describes as "the masculine heroic discourse of discovery."[16] Central to this discourse is the "imperial trope" Pratt finds in European travel accounts of the mid-eighteenth through the nineteenth centuries. Most prominent is an aestheticized landscape, as though the narrator's description is controlled by the conventions of painting. Placed in the specular position of this narrative voice, the reader, Pratt notes, is in a powerful position of control, the source of that power, the ability to both imaginatively create the scene and to judge it. What is seen by that reader/viewer is "all there is."[17] Discussing some of these reflections with the class, I recalled the critical innocence I had brought to the movie when it was first released, especially to that panoramic opening scene inside of British East Africa. Practically every facet of Pratt's "imperial trope" is present there as Baroness von Blixen's train cuts across an unpeopled landscape, rewritten from the Western perspective as indifferent or destructive. The retrospective nature of the story enforced through voice-over refrain of Baroness von Blixen, "I had a farm in Africa," is a reminder of the brevity of those two Edenic decades in the first half of the twentieth century, a slice of time Peterman's writers attempt, as members of the class noted, to refashion as a postmodern nostalgia piece.

A productive direction and one I want to give more thought to encouraging again involved attempts by members of the class to describe the affects of these textual layerings. As an audience for the catalog's representation of the movie, they noted the different kinds of representations wedged between themselves and the actual historical time and place in which the film was set. One student who had read Dinesen's memoirs, published posthumously in 1981, pointed out that the movie script had been based not only on these memoirs, (*Letters from Africa*) and on the semi-autobiographical *Out of Africa* (1937), but also on several critical works written on Isak Dinesen's fiction.[18] An important insight came out of this discussion. The movie, as all representational forms, was created through the generic and historical conventions of the time. As readers of the J. Peterman catalog, members of the class found themselves distanced not only by chronology but by virtue of having their original experience of the story of Baroness von Blixen through a 1985 media representation whose cinematic conventions for verisimilitude were by 1994 already a thing of the past. In speaking to us through the *déjà-vu*, the always already said and seen of old books, written history, movies, and old ads, *The J. Peterman Company Owner's Manual No. 29*, with its layers of intertextual referencing, provided numerous examples of pastiche, which the class had discussed when reading Fredric Jameson's famous essay on postmodernism and consumer culture.[19] The class was split, some focusing on our vulnerability to the seduction of such media, others considering what might be gained by readers in allowing themselves to enjoy the catalog's playful emphasis on textuality and its invitation to join in the game. I wanted to be sure my students considered that attempts to define postmodernism were attempts to understand the affective levels on which phenomena reach us and the habitual ways we respond as a culture, providing models for understanding how media works on audiences. At that point we were in a position to look back and reflect on what we had just done as we followed the circuitous paths of our own responses to the movie *Out of Africa*.

Peterman's catalogs open with his company's "Philosophy," stated on the inside front cover of each issue: "People want things that are hard to find. Things that have Romance, but a factual romance, about them," and closing with, "Clearly, people want things that make their lives the way they wish they were" (p. 1). In suggesting the opposition between fact and romance, then parading its deconstruction as play, the catalog clearly fits into that class of postmodern advertising the power of which comes from hybridization of commercial and popular aesthetic texts. This hybrid of motivations makes the Peterman catalogs ideal texts for rhetorical analysis. Continual foregrounding of the storytelling process creates highly conventionalized descriptions, unstable verbal scenes constructed at the moment of their description. Trained in literary and rhetorical analysis, seminar members enjoyed playing Peterman's game, noting the way merchandise begins to appear insubstantial as the reader moves virtually across countries or continents with the turn of a page, the narrative voice assuring us that what is offered are "uncompromised," "fastidious," even genuine "replicas." Items that once seemed functional, within the realm of denotative fact, suddenly slip, becoming less substantial. A small pocket atlas "not only tells you where you are, but where you wish you were" (p. 25). Similitudes turn up everywhere. The J. Peterman Silk Shirt is "exactly like a denim shirt but not denim" (p. 40). Vintage T-shirts look old but are "new." Yet we are reminded that they are "more substantial than you usually find in T-Shirts" (p. 87). The Peterman copywriter steps into the role of postmodern theorist, warning us that in this age of mechanical reproduction there can be no authentic history. Introduced as the "Real Thing," a French Officer's Rucksack is then described: "This vintage rucksack embodies the thousand little permutations which result from a few hundred years of product development (none of it computer-simulated)" (p. 33).

Because the catalog presents readers with such blatantly overcoded materials for the game of narrative analysis, members of the seminar said they felt particularly conscious of themselves as literary readers performing critical tasks. Peterman's narrator seems intent on reminding us that we are dealing not with the real but with what Barthes describes as "the effect of the real," our sense of the actuality of the object created, as it is in the novel, by the piling up of minute detail, the more contingent, the more "natural" it seems."[20] Drawing on their readings of two of Barthes's essays, the class had conceptual tools to detect how the constant play of innuendo and name-dropping in the Peterman catalog seem to be for the purpose of exposing the reader's blind acceptance of the conventions of verisimilitude. Among celebrities we hear about are Hollywood actresses and actors. But we are just as likely to encounter, on the same level and treated as somehow equally real, Fitzgerald, Gatsby and a replica of the "Gatsby Shirt." A later ad, "The Man in the White Suit," offers for sale a suit "(Actually, Off-White)" like the one Redford and Noël Coward wore in the movies. The narrator who spins out the tale seemingly imagines his reader wearing the suit, which is "almost exactly the same Bogart wore when he got married August 20, 1938. (He looked terrific. So will you)" (p. 92).

In an ad for the Mephisto M1604 Walking Shoe, the authority for the shoes' utility comes from the Peterman copywriter, whose words, it is claimed are excerpted from an earlier Peterman catalog ad in the *New York Times* (p. 31). Other media become insubstantial points of origin and thus authority for the existence of solid referents in a real world. A Vintage BBC Tennis Blouse is the J. Peterman replica of a 1920s design by a company that designs costumes for the BBC (p. 42). A similar Nabokovian sleight of hand occurs as we are informed that proof of the existence of the Russian navy is to be found on our nightly TV news, but only if the Russians appearing there look like conventional Hollywood stereotypes of Russian sailors. It is the existence of these consciously constructed media simulations of "real" Russian sailors that are the source for Peterman's Russian Navy Shirt. As they moved from page to page, students realized that Peterman's copy is stuffed full of postmodern images and other simulacra, and they had little trouble discussing these as examples of hyperreal simulation whose referents Jean Baudrillard says are no more than other unstable signs.[21] The difficult conceptual leap, however, was their imaginative capacity to conceptualize the workings of the thick intertextuality of the catalog, the campy, playful attitude encouraged by the narrative movement, and the undeniably rhetorical advertising text which never abandons its material and symbolic referents in the world of commerce.

The J. Peterman Company Owner's Manual offers at least two perspectives for cultural critics, both of which are bound complexly together. One is as a chance for readers to chart their responses to the catalog's blatantly sexist rhetoric and its play with nostalgia for colonialist settings, which are so overwhelmingly callous that to ignore them would be to overlook the tremendous power that representations exert upon us and the frightening ease of access that distributors of such representations have to our most intimate lives. This line of critique can offer a way to examine what Colin Mercer calls "complicit pleasures,"[22] our enjoyment of texts that we might under other circumstances denounce on humane or moral grounds. Several members of the class had strong reactions to what they found to be the narrator's condescending, implicitly hostile attitude toward women, this despite the catalog's gestures toward the lives of women like Dinesen and Beryl Markham, who for earlier as well as later generations could be seen as strong, independent women. The ad's romanticizing of the colonial era as the lost Edenic paradise appeared especially callous. We had just watched a movie in which a woman's overwhelming personal loss—emotional, physical, and financial—is the result of her vulnerable position in a world dominated by white European males, where both her husband and her lover in different ways are in positions of mastery over the landscape, its inhabitants, and herself. The advertisers seem unaware of or unconcerned with the semiotic processes that can occur once their media creations are made public. The class pointed out that the catalog's invitation to women readers to step into the subject position of Dinesen's character— "*Alone in Africa, 1921.* Your husband has left you; now the farm is totally in your charge. (Always was, in fact)" (p. 28)—is strikingly ironic in light of Baroness von Blixen's voice-over in the movie, "I *had* a farm in Africa," a powerful auditory metaphor of her deep emotional scarring. Reflection on our affective responses to the insertion of older popular culture forms into current media with very different aims illustrated the continued power of these representations to shape how we imagine ourselves and our relations with other people.

An equally important perspective is offered by an understanding of the pleasures readers take in the Peterman catalog despite their full awareness of its commercial imperative. Thinking in terms of resistive pleasures allows a better view of the power we have to transform the meanings of all of those mass-produced images flooding into our living areas throughout the day. Almost everyone I know who reads catalogs will point to the way they must make the time to browse. This time-out may be a space for intricate interpretive tactics. And the pleasures gained from those can be, as Michel de Certeau shows, texts for further examination of the rich signifying practices of consumption.[23] There are pleasures in appropriating words and images of the texts of commercial ads that resemble in their subversive and playful nature those pleasures of numerous other practices—talking, reading, moving about, shopping, cooking, decorating a new apartment—all of which de Certeau shows involve making a space of one's own within the official space owned by another, each a "way of using" imposed systems.

The class had begun just this critical process when reflecting on the nature of their imaginative entrances into the historical time and place of the movie *Out of Africa.* The productivity of de Certeau's theory of resistive pleasures, those many spaces we make for ourselves each day, was particularly impressed on me when a neighbor who had been sitting in on the class was looking through several of the Peterman catalogs in my kitchen. Jane responded immediately to Peterman's logo, the J. Peterman Coat, described on page 56 of the catalog as a "duster":

> Hey, a slicker. It's split. To get on your horse. Splits at the butt. I used to wear chaps with it. If you're riding 25 or 50 miles and it's cold out, you need to stay dry and warm. Everyone wore them. They're canvass duck. Broke the wind. Nothing ever keeps the rain out. Medicine Woman wears one. And the young guys wear them on the *Lonesome Dove* series, Saturday nights 6:00. Cow days are going out and the train coming in. Curtis Wells, Montana is the setting for that. I've never heard of Curtis Wells.
>
> That coat takes me back 30 years. It was great. I must have been 14 or 15 years old. We'd run our cattle from the ranch near Cut Bank [Montana] on the eastern edge of the Blackfoot Indian Reservation, near highway 21 to the Blackfoot Reservation in Glacier Park. 120 miles. This is the North fork of the Milk River country. We'd lease pasture area from the tribe . . .

The associations in this excerpt branch off in a number of directions, back to the storehouse of memories my neighbor Jane has of growing up in Montana on the eastern slopes of the Rockies, forward to contemporary media through which she tries to find analogies for her listener. Although determination of motivations is only at most approximate and largely a reinterpretation, a good part of Jane's motivation for these associations, it seemed to me, was the need to reward herself after the privations of the day she'd just spent at work. The subversive impulse was as much directed toward the monotony and frustrations of the workday as it was toward Peterman's commercial aims. With no intention of buying the J. Peterman Coat, she could still travel somewhere else by simply inscribing over Peterman's "duster" her own nomination, "slicker," a move that made the catalog "habitable" for the expression of her own desire. I noticed that my own appropriation of the Western outdoors motif in the catalog was triggered by Jane's comments and my memories of fishing several small glacial lakes off that same highway between Browning and Cut Bank. The labyrinthine paths of pleasure derived from browsing through catalogs could provide a rich store of texts for discussion and for writing assignments on popular culture. To the extent that television and video have made us much more cinematically literate than we were ten years ago, the sharpened critical reflex in students is a resource they can use to examine intertextual phenomena in other media.[24] If our shared experience of movies, television, newspapers, magazines, catalogs, and other kinds of popular culture gives us a common point of reference, a common language, for thinking about and explaining the world, then a better understanding of and facility with this would be an important form of literacy.

The Russian semiotician Yuri Lotman considers a phenomenon with some affinities to this which he calls "double replication," the encoding of one art language onto the system of another.[25] This replication can be seen, for example, when the artist turns an historical event into the subject of a painting. Lotman finds in this a dynamic principle of growth. The introduction of this external text or language into the structural field of another text brings about a transformation, an increase in semiotic existence or the text's potential for meaning or significance. This model may be useful in thinking about what happens when we respond to the J. Peterman narrator as he invites us to recall memories of a particular scene from an old movie, or to imagine one of its characters contemporaneous with ourselves. To what extent do we move in our mental voyages through these layers of old movies and TV shows? What are the pleasures of imagining the already represented, and in what way does this add significance to our existence?

In her studies of popular culture, Angela McRobbie finds that the intensification of exchanges between media, especially between commercial and aesthetic texts, makes the social act of consuming objects and symbols powerful forces in the production of culture.[26] We need, she says, to understand consumption in everyday life, but to do this we need to understand the varied forms of pleasure people gain by consuming, a pleasure that does not have to be apolitical.[27] Reflecting on their written analyses of the narratives within a retail catalog, members of our seminar began to look at some of their own pleasures and through their understanding of those to raise further questions about themselves as active and imaginative agents in the "ordinary" cultures surrounding them each day, in this way making our class dialogue and their writing serve a larger, more important critical function.

Notes

1. Raymond Williams, *Culture and Society 1780-1950* (London: Penguin, 1966), 16. First published in 1958.

2. The course, Cultural Rhetoric, was funded by the Summer Session Program at Washington State University. I taught the course in the summer of 1994 and again the following year. The grant covered the cost of the visual texts for the course—comic books, magazines, and a number of films—as well as blank video and audio tapes.

3. Terry Eagleton, *The Function of Criticism: From "The Spectator" to Post-Structuralism* (New York: Verso, 1984), 124.

4. Henry Giroux, *Disturbing Pleasures: Learning Popular Culture* (Routledge: New York, 1994). In an earlier work Giroux said we need to look closely at why people affect investments in popular culture, and he calls for a "critical politics of representation" to further social transformation. *Border Crossings: Cultural Workers and the Politics of Education* (New York: Routledge, 1992), 192–241.

5. Roland Barthes, *Mythologies* (Paris: Editions de Seuil, 1957).

6. Roland Barthes, *The Fashion System*, trans. Matthew Ward and Richard Howard (New York: Hill and Wang, 1983); originally published in French as *Système de la Mode* (Paris: Editions du Seuil, 1967).

7. In addition to contributions from popular culture, we used five major texts, beginning with *Studying Culture: An Introductory Reader,* edited by Ann Gray and Jim McGuigan (London and New York: Arnold and Routledge, 1993). Moving from foundational texts to more recent ones, it included essays by, among others, Raymond Williams, Roland Barthes, Janice Radway, Edward Said, Graham Murdoch, Stuart Hall, Phil Cohen, Erica Carter, Judith Williamson, Fredric Jameson. In addition there were essays by Barthes, Laura Mulvey, David Morley, Ann Kaplan, Hilary Radner, John Fiske, and John Hartley. We also used Ellen McCracken's *Decoding Women's Magazines from Mademoiselle to Ms.* (New York: St. Martins, 1993), *The Many Lives of the Batman: Critical Approaches to a Superhero and His Media,* edited by Roberta E. Pearson and William Uricchio (New York: Routledge, 1991), and *Nation, Culture, Text: Australian Cultural and Media Studies* (London and New York: Routledge, 1993) edited by Graeme Turner—an excellent collection on the ways in which Australian scholars are using theory in hopes of changing the civil and economic structures of their country—texts ranging from the business pages of the Sydney newspaper to discourses created by television and newspaper news coverage of the Azaria Chamberlin case. A final major text was *Film Theory Goes to the Movies* edited by Jim Collins, Hilary Radner, and Ava Preacher Collins (New York: Routledge, 1993). The grant covered the cost of films covered in *Film Theory: Boyz N the Hood, Jungle Fever, Silence of the Lambs, Thelma and Louise, Dead Poets Society,* and the *Batman* films.

8. See Charles Fuller, "From Peacocks to Porcelain, Selling the Way We Were: A Modern Classic, *Entrepreneur,* February 1992, 88–92; Gail Buchalter, "Starting Your Own Business: J. Peterman Co." *Forbes,* 26 October 1992, 222–225; Tom Peters, "Businesses Need to Put Some Life into 'Quality,' *Chicago Tribune,* 19 November 1990, sec. 4; James R. Rosenfield, "In the Mail," *Direct Marketing* 57:3 (July 1994):25

9. Holly Brubach, "Mail-Order America," *New York Times Magazine,* 21 November 1993, 55–61, 68–70.

10. Gary Trudeau, "Doonesbury," *The Spokesman Review,* 17 April 1994.

11. Marjorie Ingall, "The J. Peterman Catalog," Sassy, October 1994, 80.

12. Roland Barthes, "The Death of the Author," in *The Rustle of Language,* trans. Richard Howard (Berkeley: University of California Press, 1989).

13. J. Peterman Company, *Booty, Spoils, and Plunder,* October 1991, 26.

14. Susan Sontag, "Notes on Camp," in her *Against Interpretation* (New York: Farrar, Strauss, Giroux, 1966): 275–292.

15. Roland Barthes, *The Fashion System,* xii–14; 12.

16. Mary Louise Pratt, *Imperial Eyes: Travel Writing as Transculturation* (New York: Routledge, 1992).

17. Ibid., 204.

18. Judith Thurman, *Isak Dinesen: The Life of a Storyteller* (New York: St. Martin's, 1982), Errol Trzebinski, *Silence Will Speak: A Study of the Life of Denys Finch Hatton and His Relationship with Karen Blixen* (Chicago: University of Chicago, 1977).

19. Fredric Jameson, "Postmodernism and Consumer Society," in *Studying Culture: An Introductory Reader.* Originally published in *Postmodernism and Its Discontents,* ed. E. Ann Kaplan (New York: Verso, 1988.) Jameson finds one of the salient features of the postmodern to be what he calls the nostalgia mode, the attempt to portray the historical past by intertextual references to older periods or artifacts, in particular the

through the nostalgia film in which these references are to earlier films or other aesthetic forms which themselves were recreations of that past historical period. One of the effects of this pastiche is that we are aware of the aesthetic intentions of the earlier forms. Jameson expands these ideas in *Postmodernism or the Cultural Logic of Late Capitalism* (Durham, NC.: Duke University Press, 1991).

20. Roland Barthes, "The Effect of the Real," in his *The Rustle of Language*, trans. Richard Howard (Berkeley: University of California Press, 1989): 141–148.

21. Jean Baudrillard, "Symbolic Exchange and Death" and "Simulacra and Simulations," in his *Selected Writings*, ed. Mark Poster (Stanford, Calif.: Stanford University Press, 1988): 50–68.

22. Colin Mercer, "Complicit Pleasures," in *Popular Culture and Social Relations*, ed. Tony Bennett, Colin Mercer, and Janet Woollacott (Philadelphia: Open University Press, 1988): 50–68.

23. Michel de Certeau, *The Practice of Everyday Life* (Berkeley: University of California Press, 1984). Based in part on Roland Barthes's earlier *The Pleasures of the Text,* de Certeau's theory of subversive pleasure in everyday activities laid some of the groundwork for examining the role of pleasure.

24. Jim Collins examines the "foregrounded, hyperconscious intertextuality" of popular movies. He sees a profound change in audience competence and a "fundamental shift in what constitutes both entertainment and cultural literacy in the 'Information Age.'" From "Genericity in the Nineties: Eclectic Irony and the New Sincerity," in *Film Theory Goes to the Movies*, ed. Jim Collins, Hilary Radner, and Ava Preacher Collins (New York: Routledge, 1993): 242–263.

25. Yuri Lotman, *Universe of the Mind: A Semiotic Theory of Culture*, trans. Ann Shuckman (London: I.B. Tauris, 1990); "The Text Within the Text," *PMLA* 109, no. 3 (May 1994): 377–384.

26. Angela McRobbie, introduction to her *Postmodernism and Popular Culture* (New York: Routledge, 1994).

27. Angela McRobbie, "New Times in Cultural Studies," in *Postmodernism and Popular Culture*. See also her earlier article "Dance and Social Fantasy" in *Gender and Generation*, ed. Angela McRobbie and Mica Nava (London: Macmillan, 1984), 40.

8

Developing
Vernacular Literacies and
Multidisciplinary Pedagogies

W.F. Garrett-Petts

New Forms of Writing

Negotiating a space for new literacies is no easy task. Take, for example, Daphne Marlatt's claim at the end of her photo-textual collaboration with Robert Minden, *Steveston*: "Both photography (as its name asserts) and poetry can be seen as different forms of writing, one with light, the other with words."[1] At first glance, Marlatt's conflation of the visual and the verbal might seem to offer little more than a rehearsal of earlier analogies linking the "camera and the pencil." Marcus Aurelius Root (1864), William Henry Fox Talbot (1859), and other nineteenth-century critics, regarded photography as an ingenious but ultimately derivative medium. Joseph Pennell parodies the photographer as a once "mute inglorious Milton"[2] now transformed into an "artist"; and early North American novelists were frequently chastised for allowing their work to degenerate into "mere photograph[s]."[3] The "mere photograph" has long been treated as little more than a handmaiden to literature and painting. Unlike these early commentators, however, Marlatt, a poet and novelist, does not seek to colonize photography in the name of literature or some other art; by characterizing visual images as "forms of writing," she emphasizes the narrative potential of a medium more generally regarded as "symbolic communication without syntax."[4] Marlatt allows that photography can speak for itself; like many other contemporary authors, artists, and teachers, she explores the potential dialogue of image and text.

Certainly, photo-textual communication has become a ubiquitous aspect of popular culture—on billboards, in advertising, photojournalism, magazines, and in the new cyberspace environment of the World Wide Web. These

Figure 8–1
Reading and writing on the World Wide Web.
Reproduced courtesy of Wailan Low, Executor for Earle Birney's estate,
and by the University College of the Cariboo.

utilitarian crafts and objects of low- or middle-brow culture traditionally have held little relevance for the high art or literary community. However, recent, more "serious," hybrid art seems intent on raiding the visual techniques of popular and mass culture, using them as vehicles for cultural critique and "legitimate" aesthetic expression. These more serious art forms are more difficult to ignore. Some will no doubt point out that there is little new here, that image/text compositions have been featured in works and periods as diverse as medieval illuminated manuscripts, early Renaissance paintings, seventeenth-century shaped verse, Blake's engravings, and twentieth-century cubist collage. Others, such as Henry Giroux, see contemporary hybrid art as an indicator of "the changing conditions of knowledge production in the context of emerging mass electronic media and the role these new technologies are playing as critical socializing agencies."[5] One thing seems certain: As the technology for combining image, text, and other media becomes more sophisticated and accessible, the gap between production and reception of multimedia communication will diminish. Present-day audiences will be tomorrow's authors of relatively complex image/text productions—and understanding the rhetoric of this new electronically mediated or otherwise "hybridized" vernacular should be of concern to those of us who teach both literature and literacies.

Confronting the "Literary Bias"

Of particular interest is literary culture's resistance to including the study of things visual as anything more than a marginal (incidental) concern. Understanding the "reception aesthetics" and social politics that inform the literary and high art responses to photo-textual art should help provide a valuable point of departure for further critical discussion and classroom instruction. In addition, reflection on the nature of literary resistance to the inclusion of a visual vernacular should help frame and clarify those issues that inform literary values generally.

The act of responding to border-blurring art poses a challenge to academic specialization, the feature of German universities that so impressed Matthew Arnold in the latter half of the nineteenth century and that transformed English studies from a generalized field to an academic discipline. According to Terry Eagleton, English was considered initially "an untaxing sort of affair, concerned with finer feelings rather than with the more virile topics of bona fide academic 'disciplines,' . . . a convenient sort of non-subject to palm off on the ladies."[6] Once the momentum of disciplinary expansion took hold, English quickly established its own field for study, or garden to cultivate, replete with the obligatory appeal to specialized methodologies. Though a professional commitment to specialization still holds for most academics, recent interest in cultural studies, women's studies, and rhetoric has introduced questions not easily answered by specialist approaches. Instead, in these areas, the emphasis has shifted toward interdisciplinary and multidisciplinary inquiries—from monologues to collaborative dialogues.

Some have argued that the questioning of specialist knowledge marks a move from modernism to postmodernism. Indeed, Stanley Aronowitz, Henry Giroux, and others have called for a program of "postmodern education," a program seemingly informed by the same border-crossing impulses that characterize the convergence of photography and literature. Giroux, for example, argues against a curriculum "locked within disciplinary boundaries and recycling old orthodoxies";[7] instead he champions an interdisciplinary pedagogy based on "a new discourse that proposes radically new questions, analyses, and forms of ethical address."[8] This pedagogy is not so much an attack on specialization as it is an appeal for greater integration of specialist knowledge—an appeal for educators to combine their expertise, to collaborate on research that speaks to issues of more than specialized significance. One response would be to develop a "border pedagogy" as a "counter-text,"[9] an approach to teaching that places the analysis of cultural codes, the excavation of contending literacies, and a radical interdisciplinary dialogue at the center of the curriculum.

Of course, talking about such radical change and actually enacting such change are two very different tasks. As William Nericcio notes "[m]ost literary critics, especially those not yet bowled over by the intoxicating contagion named 'cultural studies,' are not always, or have not always been, comfortable with pictures. They will venture to a museum here, attend a film festival there, but rarely will they interrogate the 'infection' of image within the bodies of words they navigate."[10] While "excavating" contending literacies will never be easy, especially for those of us trained in a single academic specialization, classroom discussion of works that overtly challenge specialist orientations—works that speak with multiple voices and in multiple modes—can certainly help foster multidisciplinary understanding. The first step is to come to terms with the literary bias against the visual and learn to read texts of popular culture in context; the second step is to encourage hands-on experimentation that allows students, in a workshop or studio setting, to learn more about the theory and practice of integrating both visual and verbal literacies.

Visual literacy is too frequently cast as "something practised by others on us." Even many media studies programs (where one might expect a sympathetic treatment of visual culture) present visual literacy as a means of inoculating the unwary against the snares and baits of advertising, television, music videos, photography, and other forms of visual representation. Kay Ellen Rutledge, for example, casts the purveyors of visual culture as a "professional" class of "advertising experts, politicians, government propagandists, and activists . . . [who] influence our behavior and alter our perceptions by creating illusions—illusions so skillfully crafted that we easily confuse them with reality."[11] Vernacular art forms such as photography seem especially suspect, for literary culture has long valued imagination over image, what is recollected over what is seen. The association or intermixing of photography and narrative (or vernacular culture's images and high cultural texts) presents a potentially disruptive challenge to the hegemony of word over image.

Where literary culture and literacy educators feel threatened by the visual, the typical response from critics and teachers involves a defense of the *imagination*, that "wonderfully ectoplasmic term."[12] Here's what Marianna Torgovnick has to say in *The Visual Arts, Pictorialism and the Novel*, a study which invokes a rhetoric of suspicion, disdain, and moral prohibition. Speaking of the relationship between Dickens's writing and his (H. Talbot Browne's) illustrations for *Bleak House*, Torgovnick argues that "[t]he illustrations seem, finally, inadequate to the text even though they—perhaps because they—linger in the reader's imagination and often shape his later conception of the novel much as the film of a novel often influences a viewer's subsequent experience of the text."[13] The use of the word *inadequate* is revealing, for Torgovnick's observation is more a complaint about interference than adequacy. In the final analysis, according to Torgovnick, no illustration is adequate to the task:

> Illustrations severely limit the range of the reader's visual imagination as it comes into contact with the author's. Often, indeed, the author's visual imagination sprints ahead of the illustrations, suggesting more than the plates actually record and yet tempting the reader to accept the plates as an accurate and adequate representation of how people and events in the novel "really looked."

She offers the warning that "illustrations can thus lull the reader's visualizing faculties."[14]

The imagination, the mind's eye, is active, dynamic, free to "sprint ahead"; while perception is cast as limited, inhibiting, offering only a photographic temptation or visual crutch. Actual images are said to be "complete in themselves"—"mimetic, not semiotic or symbolic";[15] and the whole argument against illustration becomes an issue of morality and pedagogy divorced from theory. Remarkably, the semiotic and symbolic potential of visual images, or of the interaction between the visual and the verbal, is left unexamined. Like John Szarkowski's famous insistence on the "narrative poverty" of the photograph, Torgovnick's reading assumes the narrative poverty of the visual generally.[16]

We are exhorted to wean young, lazy, or dull readers away from a reliance on visual aids:

> Such illustrations—indeed illustrations in general— may be harmless enough, may sometimes even be helpful to readers who have difficulties visualizing as they read. But, like eye glasses improperly used, they dull the average reader's visual imagination, accustoming him to relying on illustrations and not his own faculties.[17]

Ironically, fifty years ago, as Ellen Esrock has pointed out, I. A. Richards and William Empson mounted many of these same objections, not against visual illustrations but against visualization itself (*The Reader's Eye*). For the New Critics, visualization distracted readers from proper attention to the words on the page; for the new New Critics, like Torgovnick, visual images inhibit language's ability to stimulate the visual imagination. Either way, it seems, visual and verbal are prohibited from mixing too closely.

Even when they do mix, they are too often ignored by critics and teachers. Anthologies and new editions that reprint the writing but leave out the original accompanying visual art suggest one significant aspect of the "literary attitude"—the same kind of attitude that allows Dennis Cooley to reflect "ironically," in footnote 12 of his article on Michael Ondaatje's *The Collected Works of Billy the Kid*, "my argument about photography doesn't take account of the actual photographs [in the book]."[18] We need to recognize, with Douglas Barbour, that a work like Marlatt's *Steveston* "is a collaboration [between a poet and a photographer], and that reading the poem apart from Minden's series of photographs makes for an incomplete reading of the work."[19] We also need to understand (and question) the critical presuppositions that in the same article allow Barbour to present just such an "incomplete reading," one ignoring Minden's photographs with the confident declaration, "Nevertheless, it is Marlatt's writing which interests us here."[20]

Such critical practice seems all too familiar. As Richard Kostelanetz remarks, much of the best writing depends "as much on visual literacy as on

Figure 8–2
Two pages from Daphne Marlatt and Robert Minden's *Steveston*.
Reproduced courtesy of the authors.

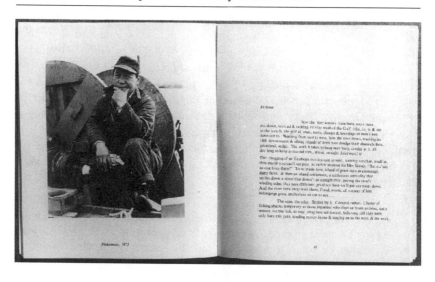

Figure 8–3
An image and text section from Michael Ondaatje's
The Collected Works of Billy the Kid. Reproduced courtesy of the author.

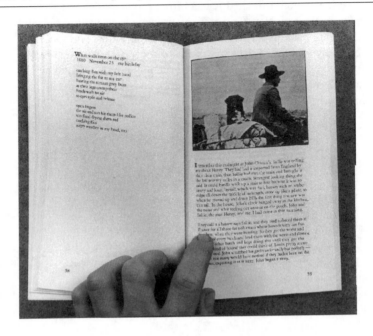

verbal literacy; many 'readers' literate in the second aspect are illiterate in the first."[21] In one respect, the literary bias (or blindness) remains a matter of class consciousness. Those who confer legitimation (universities, museums, granting agencies, academics) have traditionally placed literature, painting, and classical music above photography, film, and jazz (as, in turn, these middle-ranked arts sit above the crafts and trades of oral storytelling, advertising, and popular music). Pierre Bourdieu, whose *Photography, a Middle-brow Art* informs my own understanding of how cultural legitimacy is achieved and maintained, offers a concise rationale for singling out photography as the "in-between" art most likely to trouble the guardians of book culture: photography represents a "popular aesthetic" that is "defined and manifested (at least partially) in opposition to scholarly aesthetics"[22]—just as scholarly literacy has been defined by a withdrawal from popular discourse. Bourdieu explains that the

> position of photography within the hierarchy of legitimacies, half-way between "vulgar" practices, apparently abandoned to the anarchy of tastes and noble cultural practices, subject to strict rules, explains . . . the ambiguity of the attitudes which it provokes, particularly among the members of the privileged classes.[23]

These in-between practices, what I have referred to as forms of vernacular expression, interrupt the movement of mainstream culture; by intruding upon or resisting the mainstream, such practices offer a moment of held breath, a cultural pause, wherein we can reflect upon the normally invisible social, historical, and cultural forces that shape what we read and see.

Implications for the Composition Classroom

The advent of new, visually-based literacies invites us to read for difference— and, in the process, to learn to read and write differently. To this point I've had more to say about "literary" attitudes than I have about the teaching of composition. But while it may be argued that composition studies has long been open to including aspects of "media studies" as the subject for discussion and writing, composition instructors are not immune to the print bias against the visual. We may encourage our students to write about the forms of popular culture, but we seldom allow our students to *use* those forms as vehicles for personal and academic exploration. What I am proposing here is a little elbow room for the examination and development of alternative literacies: I'm asking (1) that we examine the print-literacy bias of the university composition classroom, and (2) that we follow Daphne Marlatt's example, admitting alternative "forms of writing" into our classrooms. Why, for example, have we chosen to let the path of academic specialization lead us away from the natural integration of literacies that we nurture routinely in the elementary-school curriculum? As Donald Murray writes,

> Children know what writers know: we write what we see. The relationship of seeing and telling, drawing and writing, is intimate, essential, and a significant aspect of teaching and researching the writing act.
>
> Yet the education profession builds walls where there should be none, isolating instructors and students of visual arts from instructors and students of language arts. We all lose when education locks us into subject-tight compartments.[24]

As composition teachers we have much to gain by building bridges rather than walls. Writing and photography offer an especially congenial pairing.

Encouraging students to examine "photo-graphic" works by authors/artists (such as Daphne Marlatt and Robert Minden, Michael Ondaatje, Walker Evans and James Agee, Barbara Kruger, Laurie Anderson, Donald Lawrence, Carol Condé, and Karl Beveridge, to name a few) can only help enhance their appreciation of how verbal and visual codes work together.[25] They will note, for example, how photo-textual documentaries are constructed, and how the collaborative efforts of artists and authors often yield contradictory or competing representations. This understanding becomes more profound when students are challenged to create their own photographic compositions. The example of media studies instruction has taught us that hands-on experiential learning forms an essential complement to "talking about" and "reflecting upon" how the media work .[26] My own experience in teaching visual and verbal literacies together suggests that composition students, especially, have much to gain from the exploration and integration of multiple literacies. Not only does such an exploration provide an opportunity for an introduction to more traditional visual concerns—page layout; the use of headings, charts, diagrams, and so on, in technical writing—but it reinforces the crucial importance of *seeing* the topic and *representing* that topic to an audience. At first, students tend to use the visual element as simple illustration (of the sort referred to by Torgovnick). With work, and by following the example of more experienced writers/artists, students learn how to combine visual and verbal expression into an integrated whole—a composition that uses the literacies of vernacular expression as complementary modes of inquiry and communication.

For many of my own students the challenge of being asked to compose both verbally *and* visually has resulted in some of their most satisfying—and best-written—work. Asking students to explore a topic visually and to, in turn, incorporate visual elements into their essays seems to make them more aware of the way language is (or can be) used. Michael Benton notes in a recent essay on teaching poetry and painting to high school students that

> Reading pictures is a more sociable activity than reading print. Pictures are usually viewed and discussed by groups of students more readily than poems are because the visual medium is more invitational. . . . Students find that the hesitant explorations of their own language are not daunted by the dominant language of the object of their attention. It is easier to talk and write about a work of art in an iconic medium different from the very one we are using to articulate our responses.[27]

Integrating visual and verbal literacies has much the same effect: When students incorporate visual representations into their essays, they open up their work to group response, "inviting" as it were both author and audience to see (and talk about) the essay's theme, organization, and symbolic logic differently. The task of integrating literacies moves writing dramatically from the private, largely invisible realm to the public, overtly visible realm.

In addition, and especially for students who experience various forms of writer's block, the sense of play that accompanies visual/verbal composition leads many to develop highly useful and creative invention strategies as alternatives to outlining, freewriting, brainstorming, and so on. Greg Ulmer's much-discussed heuristic, CATTt, suggests one such invention strategy that might be practised in a classroom setting: Ulmer takes the associative, weblike structure of the Internet as his model and recommends a new form of writing, the "Mystory," calling it the mode of visual/verbal discourse best suited to supplement traditional argumentation as a mode of academic and personal inquiry.[28]

The most important reason to emphasize the study and practice of multiple literacies, however, devolves upon our collective need to engage in an increasingly complex cultural conversation. Including the visual need not

Figures 8–4 and 8–5
A series of photo-narratives from Donald Lawrence's
Romantic Commodities exhibition. Reproduced courtesy of the artist.

Figures 8–6 and 8–7
From a series of photo-etchings by photography and literature
student Jana Sasaki: "A Personal Narrative in Image and Text."
Reproduced courtesy of the artist.

mean excluding the verbal; on the contrary, inclusion of visual materials and approaches offers an important set of reference points to help students (and their teachers) position themselves and their arguments among the rival discourses at play in any rhetorical situation. As Anthony Paré notes, "Joining a collective, or discourse community, entails joining the dialogue. In doing so, the individual adopts and adapts the views of the collective, which are embedded in and enacted by the group's discourse practices."[29] By ignoring or marginalizing visual codes, classroom instruction too often fosters an artificial discourse community, one that treats popular culture (and thus much of our lived experience) as variously trivial, irrelevant, or dangerous. By allowing room for the reading and writing of noncanonical forms, we can help put students back into the picture. We can ask directly, "What is at stake in, say, privileging the verbal over the visual?" "How do visual clichés relate to verbal ones?" Or, more generally, "How has visual culture shaped our habits of verbal response and expression?"

Model Assignments

These questions have worked themselves into a number of assignments that I now include regularly in both my first-year and senior-level composition courses. Unlike drawing, painting, or sculpture, photography seems (at first

Figure 8–8
My students concluded the year by publishing their image/text works in a student magazine. Cover reproduced courtesy of the University of the Cariboo.

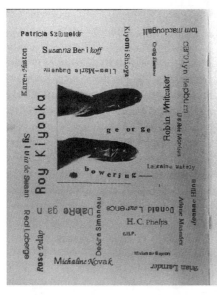

glance) an unintimidating artistic practice, and thus it is ideally suited as a means of introducing students to image/text production. Few students object to either taking their own photos or appropriating the images of others.

Description Assignments

I normally start off with one or two exercises in descriptive writing. The "verbal snapshot," where students are asked to take twenty minutes and describe a person, scene, or object in as much detail as possible, helps introduce notions of perspective, arrangement, and so on. The exercise becomes especially effective if, after the verbal snapshot is composed, the students take an actual photograph and, in small groups, compare the two. Similarly, asking students to "write the story behind the photograph" (any photograph involving people will do) helps link description and narration.

Personal Narrative Assignments

Photography offers a wonderful way of tapping into childhood memories. I ask the students to begin by bringing in a photograph of their family homes. Next, I give them a legal-size sheet of paper and ask them to draw the floor plan of the house. With photograph and drawing in hand, they then take a fellow student on a "tour" of the house. Invariably, the tour moves from simple description to the story of their homes—and thus provides a highly productive heuristic as a prelude to the writing of a more fully developed personal narrative. Family photographs, and even "hypothetical photos," photos which would have captured key moments in our lives if only we'd had a camera with us at the time, offer similar points of departure.

The Family Album Assignment

In addition to looking at individual photographs, we also look at collections of images. Here students explore their own family albums not only in terms of the family history recorded, but in terms of the organizational logic of albums generally. Asking students to compare their own album with published collections—or with collections of photographs held by local archives and libraries—encourages a sophisticated understanding of the documentary tradition. Indeed, in my advanced classes I ask the students to first research a photo-documentary work or artist and then compose an essay that discusses documentary practices "in the style" of their subject. The results are truly impressive.

The Mystory Assignment

The Mystory is perhaps the most demanding of the image/text assignments: it asks students to select an icon from popular culture (someone or something they know or admire) and explore their relationship with that icon in a variety of genres: academic, personal, popular. The result is a collage of voices and images which, if well done, offers a highly engaging essay in cultural study. Perhaps because the Mystory is a new, developing genre—actually a synthesis of multiple visual and verbal genres—my students have approached it as a playful introduction to serious research. Certainly the assignment has produced some of the best *writing* I've seen from my students.

Given the pervasiveness of new communication technologies—especially photography, film, television, and the World Wide Web—we have no choice but to teach reading and writing in the context of multiple and often competing literacies. Like some literary critics and gatekeepers of high culture, we may pretend that the visual can be separated out from the verbal once the classroom door is closed; or, more profitably, we can integrate visual literacy into the composition class and thus help develop an even *more* literate, *more* culturally aware society.

Acknowledgments

Research for this article was supported by grants from the Social Sciences and Humanities Research Council of Canada, and from the University College of the Cariboo. I'm grateful to the artists and authors referenced in this article for allowing images of their work to be included here. In addition, I wish to thank my co-researcher Donald Lawrence for both his comments on this article and for his preparation of the accompanying photographs. Lawrence, a professor of visual arts, and I had the opportunity to try out our version of border-crossing pedagogy when we team-taught a senior-level course, Photography and Literature, several years ago. That experience and our subsequent joint research has convinced me that we have a lot to learn from artists, authors, and others who treat disciplines and discourses as permeable, rather than permanent, boundaries.

Notes

1. Daphne Marlatt and Robert Minden, *Steveston* (Edmonton, Alberta: Longspoon Press, 1984), 92.

2. Joseph Pennell, "Is Photography Among the Fine Arts?" in *Photography in Print: Writings from 1816 to the Present,* ed. Vicki Goldberg (New York: Simon and Schuster, 1981), 211.

3. Pennell in Carol Gerson's *A Purer Taste: The Writing and Reading of Fiction in English in Nineteenth Century Canada* (Toronto: University of Toronto Press, 1989), 74–75.

4. William M. Ivins, Jr.,"Prints and Visual Communication" in Goldberg, 389.

5. Henry A. Giroux. "Slacking Off: Border Youth and Postmodern Education," *Journal of Advanced Composition* 14, no. 2 (Fall 1994), 349.

6. Terry Eagleton, *Literary Theory: An Introduction* (Oxford: Basil Blackwell, 1983), 28.

7. Henry A. Giroux, *Border-Crossing: Cultural Workers and the Politics of Education* (New York and London: Routledge, 1992), 1.

8. Ibid., 3.

9. Stanley Aronowitz and Henry A. Giroux, *Postmodern Education: Politics, Culture, and Social Criticism* (Minneapolis and Oxford: University of Minnesota Press, 1991), 118.

10. William Anthony Nericcio, "Artif[r]acture: Virulent Pictures, Graphic Narrative, and the Ideology of the Visual," *Mosaic* 28, no. 4 (1995): 81.

11. Kay Ellen Rutledge, "Analyzing Visual Persuasion: The Art of Duck Hunting," in *Images in Language, Media, and Mind*, ed. Roy F. Fox (Urbana, Ill.: NCTE, 1994), 204.

12. Antony Easthope, *Literary into Cultural Studies* (London and New York: Routledge, 1991), 13.

13. Marianna Torgovnick, *The Visual Arts, Pictorialism and the Novel: James, Lawrence, and Woolf* (Princeton, N.J.: Princeton University Press, 1985), 93.

14. Ibid., 93–94.

15. Ibid., 96.

16. John Szarkowski, former curator of photography at the Museum of Modern Art in New York City, has been a pivotal figure in shaping a modernist understanding of photography as a medium without narrative potential.

17. Torogovnick, 96.

18. Dennis Cooley, "'I am here on the edge': Modern Hero/Postmodern Poetics in *The Collected Works of Billy the Kid*," in *Spider Blues: Essays on Michael Ondaatje*, ed. Sam Soleki (Montreal: Vehicule Press, 1985), 237.

19. Douglas Barbour, "Daphne Marlatt and Her Works," in *Canadian Writers and Their Works: Poetry Series*, ed. Robert Lecker, Jack David, and Ellen Quigley (Oakville, Ontario: ECW Press, 1992), 225.

20. Ibid., 226.

21. Richard Kostelanetz, "Book Art," in *Artists' Books: A Critical Anthology and Sourcebook*, ed. Joan Lyons (Rochester, N.Y.: Visual Studies Workshop Press, 1985), 29.

22. Pierre Bourdieu et al., *Photography, a Middle-brow Art*, trans. Shaun Whiteside (Stanford, Calif.: Stanford University Press, 1990), 84.

23. Ibid., 97.

24. Donald M. Murray, foreword to *Picturing Learning: Artists & Writers in the Classroom*, ed. Karen Ernst (Portsmouth, N.H.: Heinemann, 1994), vii.

25. For a detailed discussion of Donald Lawrence's narrative strategies, see my article "Negotiating Personal Narrative through Text and Image" in *Artichoke: Writings on the Visual Arts* 5, no. 3, (1993), 75–81.

26. For a more detailed discussion, see Len Masterman, *Teaching the Media* (London: Comedia, 1985).

27. Michael Benton, "Education and the Sister Arts," in *The Journal of Aesthetic Education*, 30, no. 1 (1996), 36. My thanks to Michael Benton for sharing an advance manuscript copy of his article.

28. For a detailed discussion and illustration of Ulmer's approach see Michael Jarrett's "Towards Electronic Literacy: Heuretics in the Classroom," in *Integrating Visual and Verbal Literacies*, ed. W. F. Garrett-Petts and Donald Lawrence (Winnipeg, Manitoba: Inkshed Publications, 1996), 188–206. See also Greg Ulmer's *Heuretics: The Logic of Invention* (Baltimore: Johns Hopkins University Press, 1994).

29. Anthony Paré, "Toward a Post-Process Pedagogy; or What's Theory Got to Do With It?" *English Quarterly* 26, no. 2 (1994), 5.

9

Multimedia and Multivocality
(Com)Posing Challenges to Academic Print Literacy

Jeffrey Maxson

This is a report from an ethnography of a university-level basic writing classroom which investigates an unusual set of student projects.[1] These required students to create computer-based multimedia presentations that combined essays they had written with sounds and images from music videos and television news broadcasts. As such, these student projects differ from much educational multimedia in that here students are producers rather than consumers of multimedia presentations. In addition, I call this a "basic writing" class because students were required to complete it by virtue of their having failed a placement exam in written composition.[2] These were "nontraditional" students in that twelve of the fifteen class members were people of color, but more significantly they were students who forty, or even twenty years ago might not have had the opportunity to attend college.

Students produced their multimedia projects using HyperCard, software for the Macintosh computer which creates a presentation in the form of a "stack" comprised of "cards" appearing on the computer screen. Cards may contain text and graphics, and "buttons," which when selected—clicked on—with the mouse move the user to another card in the stack, or perform other operations. These buttons may also underlie a running text (as opposed to being labeled), so that selecting a particular word or phrase takes the user to another related piece of text, hence the nonlinear, hypertextual aspect of the program (an aspect which was not explored in the student projects described here). Students created these presentations in response to an assignment that asked them either to write a letter to the parents of high school students telling them how metaphors of love in music presented on MTV were "seducing" their children, or to support or refute any claim from Neil Postman's 1985 book *Amusing Ourselves to Death: Public Discourse in the Age of Show Business*, the premise of which is that television has rendered superficial the terms of public debate. Students first individually wrote five-hundred-word essays, and then worked in groups of three or four to digitize sounds and images and to combine them with portions of their essays to create the computer representations, or stacks. The students were given a template card, of which they made multiple copies, and these became the cards onto which they imported text, sounds, and images. Thus, all of their cards had a block of text on the left side—in either a scrolling or nonscrolling text box—and some contained a sound button or image (or both) on the right. The four student stacks contained from six to twenty-one cards each, and I have assigned them names according to the image that appears first in the stack ("Madonna," "Rather" for Dan Rather, and "Married" and "90210" for characters from *Married . . . with Children*, and *Beverly Hills 90210*).

In this essay, I discuss how these stacks might be used as a tool not so much of pedagogy but for the examination of our own expectations about what counts as print literacy. Certainly using materials of popular culture in the classroom builds on students' existing expertise—and I review below examples from the stacks that show students to be fine and practiced media critics. Yet I want to examine how students might use these materials in ways we might consider inappropriate, how they might challenge in productive ways our notions of what academic literacy ought to be about, or ought to remain being about, given current and future changes in the ways information is displayed and transmitted.

I am hinting here at some broad assumptions, four of which I would like to make explicit here:

1. There is a potential for dramatic changes in literacy production, consumption, and, concomitantly, education brought about by new electronic technologies. These changes will result from the differences between the representation of text on a computer screen versus on the printed page, the ease of incorporating graphics and other media into computer-generated documents, the advent of new modes of networked communication, and the development of nonlinear means of presenting text.[3]

2. There are good reasons for seeking alternatives to conventional academic language and patterns of knowledge making. First, cross-cultural studies and contrastive rhetorics show us that other cultures possess equally valid though very different means of mounting arguments and substantiating claims, even in the forms of their "logical" reasoning.[4] And feminist critiques tell us that academic knowledge-making in general is essentializing (prone to "either/or" distinctions), hierarchizing (prone to valuing one mutually exclusive term over the other), and objectifying (prone to splitting the self from the object of study, the object from what is known about the object).[5] Further, a number of recent experiments in scholarly writing

challenge the norms of academic discourse,[6] though I would argue that we offer the opportunity to challenge these norms to students as well.[7]

3. Nontraditional students, for example those populating writing courses, have ways of using language that are different from those required by academic literacy, but ones that are equally rich and valid.[8] It is unfortunate that these language ways do not serve to enrich academic language use; instead such students by and large are given the choice to conform to conventional usage or be excluded from the academy.

4. Students possess expertise in electronic technologies, including the decoding of televisual communication, rivaling that of their elders.[9] This is the most important contribution of cultural studies to pedagogy: a view of students as competent consumers of mass-cultural products, who are already—before the intervention of any pedagogy—using these materials in important ways to structure and make meaningful their everyday experience.[10]

Thus, I hypothesize that giving nontraditional students the opportunity to experiment with new electronic tools will help them express some of their language ways, and their ways of knowing, that are normally discounted. I offer up the following not to prove or refute this idea, but as an invitation to begin thinking about its possibility.

In order to accomplish this, I call on the work of media scholar Gregory Ulmer, who in building on the insights of Jacques Derrida, contrasts the type of reasoning that electronic media promote with that valorized within the traditions of orality and print literacy:

> There are three ways to organize the release of information, which are used across all media: narrative, exposition and pattern. The three modes are not mutually exclusive, but all three are present in any work, with one dominant and the other two subordinate. Thus narrative predominates in story, exposition predominates in documentary, and pattern predominates in collage. One way to construe what is happening as we move from print apparatus to electronics apparatus would be to say that the dominant forms of organizing information in print have been narrative and exposition—splitting the functions of imagination and fact between them—with pattern predominating only in the arts, at the bottom of the hierarchy of knowledge in the relations among science, social science, and the humanities. The dominant form organizing the release of information in the new apparatus, however, is pattern, whose essential form is collage.[11]

Ulmer further associates the logic of the third category, "pattern," with the bottom of various social and conceptual hierarchies: "*descriptions* of the unconscious, the right brain, inner speech, the mind of the savage, child, or even 'feminine style,' all share similar features, which we recognize to have been generated for the most part in opposition to analytico-referential reason."[12] And he characterizes collage as working through "citation or appropriation, juxtaposition, fragmentation."[13]

Ulmer's categories have inspired my classification of the connections among text, sound, and images on individual cards from the student stacks. These are described in Table 1, where they are arranged in order from most to least like written academic forms. By the first category, "citation," I mean to designate the relationship in, for example, literary studies, between a text and the primary or source text on which it comments. One example of this relationship appears in a card from the stack "Madonna." The card displays a still image from the video "Wicked Game" by Chris Isaaks, in which the singer and a woman, neither wearing any discernible clothing, embrace on a beach. The text on the card comments, "Though this may seem to be a romantic picture for those who just briefly glance at it, it is actually depressing and bitter . . . [The singer] refers to love as a 'wicked game,' and implies that it should be avoided altogether. Of course, you would never know that this is really what he thought by watching him with this woman."

In the next category, "illustration," the image stands as evidence that backs up an argument made in the text (as, in fact, citation might do in an academic text, when a writer quotes an authority to substantiate her claim), as distinct from the first category in which the image stands as the data that the text analyzes. (At the same time, these and the remaining categories are not discrete but continuous.) A card from "Married" can be seen as an example of the "illustration" category: since the image of a wok on a stove top serves to substantiate its claim that television programming attempts other purposes besides that of pure entertainment, namely instruction in cooking. This mode of providing evidence for the writer's claims is of course prevalent, if not predominant, in academic writing; however, it is most often accomplished textually, and very seldom through the inclusion of photographic images. Most often, academic prose appears as a "featureless expanse of printed pages, designed

Table 1

Categories of Rhetorical Connection in Stacks

Category	Description	Number of occurrences in all stacks
Citation	Text comments on all or part of sound or image	9
Illustration	Sound or image exemplifies, provides evidence for, or substantiates all or part of text	11
Evocation	Sound or image and text share some recognizable referent	9
Juxtaposition	Some unpredictably new impression is created out of the conjunction of sound or image and text	2

precisely not to catch our eye and thus draw our attention away from the meaning conveyed by the words,"[14] or it is interrupted only by charts and tables, which are even more densely packed with textually oriented information.

The category "evocation" is exemplified by a card from "Rather" that describes a newspaper image of war damage in the former Yugoslavia, accompanied by an image that depicts (though not clearly) a different scene. Still, the text—"shattered buildings and houses as well as civilians observing the damages"—and the image—a figure driving a burro down a European-looking street—together evoke the disruptions and displacements of normal life during war. As with the next category, this sort of connection between text and image is alien to academic writing, though not to artistic expression, especially collage.

The last category, "juxtaposition," is best represented by a card from "90210." Here the text refers to the negative portrayal in the heavy metal group Warrant's "Cherry Pie" video of love as male ownership; the image depicts (vaguely and rotated ninety degrees) a shirtless male with a barbell. The connection is unclear: if viewed as belonging to the previous category, it could be seen as an evocation of male machismo, and the text's focus on love as "ownership of a sexual object" leading to battery and rape, would then be linked to the way in which the image calls forth male displays of physical strength, as institutionalized in the practice of bodybuilding. Still this connection, though perhaps the most tenable of other possibilities, is tenuous at best, justifying my own categorization of this card.

All told, there are ten sounds and twenty-one images on the forty-six cards of the four stacks ("Madonna" is made up of six cards, "Married" has twelve, "Rather" twenty-one, and "90210" seven); of these thirty-one connections between text and sound or text and image, I have classified nine as citation, eleven as illustration, nine as evocation and two as juxtaposition. Thus, fewer than one-third of all connections are of the kind that could be recognized as belonging to traditional language uses of the academy. The large number of instances of illustration further marks these stacks as belonging to a hybrid genre between academic and more popular forms. That is, pictorially illustrated texts are more prevalent in journalistic, children's, and popular nonfiction genres, so that the stacks mediate between the strictly academic and other orders of print more familiar to students.

In important ways, though, the stacks transcend the possibilities of print literacy. The "Rather" stack in particular uses two devices that more resemble televisual than text-based means of exposition. First, the "Rather" stack displays only a brief paragraph or several one-sentence paragraphs on each card—the written analogue of sound bites. This contrasts with the other stacks' more circumspect investigations of topics in their scrolling paragraphs. And interestingly, this tendency in "Rather" jars with the tenor of much of its critique of television news, particularly as shown in its quote from anchorman Robert MacNeil that in television news "'bite-sized is best, complexity must be avoided, nuances are dispensable.'" Still the group that created the stack apparently found that lengthier paragraphs in scrolling text-boxes impeded the flow of reading from card to card, a tendency one does notice in the other stacks.

The second instance of televisual means of presentation in "Rather" occurs on two adjacent cards, which together (given a particular, though not idiosyncratic, reading) recreate the same experience of television viewing that they critique. The text of the two cards compares print with television reports of armed conflict in the former Yugoslavia. On the card, the text describes a newspaper account of the struggle accompanied by "a picture showing shattered buildings and houses as well as civilians observing the damages ." The card echoes the typographical arrangement it describes, with text situated next to a depiction of civilian hardships in the war. This is true until the viewer clicks on a button labeled "air raid", after which the assemblage is animated by the sound of air raid sirens and the television voice-over: "The air raid sirens sound daily throughout Croatia. But as serious as the warfare is, it could get much worse." The sound, in fact, provides a bridge to the next card, where the text discusses how the same story is reported on television, that is, interrupted by commercials, which trivialize the content of the news.

The text here is accompanied by an image of a woman in an apron standing behind an ironing board and holding up an iron, and by a button labeled "ironing commercial," which when selected plays the audio portion of two advertisements. The first features a trumpet-led theme resembling the incidental music of an afternoon game show, over which comes a high-pitched woman's voice marked by shrill laughter and tag questions at the ends of phrases:

> Pleated pants can present a particularly pressing—he-he—problem, hee. But ladies before you throw your hands up in despair, hm? let's try this simple technique, hm? Place the tip of the iron at the top, top of the pleat closest to the zipper and, pressing firmly but gently, hipping and hopping like so, hm? and pressing all the way down, never pushing, open the pleat. And to prevent puckering, always press on the bias, hm?

This is followed immediately by a male voice backed with a flourish from an electric piano:

> Who were you watching when Michael Jackson taught Homer Simpson how to moonwalk? *TV Guide.* Don't watch TV in the dark.

The effect of the image and the two audio clips is to overshadow the images of suffering displayed in the previous card, just as the text of this card argues that television "mak[es] important news seem absurd and irrelevant." The stack does more than just argue this point in words; it uses the technology of movement from card to card to demonstrate the process it describes.

Yet this example, quite masterful in its formulation and effect, is still very much a traditionally academically-oriented achievement; that is, one that would impress teachers and scholars of English and writing as a skillful use of mimesis to reinforce a claim. It would be much more difficult to find such agreement about "90210," for there are ways in which this stack challenges traditional notions of academic literacy in ways that "Rather" does not. First, "90210" contains the only instances of juxtaposition in any of the stacks, and only one instance of citation, the fewest of any stack. Further, the connection between the text and image on the card depicting the characters from *Beverly Hills 90210* is even more indeterminate than the instance on the card depicting the weightlifter discussed above. That is, the image of two characters from the television program—one male and one female, standing facing the viewer, smiling with arms folded and leaning shoulder to shoulder—might conceivably represent people for whom sex is the "predominate form of expressing love." But really there is no reason to believe this. Here in fact is the way Francisco, a member of the group that built the stack, describes this card in a presentation before the rest of the class:

> "Express Yourself" by Madonna, she's kinda, it's like filled with sexual connotations. So that's what we used for our basis, in our paper. We used 90210, the image, because it exemplifies like the trash that's on TV [general laughter plus exclamation from the instructor], like, like the—like the images, that—I mean, like ninety-nine percent of the kids in America will probably never attain. But they present these images on TV, so, it's a popular show.

Francisco evokes a connection here between images of love as sex on the one hand and of unattainably beautiful and affluent personae on the other as both appearing on television and serving to mislead. This linkage, though, is qualitatively different from the interrogation "Rather" opens up—in the pair of cards depicting war in the Balkans and the ironing commercial—of the economic interests that drive the pacing and sequencing of news programs. Instead, Francisco's connection more resembles the postmodern state in which signifiers become detached from what they signify and instead serve to mark a location within a cultural system of signs, as listening to heavy metal music associates one with the group "middle- and working-class white suburban males." This seems to be the case with Francisco's description and the card as well: Madonna's hit, the characters from *Beverly Hills 90210* and the ideas about casual sex (both its promotion and its condemnation), all bits of popular culture, float at the same level of specificity; none is more basic or central than another and there is no underlying meaning which relates them all to one another.

And this same tendency is manifested in the textual portion of the stack as a whole. It is couched in the form of a letter from "Father O'Brian" to the parents of students at a Catholic school. There is every indication that Francisco (the author, in fact, of the entire text) relishes the chance to inhabit this persona. The wording is hyperelevated:

> As a Catholic institution, the school feels this is an obligation with upmost per-
> tinence to the development of our students. . . .There exist even harsh videos
> however with far more alarming themes . . . Cherry pie, referring sexually to a
> woman, with claimed ownership by a male individual. . . . Again it is my duty
> to reiterate . . . Love is a splendid creation, and to defame it . . . is most tragic.

Francisco seems to take pleasure in having Father O'Brian invoke the authority of the school psychologist and the "religion department," and even recommend that parents read *Amusing Ourselves to Death*, just as it was assigned to
Francisco himself. But at the same time, this is not parody of a simple or
straightforward kind. After all, Father O'Brian condemns the objectification of
women and the numbing effect of television violence; Francisco clearly does
not mean to celebrate them. Rather this essay exhibits the flattened effect Fredric Jameson attributes to "pastiche":

> Pastiche is, like parody, the imitation of a peculiar or unique style, the wear-
> ing of a stylistic mask, speech in a dead language: but it is a neutral practice
> of such mimicry, without parody's ulterior motive, without the satirical
> impulse, without laughter, without that still latent feeling that there exists
> something normal compared to which what is being imitated is rather
> comic.[15]

In fact the other stacks also exhibit qualities of pastiche, though not as markedly as "90210." There are, for example, hyperbole,

> [Magic Johnson's] appearance on television is desperatly [sic] yearned for by
> the public (from "Rather");

stentorian dictates,

> Only through education can our children be made aware of the negative con-
> notations that are represented in the MTV videos (from "Madonna");

and other locutions which it seems only this topic could have called up,

> Watching television does not expect one to struggle through a full screen of
> text as one would have to do when one reads through pages of text in newspa-
> pers, magazines, and books (from "Married").

As with Francisco's opinion in relation to Father O'Brian's, I would not argue
that students necessarily disagree with the stance that the assignment calls on
them to take. At least the textual portions of their arguments are substantially
in agreement that television offers a more superficial treatment of current
events than print sources, and that MTV presents a narrow view of love. Yet
there is a sense in which any attempt to arrive at what students *really* believe is
futile. Instead, the examples from "90210" and the other stacks suggest that
for students, point of view or position may be largely context-dependent. This
is taking the writing students' question (or at least the question posed as such
by writing teachers), "How do I know what I think until I write about it?" to

the next degree: "How do I know what I think until I know what it is possible to say?" It seems no contradiction for them that when writing an essay in an academic setting, they "believe" the point of view that the assignment asks them to take, even when their enjoyment of television or music videos might belie this position. For them it seems easier to accept (what we teachers and scholars need barely penetrable, mostly French, theory to instruct us) that there is no unitary self that one expresses in writing, but any number of possible selves that are constructed in the act of responding to an audience.

Taken together, the stacks discourage univocal readings: At the same time that their textual portions represent quite good approximations of academic writing, their nontextual features—the very manner in which one "turns the page," as well as their sounds and images—encourage one to see them as combinations, some smooth and others not so smooth, of academic and more popular forms. Further, the stacks use means of presentation that are more televisual than print-oriented, while at the same time making a case in their textual portions for the shortcomings of those very modes. And there are ways, especially in "90210," that they transcend this sort of binary opposition to present surfaces which are not penetrable by traditional means of analysis. They are after all strange hybrids, which are not subsumed by the conventions of either print or television, but play one off the other. And while the stacks do not openly challenge the conventions of the academy, they do give them a gentle nudge. I would celebrate these students' efforts for this playful transgression, for their evocation of pleasure, and for their juxtaposition of opposites which coexist in creative tension.

Ultimately they present a challenge for us as teachers of writing. That is, with the introduction of these new tools, we do not want to be responsible for reproducing existing hierarchies in new guises. And here, as readers can see, is something *quite* new, certainly different from computerized drill and practice programs of the past, and different as well from word processors by themselves. I would argue that as teachers of writing, we, like the student creators of the stacks, are mediators between old and new forms of literacy. This, though, is not so simple or straightforward a task as merely taking the best of the old and combining it with the best of the new. Instead, it is our responsibility to live uncomfortably, on the border between old and new. We are responsible for negotiating this changeover and working—in fact, struggling—to see to it that those who have traditionally been denied access have an entry, and more, are given opportunities to experiment with these new forms.

Notes

1. For the complete study, see Jeffrey Maxson, *Multimedia and Multivocality in a Basic Writing Classroom.* Ph.D. diss., University of California at Berkeley, 1996.
2. In fact, these students were quite competent in their writing abilities, within the broad range of students classified as "remedial" or "basic" writers. On the problems

inherent in defining basic writers, see especially Andrea Lunsford and Patricia A. Sullivan, "Who are Basic Writers?" in *Research in Basic Writing: A Bibliographic Sourcebook*, ed. Michael G. Moran and Martin J. Jacobi (New York: Greenwood, 1990).

3. For overviews of all these developments with respect to literacy and literacy education, see Myron Tuman, *Word Perfect: Computer Literacy in the Computer Age* (Pittsburgh: University of Pittsburgh Press, 1992); Myron Tuman, ed., *Literacy Online: The Promise (and Peril) of Reading and Writing with Computers* (Pittsburgh: University of Pittsburgh Press, 1992); Richard Lanham, "Digital Rhetoric: Theory, Practice and Property," in *Literacy Online*, 221–243; and Richard Lanham, "The Extraordinary Convergence: Democracy, Technology, Theory, and the University Curriculum," *South Atlantic Quarterly* 89, no. 1 (1990): 27–43. For work more focused on hypertext, see Jay David Bolter, *Writing Space: The Computer, Hypertext, and the History of Writing* (Hillsdale, N.J.: Lawrence Erlbaum, 1991) and George Landow, *Hypertext: The Convergence of Contemporary Critical Theory and Technology* (Baltimore: Johns Hopkins University Press, 1992).

4. Three interesting examples of these from within the field of composition, and all addressing Chinese discursive forms, are Fan Shen, "The Classroom and the Wider Culture: Identity As a Key to Learning English Compostion," *College Composition and Communication* 40 (1989): 459–466; Min-Zhan Lu, "From Silence to Words," *College English* 49 (1987): 437–448; and David Joliffe, "Writers and Their Subjects: Ethnologic and Chinese Composition," in *A Rhetoric of Doing: Essays in Honor of James Kinneavy*, ed. Steven Witte, N. Nakadate, and Roger Cherry (Carbondale, IL: Southern Illinois University Press, 1992), 261–275.

5. David Bleich, "Sexism in Academic Styles of Learning," in *Composition Theory for the Postmodern Classroom*, ed. Gary A. Olson and Sidney I. Dobrin (Albany: State University of New York Press, 1994), 161–175. Further, the adversarial method, the situating of one's argument as filling gaps—or, more particularly, correcting errors—in scholarship that has come before, has been critiqued as driven by scholarly blood-lust (Jane Tompkins, "Fighting Words: Unlearning to Write the Critical Essay," *Georgia Review* 42 (1988): 585–590), as ignoring the emotional consequences of such attacks, and as supporting a Cartesian view of knowledge (in which knowledge exists separately from knowers) rather than a social constructionist one (Olivia Frey, "Beyond Literary Darwinism: Women's Voices and Critical Discourse," *College English* 52 (1990): 507–526).

6. Within the field of composition, see Min-Zhan Lu; Mike Rose, *Lives on the Boundary* (New York: Penguin, 1989); Patricia Bizzell, introduction to *Academic Discourse and Critical Consciousness* (Pittsburgh: University of Pittsburgh Press, 1992), 3–30; Linda Brodkey, "Writing on the Bias," *College English* 56 (1996): 527–547; Richard E. Miller, "The Nervous System," *College English* 58 (1996): 265–286; and the entire issue of *College Composition and Communication* 43, no. 1 (1993). In other disciplines, see Patricia Williams, *The Alchemy of Race and Rights* (Cambridge, Mass.: Harvard University Press, 1991); Lila Abu-Lughod, *Writing Women's Worlds: Bedouin Stories* (Berkeley: University of California Press, 1993); and Gloria Anzaldúa, *Borderlands/La Frontera: The New Mestiza* (San Francisco: spinsters/aunt lute, 1987).

7. For a fine instance of this, see Lillian Bridwell-Bowles, "Discourse and Diversity: Experimental Writing Within the Academy," *College Composition and Communication* 43 (1992): 349–368.

8. For a quantitative analysis of black vernacular English versus Standard English, see William Labov, "The Logic of Non-Standard English," in *Georgetown Roundtable on Languages and Linguistics* (Washington, D.C.: Georgetown University Press, 1969) and *Language in the Inner City* (Philadelphia: University of Pennsylvania Press, 1972). Shirley Brice Heath's ethnography *Ways with Words* (New York: Cambridge University Press, 1982) not only contrasts language acquisition and use in working-class white, working-class African American, and middle-class white communities in the piedmont Carolinas, revealing the history and strengths of each, but also demonstrates the congruence of white middle-class ways with those promoted within schools.

9. This notion is a part of popular discourses on technology and youth, often vilifying television for rendering youth passive spectators; for a counterpoint see, e.g., Jon Katz, "The Media's War on Kids: From the Beatles to Beavis and Butthead," *Rolling Stone*, 25 November 1993, 46–49, 130. For the argument that students can teach their instructors a great deal about computer-mediated literacy, see Cynthia Selfe, "Redefining Literacy: The Multi-layered Grammars of Computers," in *Critical Perspectives on Computers and Composition Instruction*, ed. Gail Hawisher and Cynthia Selfe (New York: Teachers College Press, 1989), 3–15.

10. For an overview of the contributions to composition of cultural studies, particularly of the Centre for Contemporary Cultural Studies at the University of Birmingham, see John Trimbur, "Cultural Studies and Teaching Writing," *Focuses* 1 (1988): 5–18. Joseph Harris, "The Other Reader," in *Composition Theory for the Postmodern Classroom*, 225–235, argues convincingly for the value of ordinary consumers' media interpretations, as against those of professional or scholarly critics.

11. Gregory Ulmer, "Grammatology (in the Stacks) of Hypermedia. a Simulation: Or, When Does a Pile Become a Heap?" in *Literacy Online: The Promise (and Peril) of Reading and Writing with Computers*, ed. Myron Tuman (Pittsburgh: University of Pittsburgh Press, 1992), 160–161.

12. Gregory Ulmer, *Teletheory: Grammatology in the Age of Video* (New York: Routledge, 1989), 66.

13. Ulmer, "Grammatology," 161.

14. Tuman, *Word Perfect*, 126–127.

15. Fredric Jameson, "Postmodernism and Consumer Society" in *The Anti-aesthetic: Essays on Postmodern Culture*, ed. Hal Foster (Port Townsend, WA: Bay, 1983), 114.

10

Location, Genre, and Intertextuality
Music Videos in the Composition Classroom

Rich Lane

Definition of *Composition*

As evidenced by the essays included in this collection, the definition of *composition* has expanded in recent years both within and outside the academic classroom. The explosion of mass media and technology in the past thirty years has contributed significantly to this expansion. Thus, "composition" has moved beyond five-paragraph essays, research papers, and other written texts to the more "cultural" texts of film, television, space, networked communication, and other visual and conceptual constructions that directly affect the everyday lives of students. Although instructors and even some students who are "sedimented" in traditional notions of composition continue to resist this expansive definition, many of our students will find themselves in a workplace and a world in which they will be asked to produce and consume texts that do not take "traditional" written forms and modes. For this reason, the exploration of the literacies of film, advertising copy, music videos, television production and consumption, and the news media has become an important concern for the composition classroom. As Douglas Kellner expresses in his treatment of postmodern pedagogies, "the goal [is] to teach a critical media literacy which will empower individuals to become more autonomous agents, able to emancipate themselves from contemporary forms of domination and able to become more active citizens, eager and competent to engage in processes of social transformation."[1]

While seemingly distant from learning that seeks to understand "typical" modes and structures of traditional composition, the exploration and production of cultural and "media" texts in the writing classroom can be effective as a method of learning about, reproducing, and resisting/transforming traditional notions of writing in academia and in the workplace. Since throughout most of students' early childhoods and adolescent years they are constantly and simultaneously exposed to, even bombarded with, the texts of both music and television, they have developed varying degrees of sophistication in interpreting the messages and manipulations of these mediums. However, students remain largely unconscious of their own abilities in decoding and producing this type of "composition." The introduction of music videos as text can be particularly effective in dealing with these "skills" and the issues they present for writers. In this piece, I offer the use of music videos in the composition classroom. The discussion provides an introduction to exercises designed to encourage students to think critically, practice, and perhaps transform the medium of music video, and to help students understand issues of composition concerning location, intertextuality, and genre.

Composition as a Series of Discourse Technologies

Working with any medium must follow from the context of the course being taught. This seems like a logical, almost rhetorical, assertion, but it is one that is often overlooked.

The use of a film in literature classes, or computers in writing classes, can only be effective if the exercises match the context of the course itself, and, just as importantly, its pedagogy. Thus, the use of music videos as a way of introducing constructions of discourse will have little overall effect on students whose primary learning experience within that classroom is with correcting mechanics and imitating strict modes of essay writing. My use of music videos follows from the context of a course that can be termed "socially oriented" and considers the teaching and learning of writing to be an examination and practice of a series of "discourse technologies" or, to use another term, literacies. The term *discourse technologies* derives from discussions of discourse by both feminist theorists such as Teresa deLauretis and postmodern theorists such as Michel Foucault and refers to patterns of discourse widely employed and disseminated throughout a society. These patterns can be studied in the composition classroom both in isolation and in interaction, producing understandings for students of the particular tactics, techniques, and effects of each technology, as well as how they act to produce ideologies and power relations for the people who produce and consume them.

Whereas many previous composition courses, particularly "expressive" based approaches to process, were based on the idea of the student writers as autonomous agents, the sole origins of their language and sole authorities on their experiences, a socially-oriented approach, while still very interested in the language and experiences of students, redefines both those terms. My particular course sets out specific goals for each assignment built on the belief that language use constructs social difference in all spheres of discourse. The word *discourse* is used to refer to the ways whole systems of signification, whether they be writing, speaking, or other symbolic modes of expression, exercise power and shape knowledge. Throughout the course, my students begin to gain an understanding that discourses are multiple and centered in specific contexts, such as "academic discourse," "political discourse," or the "discourse of popular culture." They come to understand that writing, as a "technology," is a practice that always takes place within discourse "communities" rather than an isolated act of an autonomous individual.[2] Through both brief and longer "composing" assignments connected with each technology, students learn about how certain discourses work, how to "locate" themselves within them, and then how to imitate and/or transform these discourses. Following Adrienne Rich's definition of the term *location*, in this course "locating" comes to mean for the students discovering and articulating their own connections with various worlds of discourse—placing themselves within "academic discourse," for example, by remembering and reflecting on the kinds of language, writing, and reading they did in high school, or placing themselves within the discourse of "race" not by proclaiming that they are or are not racists but by remembering and reflecting on their own experiences with racial difference.[3]

The primary theoretical assumption of the course is that discourse preexists "expression"; that, when we write, we are participating in and reconfiguring already-existing systems of language rather than creating unique expressions of our inner thoughts and feelings.[4] This does not mean that writers do not generate unique combinations of diverse discourses through each writing act. However, this type of course shifts the emphasis from what an individual writer is to where discourses come from, what they do, and how people become different selves through processes of engaging with different discourses. My primary aim is to help students construct an understanding of how writing reflects, produces, and even transforms social relations. My hope is that, with this understanding, students will examine and construct their own texts more critically and carefully.

One of the technologies my students and I study within the course is called "Reading, Critiquing, and Transforming the Discourse of Cultural Texts." The aim of examining the technologies of cultural texts is to help students begin to understand how these texts, already familiar and important to their everyday lives, both reflect and produce cultural ideas, values, and morals. My students and I hope, through learning to "read" these texts, that we will gain a better understanding of the texts' "agendas": their political, social, and economic assumptions. By taking a closer look at the structures, images, and languages of cultural texts, we begin to gain greater confidence in our abilities to take critical stances in relation to the texts and, ideally, to begin to produce critiques that make us more active participants in the consumption of film, television, advertising, and other cultural products. One of the ultimate goals of this examination is, through developing the abilities to read and critique, to transform the cultural practices and languages of these texts.

Critically "reading" a text, such as a music video, involves students in learning how to appreciate, decode, and interpret images. They begin to examine how images operate in our lives, and what these images communicate in concrete situations. By learning to "read" cultural texts, students learn about the construction of their own writing and how it, consciously and unconsciously, reflects and produces specific values and points of view. Understanding the assumptions that produce writing is crucial in the production of a more self-conscious and informed approach to composition and an awareness of writing as an active and influential practice.

However, "critiquing" cultural texts can often be a difficult and painful process for students. In my course, critiquing involves examining and reading the texts from a critical standpoint. I stress to students that this does not mean that only the negative aspects of the texts are examined. A critique involves choosing a perspective, examining the texts in relation to it, and then producing a text that supports, investigates, and interrogates the text from that perspective. Many students will resist this part of the process, insisting that we are "overanalyzing" the texts of film, television, advertising, behavior, and music video. bell hooks offers a useful response to this type of resistance: "One issue that surfaces when teaching the skills of radical cultural critique to students is a sense of conflict between pleasure and analysis. Initially they often assume that if you are critiquing a subject it must mean that you do not like it. . . . Students should learn how to distinguish between hostile critique that is about 'trashing' and critique that is about illuminating and enriching our understanding. . . . We must do more than express positive appreciation for [others'] work; to engage it critically in a rigorous way is more a gesture of respect than is passive acceptance."[5] As we engage in this component of the course, my students and I often talk about the "pain" of critique and of consciousness. Teachers who use cultural texts that students cherish (such as Saturday morning cartoons) must be sensitive to the struggle students encounter when asked to look at these texts more closely. Although film, television, spatial relations, and cultural behaviors are also studied during this component of the course, perhaps the most interesting and enjoyable "reading" comes from the use of a series of music videos and their relations to discussions and explorations of writers' locations within their work, the use of intertextuality, and the choice and effectiveness of various genres employed by the video directors and artists.

Ideologies of Teen Spirit: Location and Genre

We begin a two-day examination of music videos within the context of a component that examines various cultural texts, such as film and architectural space. The students have previously discussed various methods of critiquing and close-reading texts. Many of these methods are centered around a sheet containing a series of questions that help students more closely examine each text from a cultural studies standpoint.[6] The questions help the students focus their readings of videos, other texts, and ultimately their writing, on several key elements: the conditions of the texts' production, the elements and organization of production (their "composition"), the audience or readers of the texts, and the texts' ideological structures. Throughout the component, we practice reading and writing about texts with these elements in mind. We also employ readings of the different texts by anthologized authors to illustrate the focus of various critiques. Thus, the discussion combines a theoretical "look" at music videos with "practical" applications of these theories within and outside the composition classroom.

The exercise begins with students reading two fairly simple critiques of music videos by Holly Brubach and Lisa A. Lewis.[7] These articles encourage students to begin to think about music videos as texts that are not simply viewed and enjoyed, but that are also constructs and are constructed by "writers" with various cultural locations and agendas. I have chosen these articles specifically because both critique the early days of music videos and of MTV. This gives the students a chance to argue with the authors based on their own experience with videos, most of which was gained after the articles were written. More importantly, the reading presents students with an introduction to how writers' (of both videos and critiques) and audiences' (in both consuming and critiquing videos) historical locations can influence topics, the focus of those topics, and the reception of ideas by the public.

After briefly discussing the articles, we begin to "practice" cultural critique using a series of music videos. In order to illustrate the importance of focusing on a specific element or issue in students' own critiques, I begin by using videos for which I suggest a specific focus. This technique gives students confidence in their own abilities to read and critique before exploring videos on their own and choosing their own focuses and agendas. The first two videos, which are used together, are John Cougar Mellencamp's "Jack and Diane," and Nirvana's "Smells Like Teen Spirit." Since many of the students have already seen these videos in some context, I ask them about general themes found in both. As the songs and videos primarily deal with the topic of teenagers, students are asked to focus on how each video depicts teen ideology. We then review and discuss the cultural studies questions, deciding on specific elements we will target in order to create a "first reading" of the videos. In order to focus on both the ideas and composing processes of the videos, I suggest to the students that we concentrate on the "locations" constructed and implied by the videos, something that we have already practiced with other texts, in order to create discussion about their different genres. I encourage students to pay particular attention to the historical and geographical locations of the videos, their visual and lyrical depictions of teen sexuality, and their contrasting visual compositions. We watch the videos twice. As the students view them, they first take mental notes of our focus, eventually jotting down the more specific or important elements of each video. It is vital that teachers remain reflective on two things during this process: the students must be allowed and encouraged to enjoy the videos, and, within the focus, multiple interpretations must be expressed, respected, and discussed. Although a framework is provided in order to give students confidence, teachers must be particularly sensitive to student locations that are, many times, "closer" than their own locations to the videos being viewed. As teachers, we must be willing to learn from the students about the videos as much as they learn from the frameworks we create.

After viewing the Mellencamp and Nirvana videos twice, we discuss the composition of the videos in both small and large groups. The conversation intitially centers around a definition of genre, and students identify the visual and lyrical elements that "compose" each video. The constrasting genres of the two videos are obvious. For example, students are quick to identify the visual composition of "Jack and Diane" as imitating a photo album. They discuss the photo album (a series of snapshots of Jack and Diane growing up in the Midwest) as a form that they equate with traditional storytelling or fairytales. They identify the story that is told about Jack and Diane as being linear in structure, having a clear beginning, middle, and end. The examination leads to a discussion of modernist narrative forms, and how they shaped and continue to shape our sense of "real life" experience.[8] In other words, students begin to see the modernist "framing" of experience as a constructed discourse, but one which seems so natural as to call it "experience." Most students have internalized the idea that this modernist structure is, perhaps, the only way that stories, particularly "real life" stories, of our own experiences can be told. However, when contrasted with the genre of Nirvana's video, the construction of these structures becomes more understandable. Asked to identify the visual elements in the Nirvana video, students point out that the video really follows no particular "story line," and yet there is a story that is clear to them. The images in "Smells Like Teen Spirit" are fragmented "cuts" of high school students in what looks to be a run-down gymnasium. We begin to discuss the more "postmodern" feel of the video. While the story is not linear, it makes sense in creating the kind of chaotic atmosphere that the band wishes to express. Simply from this initial examination, students begin to identify different genres of music video. This examination leads students to interrogations of their own forms of writing and expressions of experience.

The next step in our process attempts to construct meaning from what we have seen. The constrasting images and lyrics provide students with very different ideologies concerning being a teenager. Students begin to understand the relation between genre choice and the messages that the videos convey. Mellencamp, they point out, chooses the images of the photo album and tells the story in a linear fashion because he wants to portray the period of adolescence as happy, worry free, simple, and the best time of one's life; he tells a modernist fairytale of sorts. He even goes so far as to express that all the fun in life really ends in one's teen years. Sexuality, during these years, is also seen as innocent and "natural" in "Jack and Diane." Students often say that they think of the Nirvana video as being more "sexual" until a second viewing, where it is apparent that the major focus of "Jack and Diane" concerns sexuality—in very traditionally gendered ways. The message here is that sex is a natural and innocent part of teen ideology. In contrast, "Smells Like Teen Spirit" uses the fragmentation of the visual images and dilapidation of the school to project the opposite message. The teen years, for the teens here, are scary, chaotic, and frustrating, ones of "imitation" of preconceived roles (perhaps the ones that Mellencamp portrays). The band sings about this sense of "imitation" as the students begin to imitate each other in a frenzied dance. Sexuality, while more overtly sensual here, seems dangerous. The images used to convey sexuality are primarily tight-sweatered cheerleaders, who ironically have the letter *A* across their chests. Students are also astute to point out that this *A* has the multiple meanings of both Anarchy and the symbol of the adultress in Nathaniel Hawthorne's *The Scarlet Letter*. These images add up to a desperate and frightening depiction of teen ideology, far from that contained in the first video. The question looms in the classroom: Why are the views of teen ideology and sexuality so drastically different?

The question can be partially answered by returning to an examination of the creators' locations. The students begin to identify both the historical and geographical differences (although there are many others) in both the artists and the teens the artists attempt to depict. The Mellencamp video, the students identify, is a product of the early 1980s, a time when most of my students were early adolescents themselves and remember bits and pieces of a time that seemed to them to be more carefree and innocent. When we explore a bit of the historical condition of the country in the early 1980s, the video's location becomes clearer. The country was going through a prosperous (or seemingly prosperous) time, as Ronald Reagan became president, and the trends were toward a return to the simplicity idealized in the 1950s. Geographically, the rural Midwest is the setting of almost all of Mellencamp's songs and videos. My students, most of whom are from the Midwest, convey that they easily identify with the characters of "Jack and Diane": "We are Jack and Diane," the students often explain. Thus, although the ideology and sexuality were explicit, perhaps more so than in the Nirvana video, the ways in which both were depicted were very "Midwest": understated, seemingly natural, and metaphorically "hidden" with images of cars and natural surroundings. These observations may seem stereotypical, but the goal is to "read" these videos for their possible locations in relation to the students' own locations, and stereotypical depiction is a technique commonly used in music videos. Again, in contrast, the Nirvana video is a product of the early 1990s, a time in which students, and the world, now feel more uneasy socially, economically, and politically. This "unrest" can be felt and seen throughout the frantic cuts of "Smells Like Teen Spirit." Even the title of the song indicates the distrust teens have begun to feel, not only about growing up but about their present state as adolescents. My students indicate that the Nirvana video has a much more urban feel to it and point out that the band itself hails from the city of Seattle, which is a more urban environment than most towns in the Midwest.

An interesting "gap" in interpretation often happens here for my students and myself. While I identify more with the experience of the Nirvana video, even though I am fifteen years older than most of my students, they identify more with the Mellencamp portrayal of teen experience. We examine how our personal location has much to do with this "gap" in both interpretation and appreciation. As a result of this initial exercise and discussion, students begin to relate the genres to the political and historical conditions under which videos are produced and become conscious of the ways their writing, reading, and viewing are affected by the historical location and choice of genre.

Subterranean Rap: The Intertexuality of Composition

A second set of videos addresses the intertextuality of what we, as viewers and writers, read and compose. This set of videos reinforces the lessons of the previous set concerning the ideological nature of written or visual texts, while questioning the idea of "autonomous" originality. The exercise is brief, and demonstrates that many if not all texts are extensions of other texts. The idea of "lightbulb" inspiration and utterly unique originality is challenged in order to help students understand that creative expression can effectively build on existing texts, leading to an original work. Students also begin to understand the different purposes for these extensions and expansions. The exercise employs a video with which most students are familiar, "I Need You Tonight/ Mediate" by INXS, and then compares it with Bob Dylan's "Subterranean Homesick Blues." Both videos use a visual and textual device that distinguishes the videos: a montage of ideas conveyed by the artists, who hold up cardboard signs with the lyrics printed on them. While the students are familiar with the INXS strategy, most do not realize that the same strategy was employed by Dylan twenty years earlier. Students begin to see how video artists borrow and expand on already existing ideas, images, and genres. The question of why similar images and techniques are used is discussed and written about by the students. Most students interpret the videos as conveying similar messages: a distrust of the "establishment" and a call for peace and individual expression. Students argue that the INXS video simply but effectively uses the visual sign-turning to resurrect Dylan's message.

However, when a third video is introduced, "Wall Street Rap" from the film *Bob Roberts* (a documentary-style parody of conservative political campaigns), students learn how strikingly similar visual techniques (the sign-turning) can be used for the critique of Dylan's message. *Wall Street Rap* parodies the first two videos intertextually, by expressing the opposite of the message conveyed by Dylan and INXS. The sign-turning here, done by a well-dressed Wall Street type politician, is in support of the status quo, visually mocking anticapitalistic messages. In addition, "Wall Street Rap" adds to the intertextual parody by coopting the "new," resistant, and primarily African American genre of rap to express a white dominant and "conservative" political statement. Through discussions of these three videos, students gain additional understanding of the ways that the composition of texts constructs various ideologies, while also beginning to think intertextually—taking "risks" in their writing through mixtures of different genres and reconceptualizing of past texts.

It is important to note that teachers must strive to remain "current" in the use of music videos in order to retain the interest of students. I often ask my students to bring videos of their own to class, to help create exercises, and to suggest ways to use videos. For example, a more recent video has been suggested by my students as illustrating the medium's intertextuality in a lighter way. They suggest using the recent Blues Traveler video "Run Around" as a way to illustrate the intertextuality between the literature and film versions of *The Wizard of Oz*.

Reflections

As a result of these discussions, students begin to produce texts with a greater attention to issues of genre, intertextuality, and location. They begin to challenge the existing depictions and notions of the composition of texts as a whole and, more specifically, of the composition of visual images. Teachers and students who have explored these exercises have expressed that they encourage all of us to think more critically about what we watch and choose to watch. Students have produced texts in both written and video forms that critique music videos, advertisements, and other visual forms from various perspectives such as gender and race. Students have also produced their own videos and commercials that express an awareness of these issues and expand on the ideas of genre, location, and intertextuality examined in the exercises. The development of these types of critical literacies is crucial to composition students, helping them understand and develop the "skills" in reading and composing that turn passive readers and writers into ones that see these activities as social actions through which they can be active and powerful participants in the processes of consuming and producing texts. Most importantly, students learn to both resist and transform various mediums of "composition" in order to establish themselves as critical citizens who powerfully participate in our culture and society.

Notes

1. Douglas Kellner, "Reading Images Critically: Toward a Postmodern Pedagogy," in *Postmodernism, Feminism, and Politics*, ed. Henry Giroux (Albany, NY: SUNY Press, 1991), 60.

2. Susan C. Jarratt, John Heyda, Rich Lane, and Shannon Wilson, *Teacher's Guide to College Composition 1994–95*. Published by the Department of English, Miami University, Oxford, OH, 1994, 4–6.

3. I use the term *location* as Rich employs it in "Notes Toward a Politics of Location," in her *Blood, Bread and Poetry: Selected Prose 1975–1985* (New York: Norton, 1985),

where she discusses the responsibility and importance of tracing personal backgrounds for both authors and readers.

4. Jarratt et al., 5.

5. bell hooks, *Yearning. Race, Gender, and Cultural Politics* (Boston: South End Press, 1991), 7.

6. The following set of questions are used to initiate discussion of the videos by concentrating on the key elements of the text:

Cultural Studies Questions:

Conditions of Production

- Where and when was the text produced?
- Does the text belong to a generic or stereotypical class?
- Does the text belong to a specific genre or mode?

Key Features and their Disposition

- What are the key elements [language, visual techniques (sound, lighting, camera shots), specific musical techniques (tone, rhythm, presentation)], represented in the text?
- How does the text organize and define the elements that it represents?

The Reader

- For whose consumption was the text produced? Under what circumstances was the text to be consumed?
- How is the reader situated vis-à-vis the representations in the text?
- What part does your social position play in your reception of the text?

Ideological Structures

- What kind of ideological work does the text perform? What social, economic, or political interests does it serve?
- What beliefs, values, attitudes, assumptions does the text address, reinforce, or subvert?

Composition Questions:

Evaluation of Cultural Critique

- Does the writer convey what's pleasurable about this cultural object? Does he or she provide interesting "decoding"?
- Does the writer establish a critical distance from the object? Does he or she discuss the way this thing communicates cultural norms and values? Who demonstrates power and agency in this scene? Does the writer expose contradictions within the object?

7. See Holly Brubach, "Rock-and-Roll Vaudeville" in *Signs of Life in the USA*, ed. Sonia Maasik and Jack Solomon (Boston: Bedford Books, 1994), 175–180, and Lisa A. Lewis, "Male-Address Video" also in *Signs of Life in the USA*, 182–189.

8. I am using the term *modernist* here as Linda Brodkey does in her descriptions of the modernist notion of writing in *Academic Writing As Social Practice* (Philadelphia: Temple University Press, 1987).

11

Tracy Chapman in the Writing Classroom
Challenging Culturally Sanctioned Assumptions

Shelli B. Fowler

With increasing access to computer technologies on college campuses, the teaching of writing is undergoing reevaluation and change. In some institutions students in composition courses can respond to each other's drafts "online" in computerized classrooms. The Internet and the World Wide Web make possible on-line connections beyond the individual classroom as interactions between students located on different campuses in different regions become possible. The potential, then, for further expanding an individual student's intellectual and experiential understanding through advanced technology, for educational engagement that moves beyond what the student's lived experience has (or has not) offered, is currently viewed as "virtually" limitless.

Yet not all institutions of higher education are currently hardwired. Not all teachers, nor all students, in college writing courses have access to computerized classrooms and the interactive connections such classrooms facilitate. There are, of course, several ways to engage students' intellectual and affective experiences without access to advanced classroom technologies. There are more readily accessible instruments of technology that can be used with relative ease in any writing classroom. Consider, for example, the boom box. A classroom with a simple electrical outlet can be transformed into a site where popular culture serves as an effective teaching tool, a "bridge" between what students often perceive as distant and formal (analytical writing skills, for example) and what students often perceive as their own familiar territory, an arena of personal expertise (popular music of various genres—rock, R&B, alternative, hip-hop, rap, etc.). I'd like to focus here on the use of popular music in the writing classroom; in particular, I want to focus on using the lyrics to Tracy Chapman's "Fast Car" as a musical "text" that works to challenge students' unexamined assumptions regarding the complexities of socially constructed identities. Tracy Chapman's "Fast Car" encourages students, as readers/interpreters of the song as text, to recognize the complex intersections of sexual orientation, socioeconomic status, and racial identity.

As a seemingly familiar "discourse," popular music is a discursive mode with which most students feel comfortable. I most recently discovered the usefulness of increased student comfort levels in relation to writing assignments that require students to engage in reexamining their assumptions about cultural identities when I taught an upper-division writing course at Washington State University in the fall of 1994.[1] The English 302 course, Writing About Literature, attempts to introduce students to the various modes of literary criticism and advanced interpretive critical reading and writing skills. Students learn (or review) the central tenets of New Criticism, reader-response criticism, new historicism, and feminist criticism, for example, and learn how various literary critical approaches may inform a reading/interpretation of any given text. Students read both primary texts and interpretive critical essays that model one or more kinds of critical approaches. As a writing course, students also learn to further refine their own analytical and interpretive writing skills. The primary texts the students read are drawn from a variety of literary genres, including fiction, poetry, and drama. The section of the course that focused on writing about poetry proved particularly problematic for the students. Many of the students expressed a general weariness when it came to reading, much less explicating and writing about, poetry. The genre of poetry seemed, to most of the students, an archaic one (regardless of the fact that most of the poetry they were required to read was contemporary), with form very often working to make the content, in their view, inaccessible.

The students' vocal resistance to poetry, as well as the difficult task of encouraging students to become self-reflective, critical readers willing to question the unexamined culturally sanctioned assumptions that we all, as readers, bring to a text, led me to bring the music of Tracy Chapman into the classroom as a pedagogical strategy. My initial goal was to find a way to make poetry more accessible to the students. Distributing Chapman's song lyrics turns the "song" into "poetry" as students visually "see" the lyrics in front of them (similar in textual format to a poem). Listening to the song makes more familiar the lyrical text, and raises the collective comfort level of the class. Students usually have a favorite song, know the lyrics to it, and feel comfortable explicating (to some extent) what the song is about; they are generally more secure in their abilities as able and attentive listeners to, and interpreters of, popular music of one form or another. The transition, then, from explicating song lyrics to explicating a poem, or moving from one genre to the other, is, perhaps, made easier for many students.

Additionally, while the students' confidence in their abilities to interpret a song was raised by playing Chapman's song and discussing it as a text, the choice of Chapman's "Fast Car" lyrics also worked to challenge the students' assumptions regarding the subject positions, particularly the gendered identities, of the two characters in Chapman's narrative story.[2] Although the textbook used in the course, Steven Lynn's *Texts and Contexts: Writing About Literature with Critical Theory*, repeatedly stresses the idea that interpreting a text, and writing about a text, involves not a single "right" answer, and is a task that is open for continual reconsideration and revision, several students seemed resistant to the idea that there could be more that one way to read and interpret a text. Prior to our discussions of Chapman's lyrics as poetry, the students read chapter 7, "Gendering the Text: Feminist Criticism," of the textbook. In this chapter, Lynn discusses feminist critical practice, and walks his readers through an interpretive reading of Samuel Johnson's 1746 poem, "To Miss ——— On Her Playing upon the Harpsichord In a Room Hung with Some Flower-pieces of Her Own Painting." In his initial feminist explication of the poem, Lynn argues that Johnson's descriptive images suggest not a simple celebration of "Stella's" artful harpsichord playing; instead, he argues that the poem's images may also be interpreted to suggest a desire "to control" Stella. He asks the reader of Johnson's poem to consider what role sex and gender play in the work, what image of women the poem conveys, and to consider how the poem depicts the gendered relationships between characters.[3] Lynn concludes that

> . . . the poem does seem to re-play that enduring story: woman as temptation, who causes man to fall. In other words, the poem seems to demonstrate once more Simone de Beauvoir's thesis that women tend to be presented as Eve or Mary, evil temptress or virginal saint.[4]

The students did not exhibit discomfort with Lynn's feminist reading of Johnson's poem in either their written responses or in class discussion. Feminist critical approaches in other English courses are common enough, as are, arguably, discussions about historically based sexism and the cultural inequities between men and women that result from a sexist system.

Lynn's "Gendering the Text" chapter also includes a section on "gay and lesbian criticism," however, and Lynn's second reading of the Johnson poem, using some of the tenets of a queer theory approach, seemed much more far-fetched and "unreal," as one student put it. In Lynn's (re)reading of the poem, he highlights the heterosexist bias of his first interpretive reading:

> If we consider my own draft above, it seems clear that I have made a revealing and unwarranted assumption: the "rash youth," I have taken for granted, is a male. Specifically, I have assumed that the youth is a heterosexual male enamored of the presumably heterosexual Stella. But the sex of the youth, as you may have noticed, is actually nowhere indicated in the poem. If it is sexist to use "he" to refer to men and women (and it clearly is), then it's similarly

heterosexist to assume that undesignated romantic or sexual relationships always refer to heterosexual couples. . . . Johnson doesn't make the sex of the rash youth clear, and he therefore opens up various other readings. Consider for a moment how the possibility that the youth is female might alter or further expand our reading of the poem.[5]

Since the students found the Johnson poem rather impenetrable in terms of its language and images and exhibited some reluctance to engage with Lynn's second, alternative reading, I brought in a CD player and the lyrics to Chapman's "Fast Car" during the next class period. After listening to the song and following along with the lyrics in front of them, the students were asked to write a brief explication of the song using the lyrics as the textual reference. Following the in-class writing exercise, our class discussion began with a focus on the song's central action and characters. Even with Lynn's warning to readers about the limitations of "revealing and unwarranted" heterosexist assumptions fresh in their minds from the previous class meeting, the students uniformly "read" the couple in the narrative of "Fast Car" as male and female. Like Lynn's first interpretive reading of the Johnson poem, "To Miss ———. . . ," an interpretive reading of "Fast Car" that views the narrative speaker (the "I" in the song) as a female and the other character (referred to in the song only as "you") as a male, is certainly a valid and supportable one. Notably, the ease with which the students referred to specific images in the song suggested that their comfort level about textual explication was much higher with Chapman's "Fast Car" than it was with Johnson's 1746 poem. After the class as a whole discussed the song, focusing on the couple's financial problems, their stay in a homeless shelter, the male character's tendency to go out to the bar and drink rather than visit with his children, and the female speaker's frustration with this scenario, her desire to "better their situation," and her ultimate refusal to accept his behavior as satisfactory in the long run, I asked the class to point out the stanza in which the "you" character was gender-identified.

There was a long, palpable pause in the class discussion. One of the students volunteered that actually only the gender identity of the "I" speaker is identified in the line that refers to her job as a cashier in a market.[6] What if we (re)read the reference to "the shelter" in that stanza not as a shelter for the homeless, but as a shelter for battered women, I offered. Another palpable pause, and then a couple of students began what turned into an engaging discussion about alternative ways to interpret/read "Fast Car." One student asserted that, yes, without a clear gender reference it was quite possible to "read" the couple not as male and female but as a lesbian couple who are trying to start over from the safe haven of a women's shelter. Another student suggested that while it isn't clear in the song what circumstances led the "you" character to the shelter, one could read the "I" (the speaker in the song) character's revelation about her father's drinking as carrying the potential of violent behavior, which would account for her being a resident at a battered woman's shelter. Unlike the collective class response to Lynn's alternative reading of the Johnson poem, the level of engagement with the issues that the song raises was markedly higher.

While none of the students had vocally collaborated Lynn's second reading of "To Miss——— . . . ," when doubts were raised in the previous class discussion, several students felt comfortable enough with the text of "Fast Car" to cite textual evidence in support of an alternative same-sex-relationship reading as doubts about the viability of such a reading were raised. One student argued that the same-sex-reading didn't work because the "you" character both drank late at a bar with his buddies and ignored his kids, citing the lines that refer to the "you" character's behavior as evidence. That objection, however, was quickly met by a student who suggested that the bar and the friends referenced in that stanza are not identified by gender, and thus, it was quite possible to read that line consistent with the same-sex reading, if one considered the fact that the bar might be a gay bar or a women's bar and that the friends referred to might be other lesbians. But, another student observed, that doesn't account for the reference to the kids, since lesbians don't have children. Yet another student, admitting that she was still pondering the feasibility of the second reading, offered that lesbians, of course, do have children, and noted that the line in the song referred to "your kids," not "our" kids, which could indicate that the "you" character was a lesbian mother staying at the shelter with her children, which might even be where the characters in the song originally met each other.

Joseph Chadwick has argued that we must include accounts of gay cultures in any curriculum that intends to move away from a monocultural toward a multicultural perspective.[7] Chadwick posits that "any research question or pedagogical strategy that does not pursue an actively antihomophobic course when issues of sexual difference arise (or that simply tries to evade those issues) must be in some degree homophobic." There is no such thing as a neutral position on the issue of sexual difference, according to Chadwick, and there is "no room for neutrality . . . since neutrality means letting the normal, institutionally and socially sanctioned current of homophobias flow on undisturbed."[8] I agree with Chadwick's assessment and intended the explicating of "Fast Car" to reemphasize Steven Lynn's discussion of gay and lesbian literary theory's contributions to interpretive critical readings of texts. What I did not expect were the ways in which an analysis of Tracy Chapman's "Fast Car" as lyrical text worked to empower the students as they wrestled with the complexities of multiple identities and the broad range of subject positions that are either located within a text and/or are informed by the location of the reader of the text. The students in the class seemed more comfortable with their alternative reading of "Fast Car," and also seemed to think that if Tracy Chapman's text raised these issues, then perhaps the task of looking for and actively engaging in reading the layers of complexities in all texts wasn't as far-fetched as some of them had initially thought it to be. Many of the students actually seemed excited about rethinking their first assumptions and about examining the cultural ideologies that led them to accept, unquestioningly, assumptions about identities. One student, who claimed he was very resistant to the idea that reading texts with an attentiveness to gender play and sexual differences was an important concept, brought up both Lynn's analysis of "To Miss ———— . . ." and the class's analysis of "Fast Car" and suggested that *maybe* an argument for a same-sex reading could be made about Chapman's song given its production in the late 1980s, but that he thought Lynn's reading was inappropriate for a poem produced in the mid-eighteenth century. One of the other English majors suggested that the terminology for naming different sexualities may have changed significantly but he doubted that the existence of different sexual orientations emerged only in the 1980s. He referred the student to Shakespeare's sonnets as further "literary proof" that sexual orientation issues have been a part of literary production long before the twentieth century, even before the eighteenth century, for that matter. The willingness on most of the students' parts to move from Tracy Chapman to Samuel Johnson to William Shakespeare and back again was, I think, facilitated by an engaged and serious look at "Fast Car" as a significant "text."[9] Further, the students moved from an awareness of how readings attentive to gender issues should also be inclusive of sexual orientation differences, to an increased awareness of how other identity issues should be considered simultaneously.

The essays submitted for the first section of the course in which students wrote interpretive analyses of short fiction were, in general, less attentive to the instructions that asked them to consider how, for example, their own cultural experiences and their own subject positions influenced the ways they constructed meaning in their interpretations of whatever text they had chosen. Although Lynn's *Texts and Contexts* encourages the students to notice the lens through which they interpret various texts, for many students that task seemed either too difficult or not relevant. The writing assignments that followed the "Fast Car" explication, however, included, overall, a significant attention to the variables of multicultural, rather than monocultural identities as the students's written work displayed a more active engagement with the variables of racial, ethnic, sexual, and class identities and began to consider what difference those variables make in any textual analysis. In a short writing assignment following the class discussions of Tracy Chapman's music, one student essay argued that "Fast Car" effectively moved the listener/reader to consider the dismal state of the American economic system and to recognize the unrealistic and yet mythical status in American culture of equal economic opportunity for all, since the text's images of working in a market as a checkout girl, even with the hope of getting promoted, would not financially enable any couple (male and female or female and female) to realize the aspirations to move into a large house in the suburbs. In their next writing assignment, students engaged in critical interpretations of the poetry of Sherman Alexie, most with an attentiveness to racial, cultural, gendered, class, and regional identities and locations, and how the complexities of location affected an interpretive reading of the poetry.

Students generally seemed to make the transition from viewing the construction of meaning as a static (and inflexible) process that holds all readers as part of a fixed, absolute, and universal group, to an awareness that a reader's way(s) of making meaning, and her/his assumptions about what is and is not important within a text, is a fluid process (thus capable of shifting), informed by specific cultural contexts, and one that is variable and continually open to (re)interpretation. In other words, the students, though initially rather rigid in their resistance to writing about poetry and toward actively considering the variables of cultural identities that affect both the production and reception of texts, seemed to become more flexible. The writing process, one with an emphasis on reexamining their initial assumptions, proved, for many of them, to be liberating work.

Notes

1. I originally discovered the usefulness of using Tracy Chapman's music and lyrics while teaching a first-year composition course at The University of Texas at Austin in 1990. The composition course did not rely on literary analysis as the means for teaching critical thinking and analytical writing skills, yet the explication of "Fast Car" helped highlight the significance of sexual-orientation issues relevant to the writing assignments about socially constructed differences in that course as well.

2. Interestingly, almost all of the students in the course knew who Tracy Chapman was, and had heard some of her music at one time or another, though few seemed to have carefully analyzed or interpreted "Fast Car." Only one student volunteered that Tracy Chapman's music was something that she listened to fairly often. Even though the majority of students were not avid Tracy Chapman fans, few had *not* heard "Fast Car" before it was played in the class. Thus, as a "text" it appeared more accessible to them than the genre of poetry in general.

3. Steven Lynn, *Texts and Contexts: Writing About Literature with Critical Theory* (New York: Harper Collins, 1994), 210.

4. Ibid., 213.

5. Ibid., 218–219. Lynn supports his second reading of the poem by arguing that the poem's caution against "pleasure" might immediately take on a different hue, for the "dang'rous hour" might be the one in which the youth is tempted to fall in love with another woman. And the odd injunction, "think not . . . / The nymph fictitious, as the flow'r" makes considerable sense, as the speaker warns the youth not to imagine that the nymph would be receptive to a lesbian encounter; or (alternatively) the speaker warns the youth not to imagine that the nymph is actually a man. The nymph is not "fictitious"; she is only what she appears to be, and falling in love with her would be disastrous for the female "youth," lesbian or not. Even though "charms thus press on ev'ry sense," the youth is being advised to resist these "New chains."

Lynn's second reading concludes with the assertion that "Johnson's heterosexism urges us to endorse 'difference' in love, attacking (in rather cloaked terms) same-sex love" (p. 220). For a full reprint of Johnson's poem, see *Texts and Contexts,* 207.

6. All references to "Fast Car" are from the liner notes to the CD *Tracy Chapman,* 1988 Elektra/Asylum Records.

7. Joseph Chadwick "Toward an Antihomophobic Pedagogy," in *Professions of Desire.* ed. George E. Haggerty and Bonnie Zimmerman (New York: MLA, 1995), 31.

8. Ibid., 32.

9. The "Fast Car" exercise could be adapted and broadened in a writing classroom equipped with computers and on-line exchange capacities. Playing "Fast Car" in the CD/ROM drive of a computer and having students choose visual images to display on screen to visually reflect their interpretive reading of "Fast Car" while they have an interactive dialogue about the text would be another way to engage in the issues Chapman's music raises.

12

Madonna, Calamity Jane, and the First-Year Composition Student

Kathryn R. Fitzgerald

A Comparative Pedagogy
for Teaching Academic Rhetoric

Notions of what it means to teach composition used to assume that the subject matter, audience and genre of the students' writing were irrelevant to the composition course's aims, which were to teach the universally valid principles of clarity, coherence, unity, and grammatical correctness. If students learned these principles, they would be able to write successfully in any context. Recent composition theory, on the other hand, has argued that a text's effectiveness, that is, its ability to achieve its aims, is contingent upon the local expectations of the audience or discourse community for whom the writing is intended. An article about the significance of the Madonna phenomenon written for *Time* magazine, for instance, would not be accepted for publication in *Feminist Studies*. Nor would a chapter from Patricia N. Limerick's *The Legacy of Conquest: The Unbroken Past of the American West* appear as a *Newsweek* story, even though *Newsweek* has published stories on revisionist American history, and even though Patricia Limerick also writes newspaper features. Each of these publications targets a different audience, embodies different aims, and employs the conventions of different genres. The differences not only affect the subject matter and points made, but also affect rhetorical choices as to paragraph organization, sentence structure, tone, and diction. The course I will describe, which I developed in collaboration with three veteran graduate teaching assistants[1] to fulfill the first-year writing requirement at the University of Utah, has the following aims: first, to introduce students to the concept that all writing is situated in local contexts that determine the rhetorical characteristics of effective writing for that community; and second, to help students to recognize the rhetorical expectations of their local context for the next four (or so) years—academic discourse—and to employ them effectively.

To convince students that all writing is local and contingent, we decided to use a comparative pedagogy premised on the notion that the differences in effective rhetorical strategies for various audiences or discourse communities are more obvious if the ostensible subject matter remains the same. Although the subject matter could be anything from representations of AIDS to analyses of the latest discoveries made possible by the Mars Pathfinder, topics from mass culture have several advantages. Besides being accessible, timely, and of high interest, such topics are addressed by academics within intellectual frameworks that serve to exemplify what the academic project is about. Academic research is misunderstood by most beginning students, who assume that the university is a glorified high school—bigger, harder, and smarter, but in essence another institution whose purpose is to disseminate the accumulated knowledge of humankind. They have no experience with the dynamics of the university as a knowledge-producing institution. As compositionist Mike Rose argues, beginning students are often mystified because they neither understand the university's stance toward inquiry nor its construction of what disciplines are and do. The juxtaposition of academic treatments of a topic with treatments in other contexts discloses the university's knowledge-making project. Becoming aware of the special purposes of academic writing, students can begin to figure out the connections between the rhetorical situation of the academic community and professors' expectations for the student's own writing.

The particular course described here investigates two topics from popular culture: the media's construction of Madonna as a pop icon and the movies' changing constructions of the American West. I should point out here that one of the problems/opportunities of a course based on contemporary work is the need to stay timely. Unless Madonna does something sensational the particular year of the course, for instance, students lose interest. The epistemological principle in effect, however, is that of the case study: constructions of Madonna and the American West serve as instances of how commercial and academic presses construct and deploy popular images. The same rhetorical principles and pedagogical methods can be applied equally successfully to any popular phenomenon that has also been treated by academics: Disney studio productions, television series like *The Simpsons, Married . . . with Children,* and *Beavis and Butt-head,* or talk shows would be equally fruitful case studies. This course does require research and preparation ahead of the autumn term to collect current articles from the popular presses, get copyright permission for them, and have student packets prepared.

The two topics of this course are each situated in a different dynamic with academic work. In the discipline of cultural studies the popular phenomenon becomes grist for the academic mill, but the popular media, more traditionally, reflect and refract the academic findings about the American West. In either case, a rhetorical approach to the readings enforces a critical stance toward both popular and academic writing. The rhetoric of the commercial press's construction of the Madonna persona reveals not only the economic basis of the Madonna phenomenon, but also the economic complicity of the press in publicizing the image. As the example of academic writing about the topic of Madonna, we use John Fiske's chapter on Madonna from his book *Reading the Popular*,[2] available in David Bartholomae and Anthony Petrosky's *Ways of Reading: An Anthology for Writers*.[3] Fiske's article extends the analysis students are able to construct themselves by complicating the gendered economic relationship between her fans and Madonna. Fiske's purposes for the article included instructing students in the practices of cultural criticism, so it serves as well as an exemplar of a discipline's research methodology and reporting. Its shortcoming in this regard is that, as an introduction to the methodology of cultural studies, it fails to turn upon itself as a critique of academic writing. However, the rhetorical approach teaches students to observe how academic writing is also constituted by and for a particular discourse community.

The rhetorical approach to the introductory chapters of Patricia Limerick's book, *The Legacy of Conquest* (also in *Ways of Reading*)[4], reveals a relationship between the academic writer, the writer's readers, and popular culture that is different from Fiske's. Limerick's audiences have consisted of at least two groups, the community of professional American historians and a wider educated reading public. By observing Limerick's rhetorical techniques for creating a credible ethos, students learn that even professionals must demonstrate their qualifications for speaking in a forum of peers, and that a variety of rhetorical techniques can be employed for that purpose. Students then read the articles in popular periodicals that disseminated the findings of Limerick and other revisionist American historians, analyzing how differences in audience and purpose affect the rhetorical strategies employed by the popular journals. Finally, they watch traditional and current film westerns to note the ways in which popular culture has absorbed and deployed the revised versions of the history of the West.

The course is divided into three major units. The first two focus on the two cultural topics and the third involves a researched paper through which students further investigate an aspect of one of the two topics. At this point, the course may seem to be a reading course in the rhetoric of popular culture and academic writing, as it is. Its primary aim—to enable students to write effectively in their academic courses—requires that they understand the rhetorical situation in which they must perform. But it also requires writing practice. The writing assignments both employ writing as a tool for learning subject matter and provide practice in genres typical of student writing across the curriculum. I will describe these assignments in greater detail as I discuss each unit.

Case Study #1: Popular and Academic Representations of the Madonna Phenomenon

Historical, analytical, and pedagogical logic all dictate that the course begin with the popular publications. Historically and analytically, the popular icon precedes and serves as the object of its academic construction (or deconstruction). Pedagogically, the popular versions of the cultural phenomenon are more familiar and therefore less intimidating or alienating to students than the language, concepts, and purposes of academic writing. Moreover, by the time students have analyzed the popular representations rhetorically, they will already be bridging the discourses, viewing the popular articles in ways formerly unfamiliar and more closely aligned with academic approaches.

We include five articles published in the mid-1980s that participated in the construction of Madonna as a pop image. Originally published in the news weeklies *Time* and *Newsweek,* in *People* magazine, and in the monthlies *America* (a publication for lay Catholics) and *The New Republic,* these articles were selected to represent a cross section of the popular press's renditions of Madonna. It came as something of a surprise to us as well as to students, who often suspect a hidden agenda, that they all promoted a positive image in one way or another. But this surprising consensus among mainstream publications about a supposedly counterculture figure provides a propitious point of entry for both rhetorical analysis and cultural critique. To provide a necessarily minimal context for the discussion to follow, here are the briefest of summaries of each article:

Newsweek. "Rock's New Women" by a team of five reporters. A history dating to the 1960s and culminating with Cindy Lauper, Pat Benatar, and Madonna, this piece is a narrative of increasing feminist presence and power in the rock world.[5]

People. "Hollywood Sizzle" by James McBride. A five-page layout divided equally between text and photos, this story describes Madonna's bad-girl persona and catalogs the economic success of her pop image.[6]

Time. "Madonna Rocks the Land" by John Skow. A rhetorically sophisticated appeal to parents for understanding of the Madonna phenomenon's symbolic import for Madonna's young adolescent fans.[7]

America. "Like a Catholic: Madonna's Challenge to Her Church" by Andrew Greeley. This analysis of the religious strains in Madonna's music and image asks Catholics to accept female sexuality as one of God's gifts rather than reject it as sinful.[8]

The New Republic. "Virgin Territory" by Joel D. Schwartz. A postmodern analysis (with little postmortem jargon) of performance as identity, pointing out that Madonna's merging of good-girl/bad-girl distinctions results in a "satirical aloofness" from questions of identity in which everything becomes pose.[9]

Our questions for class discussion of these articles guide students toward understanding the complex interdependence of content, rhetorical context, and rhetorical strategies. Questions about content tend to blend into those about context. Here are some examples:

> How is Madonna *represented* in each article? That is, what did the writer expect/want you to think about Madonna as a result of reading the article? How do the details used to describe her in each article change the reader's view? Or do they produce a cumulative effect?
>
> What differences do you see in the way each article views Madonna? Where was the article published? What do you know about the purposes of this publication? Its audience? What are the interests of the community or audience the writer is addressing? Why is each community interested in Madonna? How are the differences in the representations of Madonna related to the particular readers of the publication, to the interests of the publishers, and/or to the purposes of the writer? After explaining that *interest* is used in a specialized sense here, we ask students to consider the question in terms of who gains by the writing, who is harmed or exploited by it, and whose voices are *not* heard in the writing.
>
> Where (locate in the writing) do you "hear" the voices of the various groups interested in the representation of Madonna?

As students consider rhetorical contexts, they can also examine how each writer's rhetorical choices might contribute to the article's aims and purposes. The following questions help students to recognize rhetorical techniques or strategies:

- Whose voices are privileged in the article? Which voices are marginalized? Are there any voices that should be present but are not (silenced voices)?

- Examine the organization of the article. What kind of information appears first? What follows? Can you think of reasons for giving the information in this order?

- Compare the opening paragraphs of articles. How do they differ? Why?

- What kinds of information are emphasized? What is downplayed?

- What is the tone of the article?

- What is the level of diction in the article?

- Compare the layout of these articles, including use of photographs, headlines, and graphics. How do these choices reflect the publisher's sense of its audience and purpose?

I want to reiterate that these questions could be applied to articles on any cultural topic; I am simply using the topic of Madonna as an example. Each of the articles listed above represents a fascinating rhetorical problem and solution, but I will use an excerpt from the *Time* article to illustrate some of these questions in action. Here are the first two paragraphs of *Time*'s seven-page spread on Madonna:

> Now then, parents, the important thing is to stay calm. You've seen Madonna wiggling on MTV—right, she's the pop-tart singer with the trashy outfits and the hi-there belly button. What is worse, your children have seen her. You tell your daughters to put on jeans and sweatshirts, like decent girls, and they look at you as if you've just blown in from the Planet of the Creeps. Twelve-year-old girls, headphones blocking out the voices of reason, are running around wearing T-shirts labeled VIRGIN, which would not have been necessary 30 years ago. The shirts offer no guarantees, moreover; they merely advertise Madonna's first, or virgin, rock tour, now thundering across the continent, and her bouncy, love-it-when-you-do-it song *Like a Virgin.*
>
> The bright side of this phenomenon is that these Wanna Be's (as in "We wanna be like Madonna!") could be out somewhere stealing hubcaps. Instead, all of them, hundreds of thousands of young blossoms whose actual ages run from a low of about eight to a high of perhaps 25, are saving up their baby-sitting money to buy cross-shaped earrings and fluorescent rubber bracelets like Madonna's, white lace tights that they will cut off at the ankles and black tube skirts that, out of view of their parents, they will roll down several turns at the waist to expose their middles and the waistbands of the pantyhose.

We could start with almost any of the questions above to open a discussion of these paragraphs, but the writer's remarkable use of *voice* in this article has always struck me, so I begin there, by asking students to describe the tone of the opening paragraphs and picture the person who might adopt such a tone. These questions examine the writer's *ethical appeal*, in the terms of classical rhetoric. Students usually reconstruct the persona of a hip family friend or uncle who is close enough to address parents familiarly, even superciliously, and whose knowledge of teenyboppers is vastly superior to theirs. The first sentence, "Now then, parents, the important thing is to stay calm," establishes the superior tone of the single voice of reason in a situation about to turn ugly, like a threatening fire that has hurt no one yet, or an outbreak of severe influenza in the next county. The next sentence immediately reduces the tension with a humorous turn of phrase ("Madonna wiggling on MTV"—nothing threatening in that image) and low-key slang out of the parents' generation ("trashy outfits," "hi-there belly button.") "Pop-tart singer" is particularly fetching, a clever combination of "popular" and "tart," or whore, rendered harmless in juxtaposition by the allusion to a toaster pastry. The persona acknowledges the parents' values with the phrase "like decent girls," and then moves to establish his credibility as an authority on youth by speaking in their voice with their slang: "they look at you as if you've just blown in from the Planet of the Creeps." The author then explains the slang phrase "Wanna Be" for his hopelessly out-of-touch parents—"as in 'We wanna be like Madonna!'" Thus, through diction and tone, the writer establishes himself from the get-go as a hip friend of *Time*'s parent-readers who also happens to be an authority on their children's generation.

Reading the second paragraph as closely as the first, students discover that the writer continues to downplay Madonna's danger to the morals of the nation's adolescents by comparing their fad shopping with clearly illegal gang-related activities (they "could be out somewhere stealing hubcaps"). The unlikely comparison makes the point that, far from demonstrating deviant behavior, these young teens are functioning well in their socially approved worker/consumer roles. Rhetorical analysis becomes cultural critique with but little prompting from the instructor, who need only ask why the writer and *Time* magazine would want to downplay Madonna's perceived threat to the morals of the readers' children. What is their interest in doing so? Who gains if parents do not view Madonna as dangerous? Who loses? Who gets exploited?

This article was published a year or so before Time, Inc. and Warner Bros. merged to homogenize the news and entertainment industries and hegemonize their effects, but students have little trouble making the obvious connections between advertising dollars and editorial content. They may be interested in working out the more complex balancing act between representing Madonna as safe to parents without undercutting the allure of the bad-girl image for adolescent girls. When students have read several of the Madonna articles, they can begin to compare them on the basis of any or all of these rhetorical issues—the writer's persona, the relation of that persona to both the readers and the publisher, the privileging or silencing of various voices, the effects of choices in diction or tone, or the effects of the particular order of the information on readers.

Such analysis leads to equally interesting discoveries about the varied interests for which this pop icon was deployed. The process of analyzing the popular presses rhetorically not only denaturalizes their productions, teaching students not to accept them as transparent renditions of truth but to read them instead as interested representations of an always deferred reality, but it also teaches students the value of rhetorical analysis itself. From the popular articles, students move to a rhetorical analysis of John Fiske's "Madonna." This is an extremely difficult article for students both because of its unfamiliar concepts and its academic vocabulary. I usually assign only the first four or five pages of the article the first night, and ask students to mark the point at which they recognize that this is an academic rather than a popular article and to underline words that identify it as academic. Comparing Fiske's opening paragraphs with those of the popular articles immediately highlights the effects of the very different rhetorical situations upon the author's choice of rhetorical techniques. We ask students to identify the audience for an article like this and to consider why they would be reading this text. These simple questions about a couple of obvious rhetorical issues can lead to a complex discussion and critique of the purposes of academic writing.

A discussion of the examples of academic diction that students have underlined together with the apparatus questions in *Ways of Reading* helps students to understand Fiske's definitions and processes. His aim is to define and demonstrate to a student audience what cultural studies are, how they are done, and why they are important. Reading Fiske's article in conjunction with his raw data (the image-making articles, some of which he actually quotes), and reading them all from a rhetorical perspective, students can begin to complicate his cultural analysis themselves. They can agree that adolescent girls may find a certain individual power in appropriating the Madonna image to subvert the repressive middle-class values of their patriarchal, capitalistic elders. But students also notice, through reading the original image-constructing articles, that adolescents are at the same time exploited by the image makers who overcharge them for concert tickets, concert T-shirts, makeup, clothes, and jewelry. They begin to glimpse societal power relations that challenge their unreflective assumptions about capitalism and entertainment.

Central to this course's purposes is that Fiske's description of the methods and aims of cultural studies introduces students to the larger concept that the university is a knowledge-generating institution. Questions about how Fiske's information is organized and what aspects of it are emphasized and downplayed (rhetorical issues) lead students to recognize that the academic context includes knowledge making as well as knowledge dissemination. This discovery is of immense importance for first-year composition students. Once they understand that a purpose of academic writing is to disseminate new knowledge, they can understand many of its peculiarities as the fulfillment of rhetorical criteria for convincing the reader, a critical member of the same knowledge-generating community, of the validity of the writer's truth claims. In particular, they can especially understand academic demands for detailed evidence as they judge for themselves whether Fiske's evidence is convincing.

As students reread the article and understand it more thoroughly, they also begin to recognize some of the advantages of academic jargon. They learn that words that were originally incomprehensible serve an important function: they stand as a shorthand for very complex ideas that would take paragraphs to explain if the academic terms were not available. But an examination of diction leads to critique as well. As students consider those terms in the particular rhetorical context Fiske identifies, they may well question their rhetorical effect. Whose interests do they serve? In what ways? How do questions about interests complicate our sense of Fiske's audience and purpose? The academic jargon alienates the students Fiske seems to address and certainly excludes those very girls who are supposedly empowered through their appropriation of Madonna's semiotics. This analysis suggests a shadow audience beyond introductory students, one that consists of Fiske's peers, who would understand and approve the academic terms. Suddenly, class divisions appear at several levels that question Fiske's own complicity in the very structures of power relations he attempts to overturn.

The danger of this critical approach to academic writing is that students will become cynical about the work of cultural studies or about the entire knowledge-making project of the university. This is not our intention. It is instead to lead students to the recognition that even academic writing is rhetorically situated, conforming to certain communally constructed criteria for credibility, rather than an objective reflection of truth. To make this point, it is important to stress that cultural studies is a new field still developing a consensus about its methods and criteria. Students should learn that in this context, detailed evidence rendered in the language of the discipline in accordance with its structural and logical expectations for reasoning and writing are rhetorically effective techniques.

Writing Instruction

Though Fiske's chapter serves as an example of academic writing, it is not a model for student writing for several reasons. Most directly pertinent to our students' situation is that, like any "real" piece of writing, it incorporates descriptive, summarizing, analyzing, and synthesizing techniques that are not yet within the freshman student's repertoire. We therefore begin writing practice with the teaching of these techniques, focusing on each one individually. We start with the summary as the kind of writing with which students are already most familiar, but we don't assume that students are good summary writers (though some are). Summaries serve the secondary purpose of ensuring close reading, so I might assign summaries of two or three of the popular articles and of sections of Fiske's piece, teaching techniques for reading to find main points, for summarizing by structural unit (paragraph or section), for recognizing and eliminating supporting detail, and for explicitly stating the logical connections between ideas.

The second writing assignment of this unit is a rhetorical analysis of the student's choice of one of the popular articles or of the Fiske chapter. There are several reasons for including a rhetorical analysis at this point. Minimally, as "writing to learn," it reinforces class discussion about rhetorical strategies. But more importantly, it requires students to alter their stance as writers. When writing summaries, students must follow the lead of their source, conveying its concepts usually in the order of its organization. The difference when writing an analysis is that the student writer must take charge of the writing. Without direct instruction, students often fail to learn this distinction throughout their college careers, and professors of senior seminars are heard to complain, "All my students ever write is summary." The student writer is in charge of an analysis because he or she decides which rhetorical features to use to frame the analysis and selects the material from the text to use for support. The choice of rhetorical topics and organization are up to the student writer, not the author of the source, and the source text is subordinated in service of the student writer's points about the source's rhetoric.

The rhetorical analysis also serves as a vehicle for learning how to incorporate textual evidence into writing. Our typical first-year composition students usually need to learn how to use introductory phrases, how to document textual sources, and how to explicate textual examples. The rhetorical analysis teaches these skills in the context of the students' own writing. Handbooks provide teaching aids for these techniques, including lists of introductory phrases for quotations, MLA or APA guidelines for citation of sources within the text, and samples of paragraphs using textual evidence. To demonstrate how to explicate a quotation, I am sometimes able to find handbook examples, but samples from assigned readings and from papers written previously by students are more effective.

Case Study #2: Academic Writing and the Myth of the West

The subject matter of the second reading unit is the history of the American West. It is important to make clear to students (and to colleagues in history, should they ask) that we are not teaching a course in history, but a course in the rhetoric of academic writing. Revisionist versions of Western history simply provide another example of how the warrants, purposes, methods, and conventions of a discipline operate in its writing. The comparative pedagogical method continues in this unit as students read articles from the popular presses that, this time, operate to disseminate and critique the findings of historians. The example of academic writing is taken from Patricia Limerick's book *The Legacy of Conquest*, a particularly fruitful object for rhetorical analysis because of its positioning in its field. Limerick is often grouped with a generation of young historians who first gained notoriety in the 1980s (others included Richard White, William Cronin, and Donald Wooster) and who are generally credited with legitimating the study of the American West. As Limerick points out in her introduction, American historians, viewing the South and New England as the geographical areas critical to the nation's development, had generally not considered the West worthy of their attention. Once Frederick Jackson Turner declared the frontier closed in 1890, all that happened since became the "present" rather than history, and what happened before was relegated to the mythical realms of dime novels and the movies. Limerick and her cohorts not only insisted on treating the West seriously but also challenged Jackson's and his followers' interpretations, which had been the received wisdom of the field for three-quarters of a century. This young group of new voices faced the multiple challenges of establishing their own credibility as historians, of legitimizing a field held in low esteem, and of persuading their colleagues to hear their maverick views of it.

The central rhetorical question for the two Limerick chapters included in *Ways of Reading* is how the author establishes her credibility—the issue of *ethos*. If we open class discussion with this question, students will note that

Limerick begins by demonstrating her thorough knowledge of the major voice in the field, Frederick Jackson Turner. By examining, analyzing, and criticizing Turner's interpretations, she identifies herself as an insider in the field with the same knowledge and training her well-established predecessors (who are also her audience) have. What's more, her critique carves out spaces—the holes in the current versions of Western history—where she can insert her own perspective.

If we ask students to consider what Limerick says about her methods, they will discover that, like Fiske, she uses her discussion of methods rhetorically to establish her credibility. She argues for expanding the historians' sources from written texts to include the tools of archaeologists and anthropologists—artifacts and oral histories. She points out that no essential reasons exist for requiring historians to restrict their study to texts; the barriers between disciplines are merely traditional. In her first chapter she uses artifacts in the form of several photographs that speak to one of her central points, the continuity of Western history from "frontier" days to the present. The most famous is perhaps the photograph of miners sitting on the ground not around a campfire but around a small trash pile of tin cans. The caption reads "Miners at dinner. The men themselves might move on, but the evidence of their presence would remain."[10] The argument of her second chapter relies on an anthropological principle rather than a historical one—that the persistence of cultural beliefs, whether oral or written, is extraordinarily powerful. Thus her analysis, which diverges radically from that of the Turner thesis, gains credibility by her persuasive argument for the use of sources that were unavailable to Turner and his followers given their perception of what sorts of evidence constitute history. Close examination of Limerick's deployment of evidence by now accomplishes more than a demonstration of her use of the ethical appeal; it contributes to students' understanding of the meaning of disciplinary boundaries.

We can draw a loose parallel between the student's rhetorical situation in the university and Limerick's as a young scholar. The student is also a new, unproved voice in the discourse. Students can see that if a woman with a Ph.D. in history has to work so hard to establish her credibility with her former professors (who are her primary audience), they as undergraduates must, a fortiori, demonstrate their knowledge of the subject. Seldom does a student go away from this course still asking, "Why isn't my opinion as good as anybody else's?" They learn that a discipline's constructed conventions about how to support claims demand certain demonstrations of knowledge.

When the students turn to the popular articles about the West, they discover very different substantive and rhetorical issues at play. The academic text focuses on subject matter, with rhetorical choices made to establish the writer as an authority on the topic, but the rhetorical techniques used in the popular articles seem to be primarily audience-oriented. Writers tend to begin where they think their audience is—familiar with the West through its myths, not its history. The articles we use for comparison to Limerick's academic work are the following:

> *Journal of American Culture.* "The American West and the American Western: Printing the Legend" by Greg Garrett. Dismissing any claims films might make to historical accuracy by describing several examples of typical inaccuracies, Garrett examines the social implications of their thematic content. He traces the changes in views of the relationships between law and the outlaw, society and the individual, and optimism and cynicism to changes in the American political and economic scene.[11]

> *USA Today Magazine* "Preserving the Myth of the Old West" by Gerald F. Kreyche. Kreyche argues that the myths of the Old West are more crucial to the molding of national character and unity than are the disruptive findings of the revisionist historians.[12]

> *U.S. News and World Report.* "How the West Was Really Won" by a team of reporters. These writers both quote the revisionist historians and conduct their own original anthropological research to record some living western voices.[13]

Reversing the relationship between popular culture and cultural studies, the popular articles here respond to the historians' work as the primary sources. It is probably safe to say that this is a more typical relationship between the academic field and the popular press. To open class discussion about these articles, we use much the same questions as for the Madonna articles. Students again discover that rhetorical techniques vary with the rhetorical context. The rhetorical strategies deployed in these three articles differ from each other as well as from those of the Madonna articles. Space does not permit comparisons here, but a quick glance at the varieties of publications—an informal journal of film and cultural studies, a conservative Catholic magazine, and a news weekly— suggest the potential for difference. Rhetorical comparisons among these three and between them and the Madonna articles lead to productive discussions about the kinds of stakes the writers and publishers have in each project.

The third receptive activity of this unit is to view two or three film westerns. We require students to watch at least one pre-1980s classic of their choice, such as *High Noon*, *The Man Who Shot Liberty Valance*, or *Jeremiah Johnson*, and one postrevisionist film, like *The Unforgiven* or *Dances with Wolves*. Class discussion centers around the issues the readings have raised: How are natural resources treated in the film? In what myths or legends about the West does the film participate? Does it challenge any of the traditional myths? What values does it promote? How are women or minorities represented? What do answers to these questions suggest about the relationship between academic knowledge and the popular imagination?

Writing Instruction

We work with three writing assignments in this unit, a repeat of a rhetorical analysis, a review, and a synthesis. The rhetorical analysis can be written either to the Limerick chapters or the popular articles. Again, it reinforces both the particular points made in class discussions about the rhetorical strategies in these articles and the course's larger point that all writing is rhetorically situated. Moreover, it provides students with additional practice in making the very difficult conceptual and organizational shift from summary to analysis.

The movies provide a ready-made opportunity to work with the review genre, not only because movies are typical subjects of reviews but also because students are now prepared for the processes involved in writing reviews. We ask students to bring in reviews from the newspaper or current periodicals to study the characteristics of the genre, noting how both summary and analysis are employed. They see that writers manipulate summary to serve their purposes (pique interest, illustrate a criticism) and that they identify components (plot, acting, directing, camera work, editing, sound track, etc.) to explain the effect of the film as a whole. The point to be made for students is that none of the processes they learn in class (summary, analysis, synthesis) is used for its own sake; they all serve larger purposes.

The last writing assignment of this unit parts ways with rhetorical analysis in order to deal with another mode of writing. We call it the synthesis paper, though the name is inadequate for what we ask students to do. The term "synthesis," "the combining of constituent elements into a single or unified entity" according to *Webster's,* suggests a totalizing activity that is not what we have in mind. Instead, we ask students to find a thread, a topic, or an issue that runs through several of the readings, trace the varying representations of that issue, and come to a position of their own on the topic. We are not looking for consensus, but for critical thinking and argument. Students might, for instance, consider Kreyche's claims for the value of myth over historical accuracy, and analyze *High Noon* and *The Unforgiven* or *Jeremiah Johnson* and *Dances with Wolves* in light of the different values Kreyche and Limerick espouse. Or, depending on the films they choose to view, students might discuss any of the questions mentioned above in light of Limerick's arguments: How is the exploitation of natural resources represented? How are women or minorities represented? What changes do they see between the older films and more recent ones? Given the views of Garrett and Limerick, how would they explain the differences in the films?

The Culmination: A Researched Paper with a Difference

After completing these reading and writing assignments, students are ready for a culminating assignment incorporating many of the genres they have practiced throughout the course. Our version of the researched paper, this assignment teaches library resource skills, but it seeks to avoid some of the pitfalls of the typical research paper. In my experience, these assignments (pick a topic, research both sides of the issues, come to a position, and write a paper in which you argue for it) are more likely to result in regression than progress. Students pick a topic with which they are already familiar and about which they often already have strong opinions, find all the evidence they can, often in popular publications, to support their current opinions and just enough on the other side to meet their obligation to consider both sides, and finally write a report they could have written in high school. They learn little or nothing about the rhetoric of academic argumentation, a primary focus of this course.

Because students have been situated in two academic discourses throughout the term, they are at least minimally prepared to write an academic argument. They have been introduced to some of the questions at issue in each discipline and are aware of expectations for supporting evidence and persuasive argument. We have used two different approaches to this final assignment, and each has its advantages. The first is to ask students to pursue a question that has been suggested by class discussions, research the positions of additional scholars in the field by reading scholarly journals, and write a synthesis paper tracing and critiquing the scholars' positions. We expect this process to lead students to reaching and defending a position of their own on the issue. A student working in cultural studies might pick a cultural icon other than Madonna, or a problem in popular culture—the representation of women in television commercials or the representation of minorities in "real life" crime shows—and do their own analysis in light of what two or three experts have written on the topic. With this assignment, students conduct searches of library databases as well as a little primary research. In the field of American history, students might investigate the historical parceling out of water rights, the ecological effects of the destruction of native species like prairie grass and buffalo, or current economic issues for Indians, including mineral rights and casino gambling, and immigration questions regarding the Japanese, Mexicans, Southeast Asians or Pacific Islanders. Given their work with Limerick, they are likely to pursue historical as well as current explanations of current issues.

The second alternative is to repeat the same comparative processes for the final paper that students have been doing all quarter long. In this version of the final paper, students are asked to pick a topic treated in both popular and academic presses, much as we did in designing the course, and analyze how it is represented rhetorically in both contexts. This assignment has the double advantages of reinforcing the rhetorical approach students have been learning all quarter and encouraging students to forgo closure in their own thinking about the topic. If students are not required to take a position of their own, but are required to critique the rhetoric used in defense of others' positions, they may remain open enough to reconsider their preconceived notions, something that happens rarely with the traditional research assignment.

Our aims for this course, as I pointed out at the beginning, are to introduce students to the concept that all writing is situated in local contexts and that the writer's (publisher's, advertiser's, academic institution's) purposes and the reader's expectations set limits for which rhetorical characteristics will be effective. We want to teach first-year composition students the rhetorical strategies valued by their new community—the university—so that they can employ them effectively. For the purposes of this course, it doesn't really matter which popular topics are selected for study. The point of the contrastive pedagogy, that academic and popular publications serve different purposes for different audiences, and that local rhetorical contexts demand appropriate rhetorical techniques, will be made no matter what the topic.

Notes

1. My collaborators were Christopher Diller, Jack Vespa, and Kimberly Wilson. Without the creativity and research of these three, this course would have never materialized. More than an expression of mere gratitude, this is an acknowledgment of a productive collaborative effort.

2. John Fiske. "Madonna," *Ways of Reading: An Anthology for Writers,* eds. David Bartholomae and Anthony Petrosky (Boston: Bedford Books of St. Martin's Press, 1993).

3. Bartholomae and Petrosky, Ibid.

4. Patricia Nelson Limerick. "Introduction: Closing the Frontier and Opening Western History" and "Empire of Innocence" in Bartholomae and Petrosky.

5. Jim Miller with Cathleen McGuigan, Mark D. Uehling, Janet Huck, Peter McAlevey, "Rock's New Women," *Newsweek,* 4 March, 1985, pp. 74–77.

6. James McBride, "Hollywood Sizzle," *People,* 13 May, 1985, 40–45.

7. John Skow, "Madonna Rocks the Land." *Time,* 27 May, 1985, 30–32.

8. Andrew Greeley, "Like a Catholic: Madonna's Challenge to Her Church," *America,* 13 May, 1989, 447–449.

9. Joel D. Schwartz, "Virgin Territory," *The New Republic,* 26 August, 1985, 30–32.

10. Limerick in David Bartholomae and Anthony Petrosky, *Ways of Reading: An Anthology for Writers.* 327.

11. Greg Garrett, "The American West and the American Western: Printing the Legend," *Journal of American Culture,* Summer 1991, 99–105.

12. Gerald F. Kreyche, "Preserving the Myth of the Old West," *USA Today Magazine,* January 1991, 70–71.

13. Miriam Horn, "How the West Was Really Won," with sidepieces: "How the Myth Was Spun" by Sarah Burke and "Western Tales" (author not listed), *U.S. News and World Report,* 21 May, 1990, 56–69.

13

Examining the
Discourse of the University
White Noise *in*
the Composition Classroom

J. D. Applen

The novels of Don DeLillo are singularly representative of the kinds of organizing discourses that we use to create the world as we know it. Not only does DeLillo take time out in the run of his plots to explain the basis of his social constructionist notions of discourse, the very language of his novels conveys the distance between the words we use and the objects and ideas these words label, thus mirroring the tenuous nature of our own awkward efforts to make sense of things. Because his novels so neatly explicate much of the discourse theory that serves as the basis for most of the theoretical discussion in the field of rhetoric and composition, I contend that they can be used in the classroom as heuristic devices to allow students a better sense of the way our cultural texts operate. After a discussion of the relevant language, composition, and rhetorical theory, I will show in this essay how I have used DeLillo's *White Noise* (1985) to enable students to think and write about the different discourse communities that define the contemporary culture and the American university.

The social constructionist position claims that all the texts of our society have the value they do not because each individual is able to imbue every possible statement with meaning but because of the interdependence of individuals in society and their coordinated efforts to communicate. A signal sent and not received is an ineffective signal. A requited signal, one that is understood and responded to, is granted the status of language. Thus the words that I use when I speak or write to someone else is the language that I know he or she will understand. This is because I have been speaking and writing for some

136

time and have learned, through trial and error, how I have to say or write something to get people to understand me. When I fail to reach someone, I rearrange my sentences, reorganize my narrative or essay, employ new templates of logic and examples, and find words that work better, as I have learned to gauge the feedback my audience has given me when I succeed or fail to "make sense." However, this does not mean that the discourse I adopt is capable of describing all of the objects that exist in the world or all of the potential thoughts that humans can have; it only means that someone understands the socially constructed language that I am using.

What is important to remember when considering the social constructionist vision of language is that there are as many different ways of describing the world outside of us as there are languages. Anthropological linguist Peter Farb illustrates this with the following description of the different methods that an English speaker and a Navaho speaker would use to report the fact that "a fence is broken" within the established rules of their respective languages:

> First of all, a Navaho speaker must clarify whether the "fence" is animate or inanimate; after all, the "fence" might refer to the slang for a receiver of stolen goods or to a fence lizard. The verb the Navaho speaker selects from several alternatives will indicate that the fence was long, thin, and constructed of many strands, thereby presumably wire (the English-speaking ranger's report failed to mention whether the fence was wood, wire, or chain link). The Navaho language then demands that a speaker report with precision upon the act of breaking; the Indian ranger must choose between two different verbs that tell whether the fence was broken by a human act or by some nonhuman agency such as a windstorm. Finally, the verb must indicate the present status of the fence, whether it is stationary or is, perhaps, being whipped by the wind. The Navaho's report would translate something like this: "A fence (which belongs to a particular category of inanimate objects, constructed of long and thin material composed of many strands) is (moved to a position, after which it is now at rest) broken (by nonhumans, in a certain way)." The Navaho's report takes about as long to utter as the English-speaking ranger's, but it makes numerous distinctions that never occurred to the white ranger to make, simply because the English language does not oblige him to make them.[1]

Whereas the English speaker would be communicating well within the socially constructed rules he has learned as a speaker of English, the Navaho would find his report wanting for more information. When I have offered this passage to my students in the past, they found it to be a cogent and compelling example of how language can govern our thinking. However, they often draw the conclusion that the language that provides the most "detailed" description of an event is the "best" language. (Several students have suggested that they should be taking Navaho composition, not English composition.) I counter with the idea that all of the languages that are presently being used by the many different discourse communities in the world are working just fine, because they have proven to be successful tools that allow people within the confines of each discourse community to understand one another. Languages that do not work in this regard are either modified or abandoned.

What I want my students to draw from our discussion of this passage is an awareness that they will be encountering different discourse communities in popular culture, in their course work, and in the professions they enter, and that they should (1) learn how to use and understand these languages, (2) have an idea about how these languages are generated and adopted, (3) know that these languages change over time, and (4) have an insight into how these languages can construct meaning and channel our thoughts.

In his essay "Foucault and the Freshman Writer," composition theorist Kurt Spellmeyer uses Foucauldian theories to challenge the assumptions of scholars who "invest discourse with a static consistency, a one-sidedness which prevents beginning writers from perceiving the eventful character of language."[2] To advise our students that they will soon discover an abiding voice or discourse style that will allow them to ferret out the absolutes in their respective disciplines is to lead them on. Spellmeyer asks that we have a greater awareness of the discursive formations that contain us so that the "I" in us can speak only when we can "resist and renegotiate the terms of our participation" in discourse,[3] or as Foucault asserts, we must transgress the limits of our presently accepted discourse in a manner that demonstrates that there is something other out there, a potential world of understanding that has not been made apparent to us because we have not yet established an agreed-upon language to explain and organize it for us.

What Spellmeyer wants educators to do with their students is to give them some sense of how the clichés and "commonsense" lexical, syntactical, and logical formations that "their" prose contains and is contained by keeps them from realizing the "I" of their own subjectivity. Of all discourses, academic discourse is singularly seductive, because it affects a style that is so clinically objective and precise that it conceals "those transgressions which are essential to learning as they are to the formations of new knowledge."[4] By examining the rhetorical features of texts and the reader's position relative to them, students might better be able to understand how language makes meaning.

David Bartholomae describes the compositions that students offer us an echo of those texts with which they themselves have come into contact.[5] Bartholomae and Anthony Petrosky want students to immerse themselves in the language of the academy not because they feel it will enable them to describe the world in an unerring and absolute fashion, but so that they can "transform the roles they play" and develop "an enabling language," one that gives students a view of themselves as university writers. To do this, any text in a writing class should be understood as "an occasion for meaning, not meaning in itself, and the possibilities for meaning in any given text remain open until, as a class, we see what we have done and begin to imagine what else might be done."[6] To understand the academy, the student needs to be "conscious" of the "governing shape" of its discourse and her relationship to it.[7] Students should be asked to do more than just learn an absolute set of reasoning skills; they should learn to understand the way language constitutes their sense of self and their relationship to institutions such as the university and all institutions that produce the socially constructed texts of our society. To do so will allow students to join their professors via a shared discourse and also will allow them to become wiser consumers of any intellectual construct that they encounter in their academic, social, or professional lives.

The characters in Don DeLillo's *White Noise* are so overwhelmed by the many discordant texts that surround them, the "white noise" in *White Noise,* that they often find it difficult to discern the value of one kind of information over another. In the first section of the novel, "Waves and Radiation," bits of data percolate through every conceivable source—conversation, radio and television, advertising, the sounds of nature and street traffic, and the discourse of academia—and we see how governors, airline pilots, and disaster-control bureaucrats concoct, eliminate, and then reinvent their "state-created terminology" to elicit the feeling that they are in control. Often the texts come out of the air without any context, and we are struck with the idea that these characters are both overwhelmed by and at the same time oblivious to the chatter of this contemporary American soundscape; phrases such as "Toyota Corolla, Toyota Celica, Toyota Cressida" and "Coke is it, Coke is it, Coke is it" transformed from automobiles and soft-drink slogans into mantras that are invoked in the middle of everyday conversation.

Most students have some trouble finding the thread of this first section, as they are used to the more ordered narrative structures of traditional novels and movies. To demonstrate the value of DeLillo's technique, I like to lead them through an exercise that illustrates how the "Waves and Radiation" section is actually a reasonably accurate portrayal of how the impressionistic elements of our culture shape our thinking. In an out-of-class assignment, students make a note of every kind of information that comes to them outside of the time spent in classes. The most common examples include music from CD players waking them up from their midmorning slumber, fleeting and cursory "conversations" they have with people they have recently met in residence halls or at parties, conversations they overhear or eavesdrop on, advertising slogans such as "Just Do It," the celebration of campus teams and sports icons, and the texts of all sorts on clothing worn by their peers. While most of us like to think that this kind of noise rarely affects the core of our consciousnesses, I ask the class to consider how often their encounters with these texts supplant both the actual "texts" from the campus bookstore or library that we come to the university to think about and the "meaningful" and reflective exchanges we have with friends and family. Then I ask them to think about the effect their encounters with these fleeting texts have on the way we speak and listen, what we consider to be fashionable attire, what we deem as socially acceptable behavior, and what we think is absurd or funny. I also like to compare the elements in the lists the students generated with the "content" of one hour of MTV, a medium composed of texts of limited duration and little connective tissue.

Not only does DeLillo demonstrate the effect that the ambient texts of our culture have on us, he also demonstrates how words themselves take on a life of their own as the world becomes an array of signs in a signifying frenzy, gathering their meaning as they feed on each other's ephemeral pulse. What is lost in this is the ability of words to denote the objects that surround us; instead, words become objects themselves and they acquire a material nature that allows them to both shape and be shaped by other words that come before and after them as we read and hear them in the white noise of the 1990s.

To understand the way discourses have a material effect on the way we conceptualize our world, philosopher Richard Rorty advocates a brand of "critical thinking" that asks us to "edify" ourselves by finding more interesting ways of speaking and listening and tuning in to different cultures or disciplines with "incommensurable" vocabularies. Edification can also "consist in the 'poetic' activity of . . . [our] attempts to reinterpret our familiar surroundings in the unfamiliar terms of our new inventions. . . . to take us out of our old selves by the power of strangeness, to aid us in becoming new beings."[8] *White Noise* is rife with the play of these discursive "new inventions," such as the "mantras" mentioned above, which allow us to see our words and phrases as nothing more than a string of alphabetic characters that when "read" produce a sound that we do not associate with anything. For example, a "bike" becomes just the sound of the word *bike* and the way the four letters *b-i-k-e* look to us, not a two-wheeled form of transportation.

To get the students involved in this "poetic activity," I asked them to produce two eight-word lists, one composed of words that are unusual or relatively exotic, and one of everyday words. For example, "arachnid" and "azure" are extraordinary-sounding words, and "bread" and "blue" are common. In small groups of four students, they assembled the words from their compiled lists into "poems" of eight lines of four words each, with a double space between lines four and five. This formal structure gave the writers a template that made their work look like an ordered text, yet after they put the poems on the board and read them aloud, seeing the individual words outside their customary syntactic and lexical context allowed the class a better opportunity for noticing words as palpable objects separate from the items they designate. At the same time, some of the lines the students wrote actually had weight to them. For example, the line "bovine yellow substrate line" lacks any literal meaning, yet it suggests some "thing" to the students, evidenced by the fact that if I inverted the order of the words to "yellow substrate line bovine," they would explain that the string of words had a different sense to it, but not one that they could necessarily articulate.

My students enjoyed pointing out the way that the characters in *White Noise* are often captured by the academic-sounding logic and ritualistic trappings of their university and cultural environments, and this offered us the opportunity to be more critical of the structures of classical argumentation and the manner in which professors, parents, and the students themselves present their ideas as authority figures. In one scene in the novel, the characters Jack Gladney and Murray Siskind offer a copresentation in which they attempt to demonstrate that Adolf Hitler and Elvis Presley possess nearly identical psychological profiles, a comparison presented in a staged fashion as both professors solemnly parade before their students in academic gowns, trading off their "insights" with one another. As Jack and Murray are making their tenuous and ultimately absurd connections between the dictator and the entertainer—connections built on psychobabble that indelibly links Hitler and Presley, who both had fixations on their mothers—their professorial authority is also enhanced by a ceremonial bearing that would seem to come only from those who have committed years to the reflective and sequestered study of their disciplines. Jack tells readers during this scene that he regularly reads Hitler "deep into the night" as if he were trying to make contact with the truths found only in Scripture.

Before we begin discussing this section of the novel, I ask for two student volunteers to reenact Jack and Murray's parts by reading from *White Noise* before the rest of the class. Then we join together in groups and make our own comparisons between disparate objects or people. For example, the campus administration building and the recreation-center pool are both made of cement; they both have water in them; one has students standing in lines, and the other has students swimming in lanes. Anything can be "logically" equated with anything if we work hard enough at it.

Traditional composition theory rests on the belief that the individual needs to find her own voice by learning the rules found in composition textbooks and immersing herself in the logical constructions found in many composition readers. All too often these arguments are simplistic rehashings of the classical syllogism "Socrates was a man / All men are mortal / Socrates is mortal," and this does little to prepare our students for the array of texts that will come their way. In contrast, contemporary writing theorists have stressed a more dynamic nature between the writer and reader. Rhetorician James Raymond has suggested that we teach our students to more closely examine the assumptions inherent in the words used to construct the literal "logic" of statements based on classical argument. What is most important, according to Raymond, is that students learn to identify the nuances and assumptions, both explicit and implicit, that the presumed reader of the text is expected to share, and to locate the paradigms, if any, that form the basis of the argument. Thus, the ultimate question to ask in analyzing a piece of persuasive writing is not "Are its arguments valid?" as the traditional rhetorics suggest, but rather "What would a reader have to believe in order to find the arguments persuasive?"[9]

To work through Raymond's point, I asked my class to analyze some of the most ubiquitous texts present in their university culture, public-address announcements concerned with substance abuse. I wrote the sentence "Drinking and driving is not a game, because there are never any winners" on the board (a statement aired on the local radio stations that catered to the university market), and asked the class to theorize about the assumptions the writers of this message had about students. Does it imply students have a strong desire to be winners? Why did the writers use the game analogy? Do students have a strong need in our competitive culture not to be identified with "losers"? Playing the devil's advocate, I asked whether the word *never* was in fact an accurate term in this context. While this public-address announcement seemed effective, students were not able to agree even within the confines of their reasonably select discourse community on the many layers of textual play that allowed them to be affected by the message (if they were affected at all). Using the same criteria, we contrasted the "Just Say No" antidrug campaign of the 1980s with the quasi-syllogistic reasoning of the ad that starts with a shot of an egg, followed by a view of a frying pan full of sizzling grease, and ending with the eggs burning in the frying pan accompanied by a hard-boiled announcer instructing listeners, "This is your brain. These are drugs. This is your brain on drugs." Beyond identifying the assumptions writers make about readers, I asked the students to identify just what they thought their position was relative to the speaker/writer of these public-address missives and how these figures tried to establish their authority. To generalize, most of the students were of the opinion that the "Just Say No" message was probably better for students much younger then they, as it sounded more "parental" and because it reduced a complex problem to a simple solution. Students also asserted that they were more likely to be moved to action by the two other messages discussed above, as they "sounded" logical, but were very much in agreement that these statements were not logical at all; instead these messages were cleverly concealed efforts to either shame or command them.

Continuing with the discussion set up by the scene with Jack and Murray in *White Noise,* I ask my students to describe how some of the professors on their campus present themselves in an effort to establish some sense of authority or ethos, and we work through a series of factors in our discussion such as attire, speaking style, the physical distance between the professors and their students in large lecture halls, and whether they choose to use podiums, audio/visual equipment, and/or "revered" texts. As instructors, I think we sometimes forget what it feels like when one first arrives at a university. Undergraduates are confronted with an array of socially constructed words and phrases that signify both the university hierarchy and the kinds of theoretical methodologies that will be granted the status of power. Students are given syllabi by their graduate assistants, lecturers, and professors of all rank who speak of office hours, seminars, blue-book examinations, multiple regression analysis, and socially constructed texts, and they come to know that in some mysterious way their lives are affected by provosts, registrars, deans, ex officio regents, ombudsmen, and emeriti. While those of us who work within the structure of universities have come to understand that our leaders and methods are fallible,

I think our students—much like the students in *White Noise*—too often lack the critical skills needed to examine the way we employ the texts we have taken for granted to establish our authority.

In addition to offering humorous insights into the way texts, classical logic, and the authority ascribed to university scholars affect the way we go about our duties as students and scholars, DeLillo takes aim at the manner in which the university community constructs the institutional areas of study that we will turn our energies toward. Jack Gladney is not only a professor of Hitler studies at College-on-the-Hill, he is the progenitor of the discipline: "I invented Hitler studies in North America in March of 1968. It was a cold bright day with intermittent winds coming out of the east."[10] While university disciplines are not built in a day, DeLillo's parody does offer us a model that illustrates the caprice with which language-using people produce disciplines; these disciplines are not always hard objects that we can physically bump into and bang our knees on, but abstractions born of socially constructed language. Even physical elements in our universe are not really taken in as accepted objects of study until someone finds a way of describing them with a socially acceptable language. For example, the statements that were produced by Newton in his positing the theory of gravity needed Newton's attendant "invention" of the discourse of calculus to explain these "laws" in a palatable way to other scientists of his age.

To demonstrate how this can be understood in the context of the contemporary American university, I offer a brief overview of my field—rhetoric and composition—which has had an irregular presence in the life of the academy. The skills of oratory were an essential element in education from the age of the Greeks, yet in the latter half of the nineteenth century, oratory was shoved aside to assume an ancillary role in English departments that were more focused on the study of literature. Ironically, language skill is now back in "fashion" because in large part scholars in rhetoric and other fields have offered a series of academically seductive arguments to demonstrate how their textual maneuvers have had much to do with the construction of the objects they build their disciplines around. This is not to say that new disciplines such as women's studies, materials science engineering, and remote sensing, which presently enjoy the status of degree programs at the University of Arizona, are not of value, but that the reason they have become objects of study is that their value is cast in a discourse sanctioned by universities. I also like to suggest to my class that there are other areas of potential knowledge in our world that have yet to find our attention because so far we have not attributed a discursive array of signifiers to them.

In DeLillo's novel, Jack Gladney positions Hitler studies within the academy by adopting the jargon found in undergraduate catalogs to articulate the realm of his enterprise and the prerequisite skills of his students:

> They were all Hitler majors, members of the only class I still taught, Advanced Nazism, three hours a week, restricted to qualified seniors, a course of study designed to cultivate a historical perspective, theoretical rigor

and mature insight into the continuing mass appeal of fascist tyranny, with special emphasis on parades, rallies and uniforms, three credits, written reports.[11]

DeLillo parodies this established edifice of study by placing it in the bedrock or "theoretical rigor" of more established academic tradition. By placing "emphasis" on things such as "parades, rallies and uniforms," he delineates the artifacts students and professors will be asked to think about when thinking about "Hitler." With these emphases, other potential objects of the field will be overlooked, as Gladney's Hitler studies provides something other than the horrific traces of Hitler we usually associate with the dictator. In *White Noise*, Hitler becomes the source of an industry in which academies throughout the world take up Hitler studies, give rise to huge networking systems based on individual personalities in the field (as J. A. K. Gladney has become), acquire and produce refereed journals, and hold conferences with "three days of lectures, workshops and panels. Hitler scholars from seventeen states and nine foreign countries."[12] Murray puts this in perspective for Jack as he lauds his achievement: "You've done a wonderful thing here with Hitler. You created it, you nurtured it, you made it your own. Nobody on the faculty of any college or university in this part of the country can do so much as utter the word Hitler without a nod in your direction."[13] No mention is made that a new department has been established that would allow people to understand how our civilization might be better able to identify and counter the "mass appeal of fascist tyranny" in the future. What is important is that Hitler has been turned into employment opportunities for academics and that Jack has become a university superstar. If Hitler were to come back to life and walk into a "HS" convention, he would be of only secondary interest to the participants, perhaps even shouted down as a fake if he were to offer a speech that challenged the institutional notions of what he actually said.

In two English composition sections I taught at the University of Arizona, I asked my students to write their own analyses of any university document, informed by DeLillo's vision of the College-on-the-Hill. To prompt my students' thinking, I gave them a list of questions from James Porter's essay "Intertexuality and the Discourse Community,"[14] general questions such as What are the syntactic characteristics of the text? Does it employ a technical or specialized jargon? What is the tone? What stance do writers/speakers take relative to audiences? What are the beliefs, attitudes, values, and prejudices of the addressed audience? What constitutes "validity," "evidence," "proof" in the forum (e.g., personal experience/observation, testing and measurement, theoretical or statistical analysis)? I told the students that they could use a journal article from the library, a syllabus and set of instructions from another class, a textbook, a campus publication (e.g., *The Daily Wildcat, The University of Arizona Graduate Catalogue*), or any other document that was generated in their university community. My motive was to give the students more critical insights into the way the texts of their university's discourse community influenced them.

One of my students, Michael Clifton-Harter, was intrigued by the scenes in *White Noise* that satirize the "authoritative method" scholars use to portray their work, scenes such as Gladney's description of "Advanced Nazism," given above. Taking DeLillo's lead, Michael examined University of Arizona undergraduate catalogs from as early as 1915 through to the present and noted that there was usually an increase in the amount of words used in course descriptions and that the language employed to describe the substance of the courses grew more complex over time. Contrasting the course descriptions for History 408 (The Renaissance) in the 1980 and the 1993 catalogs, for example, he found that "words such as 'social, economic, cultural,' and 'religious' were replaced with power words such as 'schism, secularization, exploration,' and 'imperialism'." One of the points Michael draws from his study is that it is the "intellectuals who classify, group, and enlist new ideas on the subject that increase the volume of material one must learn about the subject," and he further points out that "the subject matter doesn't change, only the interpretations and ideas about it do."

After making a connection between the "merchandising possibilities that [Jack] and the chancellor forsee" with Hitler studies, another student in my class, Kirsten Schlueter, analyzed *The University of Arizona's Viewbook*, a brochure-styled description of campus life sent out to potential first-year students in the state. Below she offers her insights into the way universities market themselves as vehicles of prosperity and fulfillment:

> Promises of success are common throughout the viewbook. In fact, a form of the word "success" can be found in almost every spread. Words such as "accomplishment" and "development" that suggest achievement are also prevalent. Individual colleges seem to compete to present themselves as the best preparation for a successfulfuture. The College of Agriculture boasts that "Of approximately 100 million jobs in America, one-fourth relate to programs taught [here]," and the College of Arts and Sciences states that "graduates of the department learn to market themselves." Even the college within the University promises success in order to convince. Promoting the Humanities sector, Dean Annette Kolodny writes that "cross-cultural literacy represents our best chance of peacefully crossing new frontiers between peoples and nations on an increasingly shrinking planet." Implied is the notion that a major in the Humanities prepares a student for success in future job markets.

What I like about this observation is the way Kirsten moves beyond commentary on content and discusses the rhetoric of "success"; here she demonstrates an awareness of the public relations discourse that all major universities and colleges use to compete for qualified students. Equally satisfying is Kirsten's implicit awareness of a dean's use of jargon in the celebration of her interests.

By having our students examine the way their own "consciousnesses" are affected by the many texts that surround them, I think we can provide students with some theoretical insights into the way discourse acts on all of us, thus enabling them to become wiser interpreters of their university and popular cultures. I have found that a careful reading of *White Noise* offers a clear and engaging presentation of these insights because the novel is rife with characters whose actions and "thoughts" are a function of the whirling complex of texts that produce their socially constructed realities. As Jack Gladney tells readers, "Remarks existed in a state of permanent flotation. No one thing was either more or less plausible than any other thing. As people jolted out of reality, we were released from the need to distinguish."[15]

Notes

1. Peter Farb, *Word Play* (New York: Knopf, 1974): 195–196.

2. Kurt Spellmeyer, "Foucault and the Freshman Writer: Considering the Self in Discourse," *College English* 51 (November 1989): 717.

3. Ibid., 718.

4. Ibid.

5. David Bartholomae, "Inventing the University," in *When a Writer Can't Write*, ed. Mike Rose (New York: Guilford Press, 1985), 143.

6. David Bartholomae and Anthony R. Petrosky, *Facts, Artifacts, and Counterfacts: Theory and Method for a Reading and Writing Course* (Portsmouth, N.H.: Boynton/ Cook, 1986), 285.

7. Ibid., 285.

8. Richard Rorty, *Philosophy and the Mirror of Nature* (Princeton, N.J.: Princeton University Press, 1979), 360.

9. James Raymond, "Enthymemes, Examples, and Rhetorical Method," in *Essays on Classical Rhetoric and Modern Discourse*, ed. Robert J. Connors, Lisa S. Ede, and Andrea Lunsford (Carbondale, Ill.: Southern Illinois University Press, 1984), 150.

10. Don DeLillo, *White Noise* (New York: Viking, 1985), 4.

11. Ibid., 25.

12. Ibid., 33.

13. Ibid., 11.

14. James Porter, "Intertextuality and the Discourse Community," *Rhetoric Review* 5 (Fall 1986): 34–46.

15. DeLillo, 129.

14

Everyday Exigencies
Constructing Student Identity[1]
Beyond the College Application
and Composition Assignment

Laura Gray-Rosendale

Like many composition teachers, I've found that the concept of rhetoric frequently seems too remote from students' everyday lives to appear immediately useful to them. As critical contemporary scholarship in composition and cultural studies has begun to evidence, students' application of rhetorical reading strategies to cultural representations such as television, advertisements, and films can be a critical method for engaging students' interest and making rhetorical reading strategies more practical.* This scholarship has revealed the extent to which these cultural representations advance certain gender identities[2], racial identities, and class identities to students for their ready consumption. Becoming resistant readers of such texts and the "economic, social, and political conditions within which the signifying practices of culture take place"[3] entails apprehending how these constructions are maintained and reproduced as well as discovering ways in which students themselves may combat them effectively.

However, this important research has centered less upon the fact that, equally importantly, these rhetorical reading practices can aid students in making sense of the more seemingly mundane events of their everyday lives, which also significantly impact how their identities are being constructed for them, events that are perhaps more insidious precisely because they are apt to be ignored. In my classes I couple the application of rhetorical reading strategies to cultural events with the application of such strategies to students' "everyday" activities within both speech and writing: quarrels with parents over what one should do over spring vacation, arguments with roommates

147

over controversial issues, or occasional editorial submissions to campus news-papers. What I provide here are some examples of how my students and I have utilized rhetorical reading strategies within our classroom in an effort to reveal yet another way in which students' identities and language choices are con-stantly being prescribed for them. I examine how we have utilized such tech-niques to shed light on two events in which all of our students have engaged, one clearly elucidated by the approaches offered by rhetorical reading: the college application, and the composition assignment. By setting forward such examples I hope to also probe the complexity of students' own identity con-structions and transgressive responses to rhetorical constraints.

The College Application as a Cultural and Rhetorical Situation

Have you ever been convicted of a felony?

Have you ever been suspended or expelled from school?

Is English your first language?

Do you wish to identify yourself as having a diagnosed learning disability?

These somewhat invasive questions, which make up the bulk of those now appearing on college admissions applications across the United States, do not seem to present our first-year composition students with practical "rhetorical situations." These are occasions which, as Lloyd Bitzer claims, "operate as mode[s] of altering reality, not by the direct application of energy to objects, but by the creation of discourse which changes reality through the mediation of thought and action."[4] Instead, in many ways these questions strategically control the kinds of responses open to student applicants. Unless a student applicant is willing to write in an illegible, microscopic script or to go outside the very small spaces provided for his or her responses, he or she is forced to answer yes or no to questions that might otherwise require a great deal more explanation.

In my classes, students bring examples of various college and sometimes graduate applications to class, and we examine them as a group. First we turn to questions like those mentioned above. As my students have determined, this essentially yes/no format sets the tone of the application process early on, per-haps unintentionally leading the student to assume that the rhetorical con-straints set up by the later request for a "personal statement" are similarly prescribed. Immediately, students' identities are being determined for them, classified according to their criminality, expulsions, language abilities, and learning disabilities, for the institutional purpose of categorizing them and quickly making decisions about their college "acceptability."

Perhaps aware of the impact of such questions, we have noticed that the writers of this administrative document soften the blow a bit, also employing motivating prompts. The personal statement section in the Syracuse University admissions application, for example, asserts that students might add "pertinent biographical information" or "other facts that may not be covered in the rest of the application."[5] These prompts indicate to the student that despite the ways in which the earlier questions sought to limit his or her answers, the application may also, perhaps in spite of its own indications to the contrary, indeed still provide significant ways to reframe exigencies, constraints, and audiences.

Certainly the personal statement's set of concerns is wider than that of the other sections of the application. Yet, as my students have asserted, the personal statement too has the markings of a rhetorical situation with very prescribed limitations for response. These limits—even though they are accompanied by "open-ended" prompts—may still unwittingly lead students to answer with the same terse responses required by the earlier questions. The personal statement clearly proffers certain meanings and responses that seek to control and delimit the kind of student identities the students reveal to the Admissions Committee. However, as my students have elaborated, students also have the opportunity, if they are cognizant of the rhetorical constraints, to exercise a critical "power of response" as perceivers and interpreters of this situation.[6] Just as much as their identities and responses are delimited by such rhetorical constraints, students can and already do utilize discourse to modify the nature of such constraints and the oppressive social formations which can render them possible. Rather, they have choices about which events in their lives they decide to communicate, how they choose to frame them, and what they choose to leave unsaid, and they can create certain kinds of meaning out of the information they offer the Admissions Committee. In other words, students maintain the power of rhetors: the power to construct interpretations and to proffer various levels of significance. Within certain limitations, the students can be rhetors who determine how they want to characterize the situation and, therefore, the manner, mode, and shape of their various responses to it. In this way it can become clearer to students that their identities are not only prescribed for them but they also have the capability of constructing them themselves.

Constructing Student Identity: The "Personal Statement"

This is your opportunity to tell the Admissions Committee more about yourself. You may wish to comment on pertinent biographical information, academic/extracurricular experiences, or other facts that may not be covered in the rest of the application but that you feel are important for the Admissions Committee to be aware of before they review your application. Use this form (front and back) or a separate sheet(s) of paper.[7]

While the personal statement is billed as an "opportunity" for the student to "tell the Admissions Committee more about yourself," instructions regarding the statement, my students have recommended astutely, simultaneously intimate two contradictory things to the student applicant: (1) construct a "self" appropriate to the academic community—there is a need to fabricate a fleshed-out self, a self who is missing from the answers to earlier questions such as those dealing with felony conviction and suspension from school (the implication here is that failure to construct this self may mean that a decision about one's acceptance to the institution cannot be made), and (2) construct a self in opposition to the academic community—there is a need for the student to explain, in a relatively open forum, who this self is in contexts other than academic.

Given this awkward tension within the language of the document, the student is likely to read the words within the next sentence, "You may wish," with some understandable trepidation. Who, after all, should this "you" be? As my students have commented in class, the tentative nature of "may wish" is likely to also lead the student to wonder whether it is mandatory to comment on "biographical information, academic/extracurricular experiences, or other facts," or whether he or she has free reign to cover those things that the other application questions could not describe, as he or she wishes. Whichever option the student applicant chooses, if the student assents to the constraints of the rhetorical situation it poses, the student is effectively limited by the binary opposition proffered: the student is asked to conceive of the academic and the extracurricular only in a bifurcated relationship to each other.

This rhetorical situation, then, as my students have asserted through close readings of college applications in our class, presents itself clearly as having two exigencies that are contradictory: (1) the student must overcome the lack of information that the Admissions Committee already has with which to make a decision (or must struggle against the fact that the previous questions on the application did not invite rhetorical discourse), and (2) the student must enthusiastically write about other more personal aspects of his or her life which are of interest to him or her. The first exigency entails that the student make up for the flaws within the application document itself (perhaps going back to some of the earlier questions posed and elucidating answers), while the second implies that the student write what he or she wants to, as he or she wishes. As my students have indicated, the student applicant's responses are constrained by a number of disparate things, including the need to remain within the space and word limitations, the necessity of constructing several conflicting "selves," and the requirement of staying within the rubric of the academic/nonacademic relation delimited by the document. My students contend that the conception of audience that the occasion propounds is similarly conflicted: the audience of the Admissions Committee is both an interested group who wants to be "told" about who the student is (and wants to respect student "wishes"), and yet a group of rather distanced observers whose major role is to "review one's application," or to judge, assess, and evaluate the student's qualifications.

When we as a class looked closely at the possibilities delineated by this document, it became evident that if the student merely responds to these tensions in the ways they are constructed by the question itself, it is more than likely that he or she will produce a fairly confusing document that will not fulfill its rhetorical purpose (to gain acceptance into the college). Instead, such a document is likely to evidence the following structural problems: (1) a nebulous sense of what is at stake within writing the piece, (2) a quandary over which constraints to take seriously and which ones to ignore, and (3) a confusion over who is really reading the personal statement. The result of this conflictual situation, according to my students, is this: if he or she answers the question as posed, he or she is likely to also fail to answer the question in a manner deemed appropriate by the Admissions Committee itself.

Though we have engaged in such critical analyses in my classes, we have also attempted to take an important next step. It is not enough to criticize the ways in which such documents construct debilitating notions of student identity. As much as identity and subjectivity are constituted by larger systemic forces, students also can exercise crucial roles in counteracting as well as constituting such forces themselves.[8] Given the rhetorical nature of language, the student can assert a level of agency that the document itself seems to render impossible. As my students have shown me through their own rhetorically sophisticated responses to these applications, they do have some important control over the nature of their varied identity constructions within the composition of this document. Not only are the students merely responding in preformulated ways but actually constructing their own temporary conceptions of identity through the document.

My students have proposed some interesting new potentialities: What if the student does not merely respond to this rhetorical situation as it is constructed by the question? What if he or she does not cooperate with the rather fixed constraints of the question, but instead uses her or his "power of response" to interpret the question's meaning, to make distinct choices between possibilities, and to manipulate the cultural and rhetorical situation in her or his own inventive ways? In order for this to be possible, the student must first recognize the myriad tensions at work within the rhetorical situation itself, and then carefully think through how to utilize her or his "power of response" as a rhetor in the most effective and convincing ways possible.

Instead of simply cooperating with the very narrow limitations that the question poses, thinking rhetorically about their own power of response, my students have contended, would encourage them to reconsider the constraints of the personal statement, questioning the very nature of the questions delimited: To which exigency do I want to respond (or do I want to provide my own exigency, one not offered by the questions offered?)? Who do I want to be to this Admissions Committee at this point in my application? What can I say or not say that will help me to appear to be that person? What can I use as "biographical information"? Which bits of biographical information connect to points I've made earlier in the document? Which ones do I need to highlight here because they haven't been mentioned elsewhere? In what activities do I engage that transcend the boundaries provided by bifurcating the academic and the extracurricular, as well as call this opposition into question?

But my own students have noted that there is yet another step that must be taken. The student must also consider how her or his response, which may no longer cooperate with the rhetorical constraints of the question, will be read by the committee. She or he must translate her or his answers into a discourse that the Admissions Committee will accept. In other words, she or he must also ask herself or himself: How can I help the Admissions Committee to understand what I want them to perceive about me in the ways I want them to? Which constraints do I not have the power to manipulate (the length of the essay, the fact that it is required)? How might it be most beneficial for me to present what the Admissions Committee needs to be "aware of as they review" my application? Lastly, what construction of the Admissions Committee's identity is most interesting and persuasive to respond to here?

Such critical inquiry fostered by a study of rhetoric, my students and I have discovered, then, centers on questioning the questions and examining ways to deal creatively with rhetorical constraints, leading students to become more adept, active interpreters of their rhetorical situations. Rather than being merely confronted with a document that demands that they "fit the bill," students may instead come to comprehend that they have an empowering decision to make. To which aspects of this rhetorical situation do they most want to respond and how?

Challenging the Limits of Student Identity: Lea's "Personal Statement"

I have used this exercise of reading applications rhetorically at various stages within my courses in rhetoric and with many of my students at various academic levels. What follows is one such student response to a rhetorical reading of the application process which is particularly telling about the importance and difficulty of how students construct their own identities in response to school applications. Lea is a student with whom I worked four years ago in Syracuse University's Summer Institute "basic writing" program, and whom I have kept in touch with for a while. Now a counselor for Summer Institute, Lea recently approached me for help with her personal statement in her application for a graduate degree in psychology.

Like other students who come through the Summer Institute program and are funded by New York state programs, Lea has had to cope with a great deal of adversity on her way toward getting an education. Lea's interest in psychology came initially from a genuine need to make sense of a difficult and abusive childhood in foster care. This initial probing led her to take part in a theatre group concerned with sexual abuse issues on campus, and to become a peer counselor.

Initially, Lea was understandably rather conflicted over the assignment of writing a personal statement. Though the personal statement asked her to identify why she was interested in pursuing a master's degree in psychology, to more fully elucidate this she would have to be more "personal" than she thought the committee's prompt implied. Despite the fact that Lea had much to relay, she was trapped between the knowledge that the personal statement ought to, as she put it, "sell herself," and her own desire to reveal a more complex version of "who I am," which fell outside the conventions offered her within the prompts utilized by the personal statement.

Though more specific than the personal statement assignment for undergraduate application which we have examined, the one for graduate application at Syracuse University reads as follows:

> Using the space below, provide a statement of your general academic plans. Describe in about 500 words your main academic interests, why you wish to study for the degree you've chosen, why you wish to study at Syracuse University, how you expect to finance your studies, and your plans for the future after you finish your degree.[9]

Requesting students consider their future goals beyond a degree that they have not even started is yet another rhetorical challenge. It may indeed be almost impossible for these students to consider such educational opportunities without additional support. Asking for the applicants to address academic concerns alongside financial ones may be difficult for many students, particularly those who, like Lea, do not have any outside resources from which to draw.

Though by no means a "final response" to this task, the temporary student identity that Lea creates in the following draft reveals her willingness to work within the rhetorical constraints offered by the assignment, while still resisting them enough to assert the various shifting "selves" she wants and needs to advance. Toward this effort, Lea's introduction is necessarily fairly conventional:

> Psychology has always been one of my primary interests. I have always been intrigued by the inner-workings of the mind. While an undergraduate in psychology, I have been able to study this in fairly general terms. I look forward to taking the next step by applying what I have learned in more practical and thorough ways in graduate school.

However, what Lea does next is to set forward a construction of her student identity which, though not incompatible with the one the question itself affords her, complicates and augments that identity a great deal. Here Lea employs her knowledge of the rhetorical situation to her advantage. For instance, in support of her stated intent to "get my Ph.D. in the field of child and adolescent psychology," Lea explains further that her own troubling family history is what drives her: "as a teenager, I saw how the system worked first-hand. I was placed in group homes after family problems. I don't like the way the system works." For this reason, Lea intimates that she sees herself pursuing the following career goals: "I would probably start out in the public sector working at a clinic. Eventually, I would like to open up my own set of group homes for kids in crisis which would be separate from those run by the government." By making the somewhat risky move to legitimize her candidacy with personal experience and a desire to challenge existing social programs, Lea constructs her student identity not as one who is distantly interested in the intellectual issues presented by the field of psychology but as one who is already very personally involved with them.

Lea's next step renders this new student identity abundantly clear as she exposes her choice at a very young age to become an "independent student because of family problems" and her need to "carry a full load of classes" as well as work more than "twenty hours a week" to support herself financially through school. Competent and driven despite serious obstacles that would have derailed many in her position, Lea's choice to delve into her personal history within her document effectively breaks down the binary relationship between the personal/academic. Rather than express a passing interest in the scholarship of the field, Lea explains that she is a good candidate for a degree in psychology precisely because of her constant volunteer work, her work with Habitat for Humanity preparing houses for construction, her mentorship of countless foster children, her background in tutoring, and her work with Every Five Minutes, the campus group that educates the community about rape issues.

Lea concludes by fulfilling the final terms of the personal statement, by elucidating her difficult financial situation and her avid willingness to "take out loans and work my way through," if necessary. But importantly, Lea closes the piece with the new construction of student identity she has been building through the various identity constructions she has already taken up within her text. Her desire to be accepted into a master's program in psychology is multifaceted, and it is not a fly-by-night scheme: "getting a Ph.D. is a goal which I set for myself in high school." And, as she describes it, Lea has kept her eyes focused on this goal in spite of very difficult circumstances, including being consistently dissuaded from pursuing such a degree by friends and family. Having a personal awareness of where the troubled children she hopes to someday counsel have been, Lea indicates that implicitly that she will be a stronger counselor and advocate for them and their needs precisely because of her own experiences. As she concludes, "A lot of people told me I would never get anywhere, and I need to prove them wrong."

Clearly Lea's academic and personal profiles do not fit the traditional constructions of student identity expected by the committee. Sensing this, Lea makes an important and resistant rhetorical decision: Lea answers the questions the committee requires while challenging the very tenets of the questions themselves through the nature of her own response. Moreover, she advances information to the committee which their questions do not address but which might still encourage her admittance. This forces the committee to consider her as a person who is already very much engaged in thinking through psychological issues, a person with well-cultivated leadership abilities, and a person who has a great deal of experience caring for others, skills that are critical for anyone working with patients, particularly the patients with which Lea wants to work.

Since Lea's interpretation of her rhetorical situation is rather innovative, the committee is forced to act differently from the way it might have otherwise acted. No longer can it merely remain a distant audience, a strict evaluator of academic qualifications. It must instead also perceive Lea as a complicated, personally invested individual, one whose own experiences will make her a stronger candidate for becoming the kind of counselor she hopes one day to become. As a result, Lea is able to utilize a fairly traditional, institutionalized assignment as a way to volunteer a rather bold political statement about how she perceives her intellectual as well as critical intervention in the field of psychology and in society at large. Using her knowledge of the rhetorical situation at hand, Lea is thus able to make this assignment more subtly and more persuasively.

Teaching to the Everyday Exigencies: Foregrounding Students' Power of Response

Attention to how students can challenge and resist the many identities constructed for them as well as how they can exercise their power of response should increasingly become a greater part of the process of writing education. Not only should issues of race, class, and gender—which are debilitating to students—be pushed against, but also the static conceptions of even those identities that our scholarship makes available to our students. In addition to students' critical awareness of the ways in which they can use their knowledge of rhetoric strategically, teachers should continue to direct students' attention to the rhetorical situation set up by any writing assignment they are given.

Any writing assignment, like the personal statement we have examined here, necessarily sets up rhetorical constraints also. Take, for example, a final paper assignment I have used in a sophomore- and junior-level class in Composition and Cultural Studies, "Rhetorical Analysis: Critical Perspectives on Advertisement, Television, Print, and Film," in which students read Mark Crispin Miller's *Boxed In: The Culture of Television,* Roland Barthes's *Mythologies*, and Sonia Maasik and Jack Solomon's edited *Signs of Life in the USA: Readings on Popular Culture for Writers* [*], offering critical analyses of these writers' arguments:

> I would like you to draw upon some of the work that you did earlier this semester, and to produce a piece of cultural criticism using the rhetorical methods and styles of either Roland Barthes or Mark Crispin Miller. Broadly

speaking, this means that you should choose a cultural text and perform the type of reading that Barthes or Miller might. Ask yourself the following: What types of texts do Miller and Barthes choose to read? What features do these texts share? What analytical methods do these thinkers use to make their observations, and what kinds of observations do they make? What kinds of conclusions do they make based on these observations? All papers should be word-processed, double-spaced, with one-inch margins.

Clearly this assignment, which asks students to make an argument within the genre of cultural criticism, prescribes certain limitations within which the student must work in order to advance a "successful" response to it (i.e., the model texts, the generic conventions of "cultural criticism" required by the assignment, the types of observations that can be made, and the format of the text). The students' identity is likewise fairly prescribed. The student must act as a cultural critic, utilizing certain analytical methods and offering certain kinds of observations.

After calling attention to the fact that I had constructed such constraints, however, I allowed my students to assert the various ways in which one could respond strategically to this assignment. Within such limitations, they determined, the student must ask, What are my possibilities for a creative, critical response to this assignment? Or, How can I devise an identity or ethos for myself within this assignment which, while it fulfills the assignment, is also commensurate with how I want to be perceived?

Taking the teacher's cue further than I myself had imagined, one sophomore African American student, Preston, provided a very different student identity from that which the assignment would seem to afford him on the surface, yet still in keeping with its guidelines. Sensing that the cultural critic's work discussed within this assignment was itself indicative of cultural, academic norms that were open to criticism, Preston's response paper, "More Ideology, Less Critic" does not choose the conventional cultural text for analysis (i.e., a television show, film, or advertisement). Instead, he takes texts within the genre of cultural criticism themselves to be cultural texts worthy of careful, critical, cultural analysis.

As a result, Preston advances a decisive metacritical reading, a cultural criticism of the generic features of two chapters which purport to be part of that genre, Miller's "Getting Dirty," an analysis of gender in a Shield deodorant soap commercial, and Barthes's "World of Wrestling," a cultural analysis of the wrestling ritual. This strategy enables Preston to claim that while cultural critics argue against many larger social forces, the very topics they choose and the ways in which they put forward their arguments sometimes serve to imitate, even sometimes to perpetuate, such forces. This keen rhetorical strategy enables Preston to assume the identity not of one who merely imitates the models of cultural criticism but of a peer, a fellow cultural critic capable of criticizing the critics and the generic traps of cultural criticism altogether. For instance, Preston remarks astutely that "Barthes' essay rarely uses personal pronouns and distances the reader. In fact, Barthes writes about the attitudes of the 'public' as if his readers were not themselves members of society."

This rhetorical choice on Preston's part also alters his audience's positionality. Now his audience must perceive him as a colleague, part of an ongoing conversation, rather than as one who can be judged readily as an outsider. Preston's aim, as he articulates it within the paper, is to "compare Miller's and Barthes' ideologies and show how they shape the texts they write." In an effort to expose these writers' implicit "ideologies," Preston plans to "point out specific examples where the texts identify Miller's modern outlook on cultural happenings and Barthes' historical view of today's cultural rituals." His paper, an inventive rearticulation and revisioning of the teacher's assignment, accomplishes just that. Through using his power of response in answer to this assignment, Preston reframes the very questions the assignment poses, the student identity the assignment asks him to adopt, and the conventions of cultural criticism to which he was asked to adhere.

In order to foster this kind of rhetorical inventiveness whenever possible, my students and I assert that composition teachers interested in bringing cultural criticism into the classroom take some time to provide rhetorical readings of their own "teacherly" texts, revealing (1) what the rhetorical constraints of the assignment are, (2) what issues the assignment's constraints don't apparently address that students might want to bring to bear upon the assignment, and (3) what methods that students might be able to use in order to bring those aspects to bear upon the assignment in ways that would cooperate with the assignment's terms. In such discussions I have often found that students point to constraints we, their teachers, never intended to impose on them. As a result, we can more effectively address how teachers can become better writers of assignments; consequently, we can become better constructors of rhetorical situations ourselves, and students can productively deliver responses to their everday rhetorical situations and their assignments which resist student identity constructions they might want to contest.

To encourage students to fully acknowledge their power of response, identity construction, and audience development in the face of any assignment given is to encourage them to become skillful rhetorical thinkers in ways that enable students not just to address a preconceived audience from the position of a "student." By reconstituting the limited identities often prescribed for them by an assignment or other rhetorical situation, they can similarly reconstruct their audience's identity in new and inventive ways. The practical application of cultural studies in composition to students' own everyday rhetorical situations will inevitably help them to think about their positions more politically, more strategically, and with a greater sense of their own rhetorical agency. This can facilitate students' ability to challenge certain kinds of institutionally prescribed notions of student identity, and thereby the oppressive myths about students to which institutions often ascribe. Such thinking has relevance not only to the writing classroom, but also to students' lives outside the academy, enabling them to be more careful and thoughtful consumers of products, more critical readers of situations they encounter, and more critical constructors of the rhetorical situations they may themselves set up for other people in their home lives, jobs, and in their writing. In some real sense, then, the power of response offered to students by the rhetorical situation is the power to offer politically transgressive readings of such situations themselves, ones which our political frameworks may not as easily afford them.

Notes

1. Thanks to Ken Lindblom and Steven Rosendale for their many insights and thoughts on this project. Thanks also to Lea Ockert and Preston Ratliff for allowing me to cite their work.

*   Footnote: See, for example, Gary A. Olsen and Sidney I. Dobrin, eds. *Composition Theory for the Postmodern Classroom* (Albany, NY: SUNY Press, 1994), and Lad Tobin and Thomas Newkirk, eds. *Taking Stock: The Writing Process Movement in the '90s* (Portsmouth, N.H.:Boynton/Cook, 1994).

2. My use of the term *identities* here takes its cue from Kenneth Burke's notion of identification. According to Burke, one's identification with something always necessarily requires partisanship. In cultural texts, our students are being called upon to take up certain partisanships over and against others. Burke calls this part of the process of identification "consubstantiality" or the maintenance of "common sensations, concepts, images, ideas, attitudes" (see Kenneth Burke, *A Rhetoric of Motives*, [Berkeley: University of California Press, 1969], 21). Students are called upon to be joint participants who possess similar principles or qualities. Importantly, though, Burke also points to "division" and "difference" as part of identification. Through examining their differences from the identifications cultural texts are asking them to adopt, students can and do resist certain identifications in favor of others and come to realize that identification is itself never complete but rather contains difference within it.

3. James Berlin and Michael Vivion, *Cultural Studies in the English Classroom*, (Portsmouth, N.H.: Boynton/Cook, 1992), xii.

4. Lloyd Bitzer, "The Rhetorical Situation," *Philosophy and Rhetoric*, 1 (1968): 4.

5. Syracuse University, Undergraduate Application for Admission and Financial Aid Guide For Use 1995–96. June 1995.

6. Richard Vatz's "The Myth of Rhetorical Situation" (*Philosophy and Rhetoric* 6 [1972]: 154–61) correctly criticizes Bitzer's landmark work on rhetorical situation. Though Bitzer offers a critical focus on the rhetorical situation, this leads him to neglect the critical nature of the rhetor's own perceptions or interpretations of rhetorical situations in dictating the kind of responses that might be considered appropriate. As Vatz puts it, "no situation can have a nature independent of the rhetoric with which he [the rhetor] chooses to characterize it" (p. 154). These interpretations evidenced through language are also necessarily shaped by other institutional and cultural forces.

7. Syracuse University, Undergraduate Application.

8. Composition research's recent reliance on social theories drawn from literary studies alone has obscured this possibility. Poststructuralism, feminist theory, and Marxist theory, while very useful in exposing the systemic forces that shape our students' identities and their writings, are perhaps too global to account for the moment-to-moment interactions that students have with each other or with their own texts. Because of such global analyses, students' expression of agency and actual actions are often overlooked. Importantly, as much recent work in interdisciplinary discourse anlaysis has asserted, people also constitute their social relationships to each other and larger social functions through their interactions themselves. We are not, then, just at the whims of social forces but, through our own language choices, construct our relationships to such social forces as well as help to constitute the forces. See, for instance, Richard Buttny's *Social Accountability in Communication* (London: Sage Publications, 1993), George Psathas and Paul Have, eds., *Studies in Ethnomethodology and Conversation Analysis* (Lanham, Md.: University Press of America, 1995), and Deirdre Boden and Don H. Zimmerman, eds., *Talk and Social Structure Studies in Ethnomethodology and Conversation Analysis* (Berkeley: University of California Press, 1991), Donal Carbaugh, *Situating Selves: The Communication of Social Identities in American Scenes* (Albany, NY: SUNY UP, 1996), Jonathan Potter, *Representing Reality: Discourse, Rhetoric, and Social Construction* (London: Sage Publications, 1996), and Howard Nathaniel Bonghey, *Ordinary Social Occasions, Sandcastles, and Structural Reproduction: A Sociology of Everybody's Social Life* (Middletown, NJ: The Caslon Company, 1995). Deborah Brandt's composition research in *Literacy as Involvement: The Acts of Writers, Readers, and Texts* (Carbondale, Ill.: Southern Illinois Press, 1990) volunteers a very useful intervention in this tendency within contemporary composition research.

9. Syracuse University, Application for Graduate Study Scholarship and Research 1995–96.

10. Mark Crispin Miller. *Boxed In: The Culture of TV* (Evanston: Northwestern University Press, 1988), Roland Barthes, *Mythologies* trans. Annette Lavers (New York: Hill and Wang, 1983), and Sonia Maasik and Jack Solomon eds. *Signs of Life in the USA: Readings on Poluar Culture for Writers* (Boston: Bedford Books of St. Martin's Press, 1994).

Contributors

J. D. Applen received a bachelor of science in biology from San Diego State University, and a master of arts in creative writing and a Ph.D. in English from the University of Arizona. His professional interests include writing-across-the-curriculum and the application of poststructuralist theory to the teaching of composition. Applen has taught an array of writing courses, from basic writing to technical writing. He has given papers at several conferences nationwide and is the co-editor of "A Student's Guide to Composition" at the University of Arizona. Applen is a manuscript evaluator for St. Martin's Press and a reader for the AP and GMAT examinations offered by the Educational Testing Service. He lectured at the University of California at Santa Barbara, where he was teaching several linked courses with the Departments of Engineering and Biology. Presently, Applen is an assistant professor in the English Department at the University of Central Florida in Orlando.

Lynn Burley is a fourth-year Ph.D. student at Purdue University majoring in linguistics with a minor in composition and rhetoric. Her dissertation research is in the grammatical relations of Hocak (Winnebago), a Native American language.

Gail Corning is a doctoral candidate in the Department of English, University of Waterloo, in Waterloo, Ontario, Canada. Having completed all other program requirements, she is now writing her dissertation on "The Rhetoric of Narrative and Memory: Re-membering History and Self in Toni Morrison's *Beloved*." She has presented papers at several conferences and is published in *PRE/TEXT*.

Her department has currently nominated her for the Warren Ober Award for Outstanding Independent Teaching by a graduate student in the Faculty of the Arts.

Kathryn R. Fitzgerald is the coordinator of Writing 112 and a lecturer in the University Writing Program at the University of Utah. She received her doctorate from Utah in June 1994. She is the co-editor of two books, *Contact Zones: Ways of Writing, Being and Knowing in the University* (with H. E. Bruce, S. L. Schneider, and A. M. Vogt) and *The Student Writer* (with Jamie McBeth Smith) and the author of several articles. Kathryn Fitzgerald has also presented at several CCCC conferences and is a regional editorial advisor for Prentice-Hall, Inc. She is also a certified ESL instructor and has designed and implemented ESL courses for business.

Shelli B. Fowler is an assistant professor with a joint appointment in the Departments of Comparative American Cultures and English at Washington State University. Her teaching and scholarship are focused in the areas of African American literature and critical pedagogy. She is currently at work on a co-edited composition anthology for Houghton Mifflin, *Site Visits: Itineraries for Writers.*

Ann Garnsey completed her doctorate in English at Washington State University in May 1997. Her doctoral research focused on issues of race, particularly whiteness, in contemporary American literary and other cultural texts. As a teacher of writing and literature, Garnsey attempts to maintain bridges between her scholarly interests in theories of race and gender and the pedagogies she practices in the classroom. She is an Instructional Designer for the Extended Degree Program at WSU where she assists faculty in reconceiving their courses for a distance learning environment.

W. F. Garrett-Petts is an instructor in the English department of the University College of the Cariboo, a two-year program in Kamloops, British Columbia. He received his doctorate in 1992 from the University of Alberta. Garrett-Petts has taught at UCC, the University of Alberta, the University of Victoria, and the University of British Columbia. He is the author of several articles, and co-editor of two books *Integrating Visual and Verbal Literacies* (with Donald Lawrence) and *Critical Issues in Canadian Literature: A Dialogue* (with Henry Hubert). Garrett-Petts is also preparing the text *Contesting Literacies: Reading Visual and Verbal Narratives.* He has presented papers on rhetorical theory, postmodernism, and writing at conferences in the United States and Canada, and is a reviewer for *Mosaic, An Interdisciplinary Literature Journal* (Canada), *The American Review of Canadian Studies*, and a proposal reviewer for CCCC.

Laura Gray-Rosendale is an assistant professor at Northern Arizona University, where she teaches graduate and undergraduate courses in composition and rhetoric. Her essay "Survivor Discourse: Transgression or Recuperation" co-authored with Linda Alcoff, appears in *Getting A Life*, from University of Minnesota Press. She has also written various articles in composition and rhetoric.

Rich Lane is an assistant professor of English at the University of Utah. He specializes in composition and rhetoric and teacher education. The proud father of a newborn son, Maxfield, Rich teaches courses in first-year composition each semester, as well as graduate and undergraduate courses in advanced writing, rhetoric, and secondary teaching preparation. He received his Ph.D. from Miami University of Ohio and was part of a five-member team that constructed the curriculum for Miami's first-year composition program. Rich has given workshops and presentations at CCCC conferences since 1992. He also has presented at conferences concerning twentieth-century women's writing. Before going on for his Ph.D., Lane spent eight years teaching high school in Washington, D.C.

Jeffrey Maxson recently finished his dissertation "Multimedia and Multivocality: Some Challenges to Academic Print Literacy" in the Department of Education at the University of California, Berkeley. He is an assistant professor in the College Writing department in the College of Communication at Rowan University.

Diane Penrod is an assistant professor in the College of Communication at Rowan University, where she teaches courses in the College Writing department and the Communications Studies department. Diane received her doctorate from Syracuse University's English department in August 1994. Her research areas include media literacy and the intersection of cultural studies and composition. She is at work researching two books, an examination of the inroads women have made writing in a technological culture and a cultural studies reader for composition/media studies entitled *Official Narratives/Counternarratives: Stories from the Daily Presses.* Diane is also a member of the executive board of the *New Jersey Journal of Communication* and is editing an upcoming special issue on political rhetoric for the journal.

Sanford Tweedie, assistant professor in the College Writing department at Rowan University, has published in a variety of genres and journals, including *College Composition and Communication, Perspectives in Biology and Medicine,* the American Occupational Therapy Association's *Education SIS Newsletter, The Cream City Review, Wisconsin Review,* and *Hawaii Review.* He teaches, too.

David M. Weed received his doctorate at Syracuse University in June 1996. His dissertation examines the intersection of male sexuality and class in mid-eighteenth-century novels and autobiography. He has published reviews, and his essay on Robert Bly's *Iron John* is forthcoming in a revised issue of *Masculinities,* "Pro-Feminist Men Respond to the Men's Movement." Weed is a three-quarter time instructor in the Department of English at Washburn University, Topeka, Kansas.

Kay Westmoreland is an assistant professor in the Department of English at Washington State University, where she teaches graduate and undergraduate courses in cultural rhetoric, technical and professional writing, and American literature. She has published on the connotative semiotics of Roland Barthes and the teaching of professional writing. Her research interests are in rhetoric and culture with emphasis on media cultures and consumer practices. Her present work includes a study of Bobbie Ann Mason's fictional exploration of the social and personal dynamics of an early historical media event, and a study of the Internet cultures surrounding the film *Pulp Fiction.*